SOUTHAMPTON

THE POSTCARD COLLECTION

Anne Scorey

Peter Wardall,
Ben Waring and Rod Andrews

AMBERLEY

First published 2018

Amberley Publishing
The Hill, Stroud, Gloucestershire, GL5 4EP
www.amberley-books.com

ISBN 978 1 4456 7757 6 (print)
ISBN 978 1 4456 7758 3 (ebook)

British Library Cataloguing in Publication Data.
A catalogue record for this book is available from the British Library.

Origination by Amberley Publishing.
Printed in Great Britain.

CONTENTS

INTRODUCTION

It feels like only yesterday we were writing our previous book, *Southampton Memories: People and Places*. Through our Facebook page of the same name, we have so far spent some six years curating thousands of postcards of Southampton and its suburbs. *Southampton: The Postcard Collection* showcases our favourites.

In decades past, a plentiful volume of post would fly back and forth between individuals. Quick-written conversations were very much possible by taking advantage of multiple postal deliveries per day. An example of this type of postcard sits on my desk as I write this introduction: 'I will write again when I have your reply, I hope this afternoon' signs off one half of an Edwardian courting couple to her intended.

How many of us nowadays find the time to purchase a postcard, sit and write a few lines, buy a stamp and then find the nearest postbox? A simple text message or email will achieve the same result almost instantly and at a fraction of the cost. In this era of instant communication via digital devices and social media, our family and friends are no more than a swipe or a click away. Faced with such technological competition, postcards as a means of communication must now be considered a dying medium. The practice of sending them decreases year-on-year.

It is fascinating to look back at some of the excellent examples that have survived the ravages of time. Those of us with an interest in historical postcards tend to find ourselves falling into one of two categories.

Firstly, some pay attention to what is written on the reverse of a postcard. From the innocuous 'wish you were here' to the apocalyptic 'today we go into battle', it is perhaps not too far a stretch to consider every such greeting a time capsule in its own right.

To think of the knowledge and experiences the sender of a postcard chose to impart in the small available space is to consider that each serves as a memorial to a life lived. Those few sentences impart information that would otherwise likely have been lost to the hands of time.

As a source of social history, these messages are unparalleled. No longer was the recording of historical events restricted to the official version of the story; the world in which the balance of power was held by newspaper editors began to diminish. With ready access to an affordable and efficient medium such as postcards – almost a throwaway item – individuals' reactions to historical events, or just the mundane aspects of everyday life, came to be more widely recorded.

This gives us an additional tool with which to develop our understanding of the events, experiences and lifestyles known by the people who have gone before us; to understand their feelings about world events, or to learn of some aspect of their daily lives that they may have considered almost dull, yet to us proves fascinating. It is no wonder that some seek out such details as a motivation for collecting postcards.

The second type of postcard enthusiast, and this is by far the larger group, consists of those who enjoy seeing the image on the front, who marvel at some old-fashioned scene depicting people going about their lives among historic cars, trams and buildings. Such glimpses serve as a portal to another world, often one which has long-since been swept away in the name of 'progress' – a subjective term, if ever there was one. *Southampton: The Postcard Collection* focuses on this very aspect.

In writing this book, we've split the postcard views into chapters based on geographical areas. Thus you are transported, area to area, around this great port city we call home. Starting at the waterside, we progress through the docks area and into town, taking in the suburbs of Northam and Chapel. Next we travel across to the east of the River Itchen, encompassing areas such as Itchen, Sholing, Woolston, Weston, Bitterne and some of their surrounding landmarks. We then head to the northern parishes, offering views of Portswood, Swaythling, Banister and The Common. Our tour concludes with a look at the western parishes, with Freemantle, Millbrook, Shirley and Redbridge being well represented.

There is a great deal of history to be found on the pages of this book, and some of the images herein are very seldom seen. The question is, will you enjoy reading the book as much as we have loved writing it? Answers on a postcard, please.

CHAPTER 1

WATERSIDE

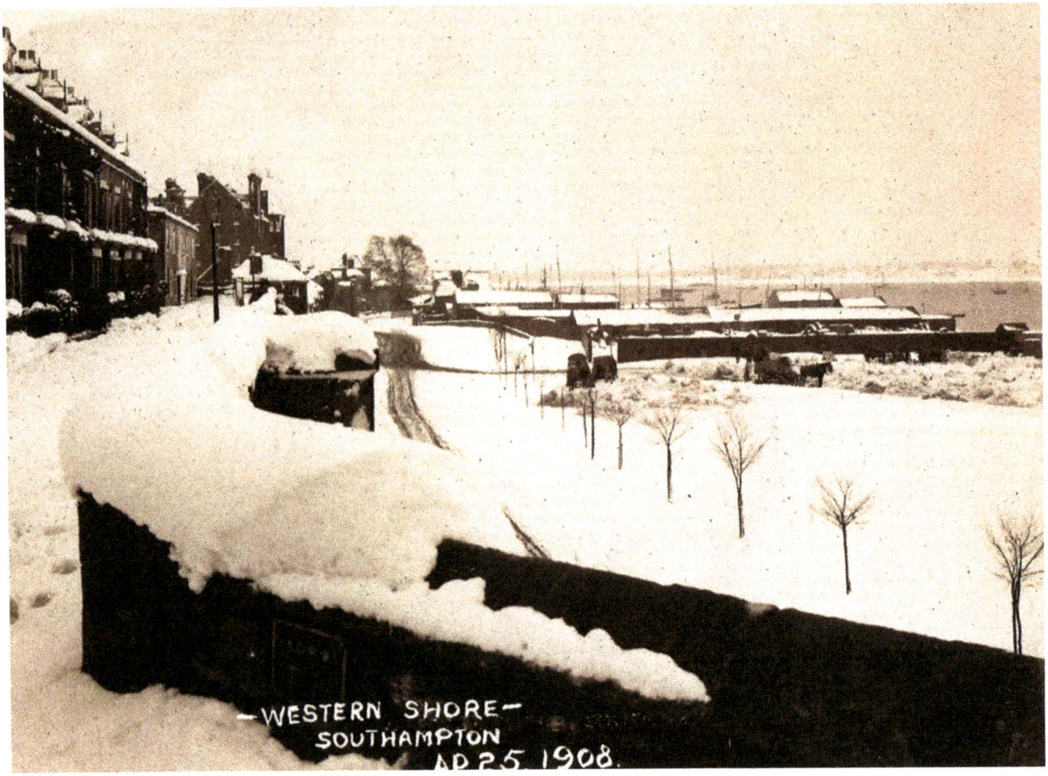

Western Shore, 1908

The 'freak' snowstorm of April 1908. Quite a few local photographers braved the elements to take images around the town. This view, from Forest View, shows street cleaning crews depositing cleared snow on the tideline of Western Shore.

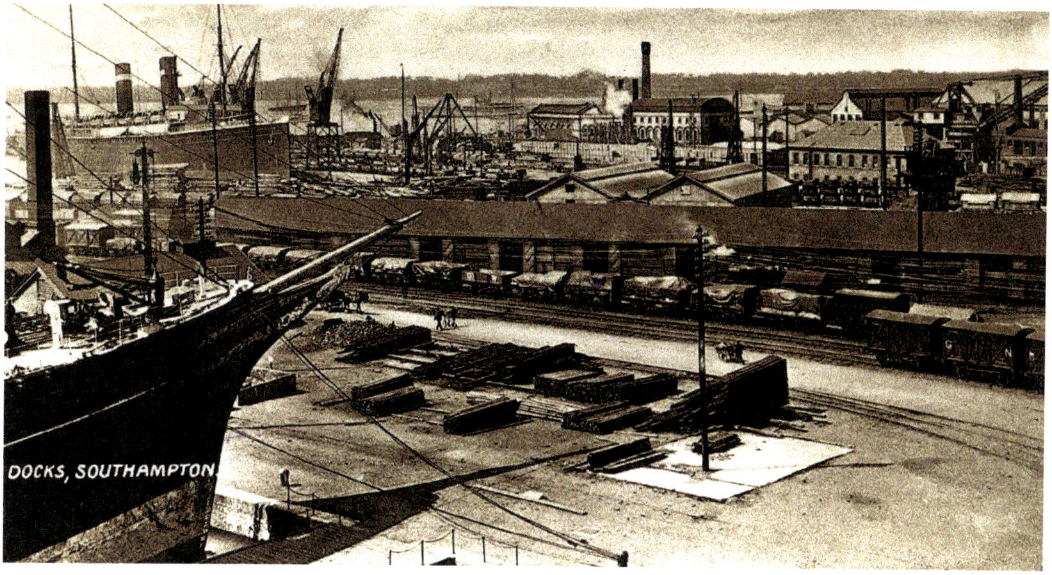

Eastern Docks

Within a very short time of its construction, the Eastern Docks became the driving force of the town. It was a major employer, a gateway to the world and, in effect, a self-contained township in its own right.

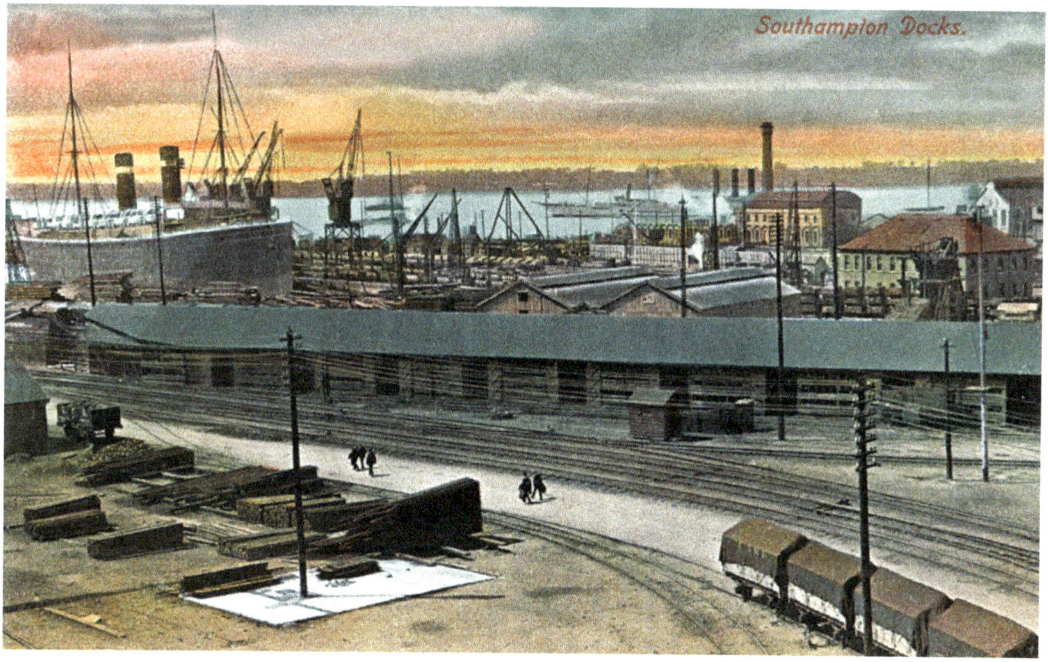

Eastern Docks, *c.* 1900

Here is a very similar view of the Eastern Docks, with an unidentified Red Star steamer to the left. This postcard benefits from the practice of colourisation, at this time still in its infancy. The original photograph would have been sent to a specialist in this art form, usually overseas, who would enliven the scene with colour.

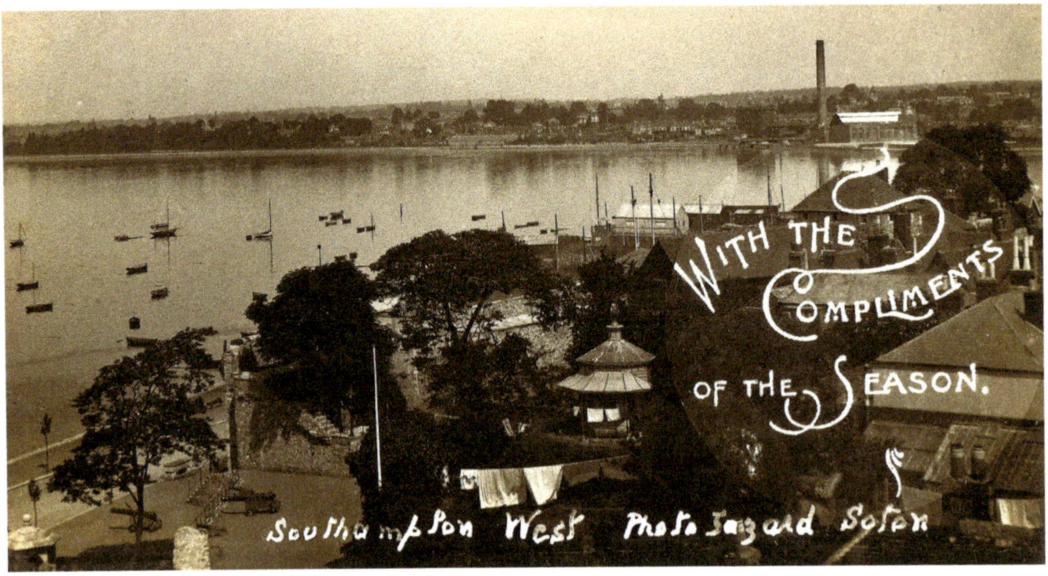

West Bay, late 1800s to early 1900s

The wide sweep of West Bay can be seen in this early greetings card. The houses in Bugle Street that backed onto the shore had a wonderful view upriver to Redbridge. To the right the boatbuilding yards at the West Gate can be seen and further round the bay the town's electricity station and the West railway station. In the foreground is a domestic scene, the garden of a Bugle Street house complete with ornate summer house and washing line.

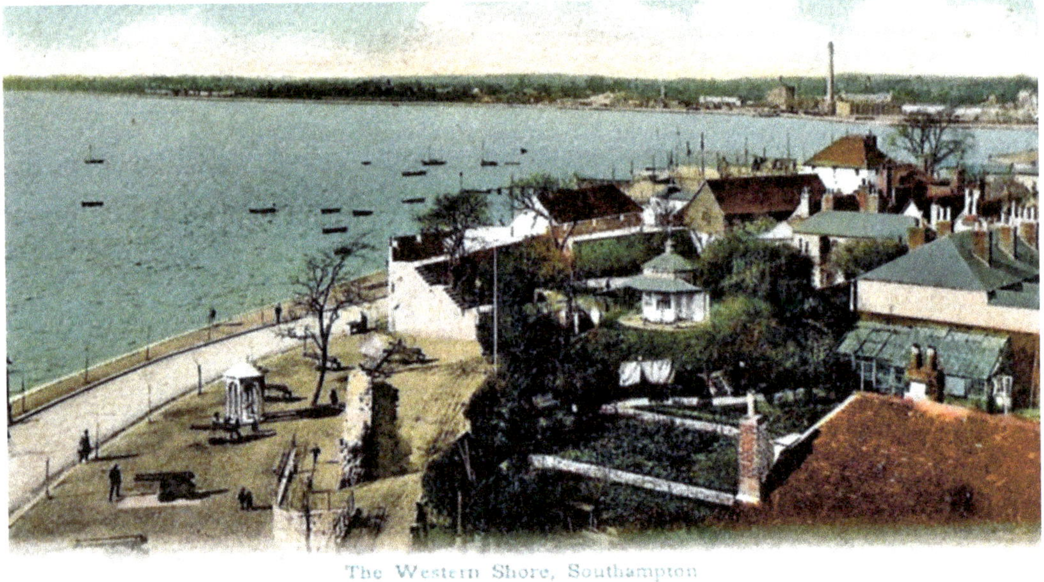

West Bay, late 1800s

This tinted version of the previous black and white postcard illustrates perfectly the rapid advances in postcard printing in the 1800s. The introduction of the one-penny stamp in the 1840s was the first impetus for the advent of postcard popularity. By the late 1800s hand colour tinting and improvements in printing techniques ensured the coloured postcard had arrived.

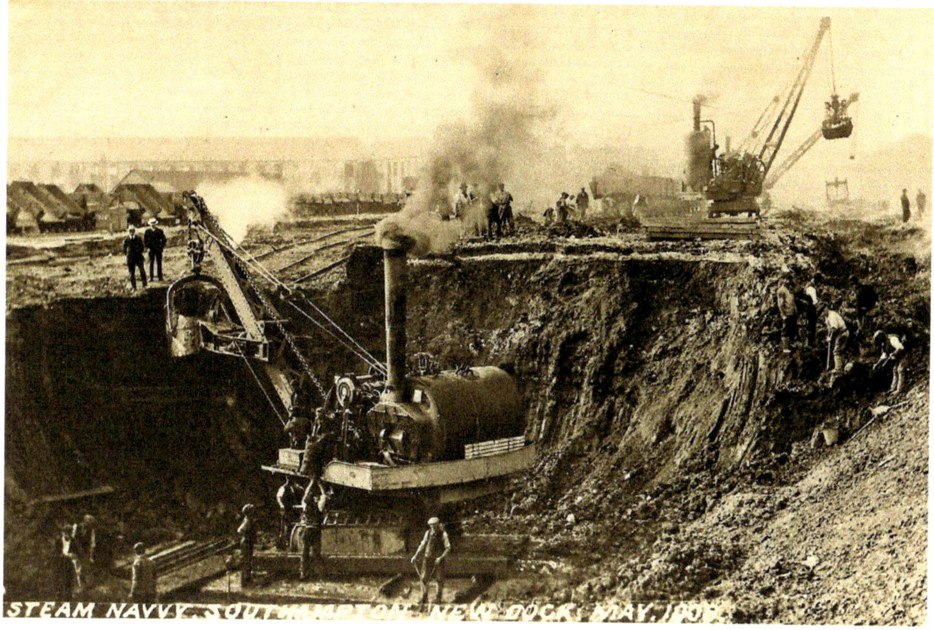

Steam Navvy, 1909
For centuries, seaborne trade in and out of Southampton loaded and unloaded at the town's quays. In 1836 the Southampton Dock Company was formed and 216 acres of marshland east of the Town Quay was purchased. Here the Eastern Docks were constructed. As seen in this 1909 postcard, the docks' continued expansion relied heavily on a combination of man and steam power.

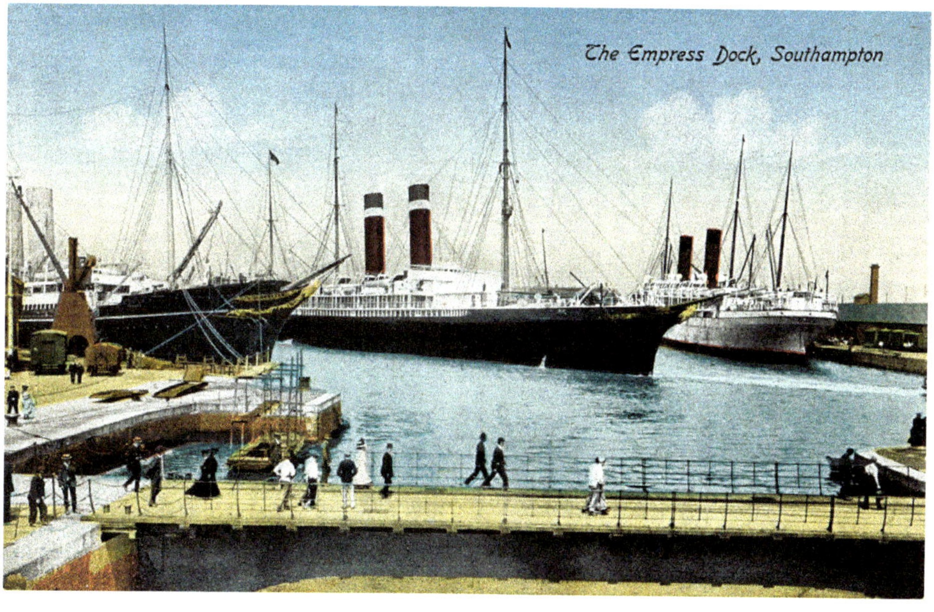

Empress Dock, *c.* 1910
Empress Dock showing the *New York*, the ship *Titanic* nearly hit when leaving Southampton on her fateful maiden voyage two years later.

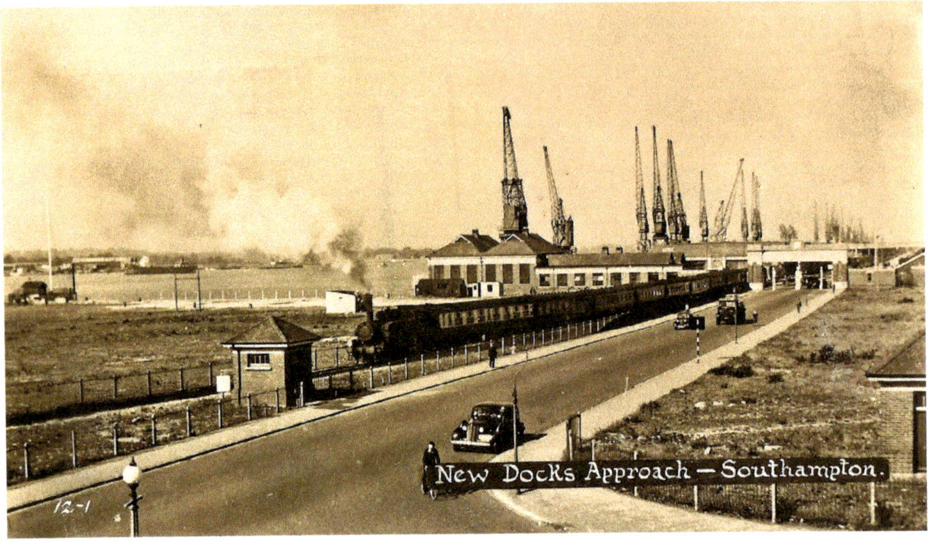

Herbert Walker Avenue, 1930s

Herbert Walker Avenue leads into the new Western Docks through Dock Gate No. 8. The new dock was built on reclaimed land and provided much needed work during the period of depression between the wars.

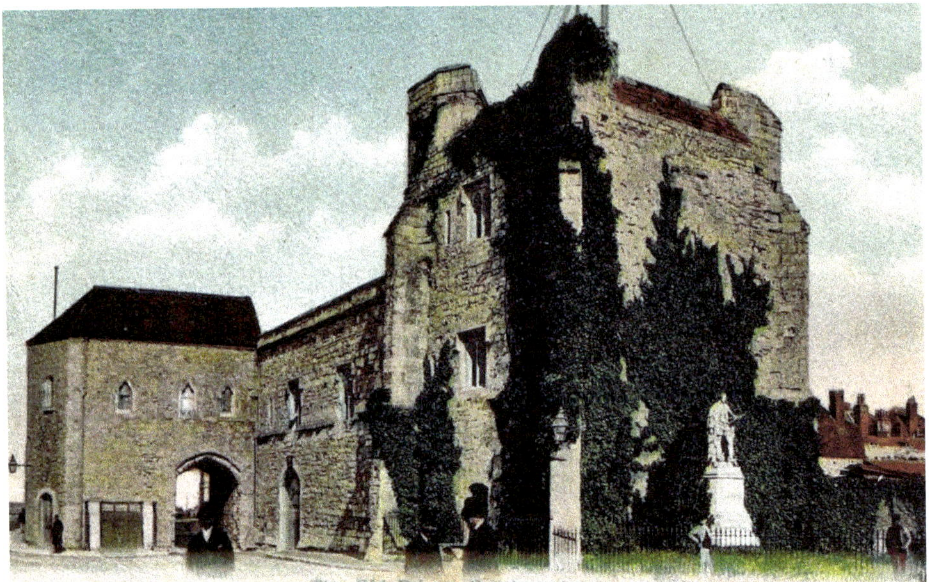

God's House Tower

God's House Tower was the southerly gate to the salt marshes to the east of the medieval town. This defensive position on the town walls was built in the early thirteenth century. It took its name from God's House Hospital, immediately to the rear of the gate. The building has been a garrison, a store, a prison and a museum. To the right the ill-fated statue of Prince Albert can be seen. Originally planned to stand in a location elsewhere, this spot under the tower was second choice. Anti-German sentiment during the First World War caused the statue to be taken into storage. It is said a group of soldiers destroyed the statue.

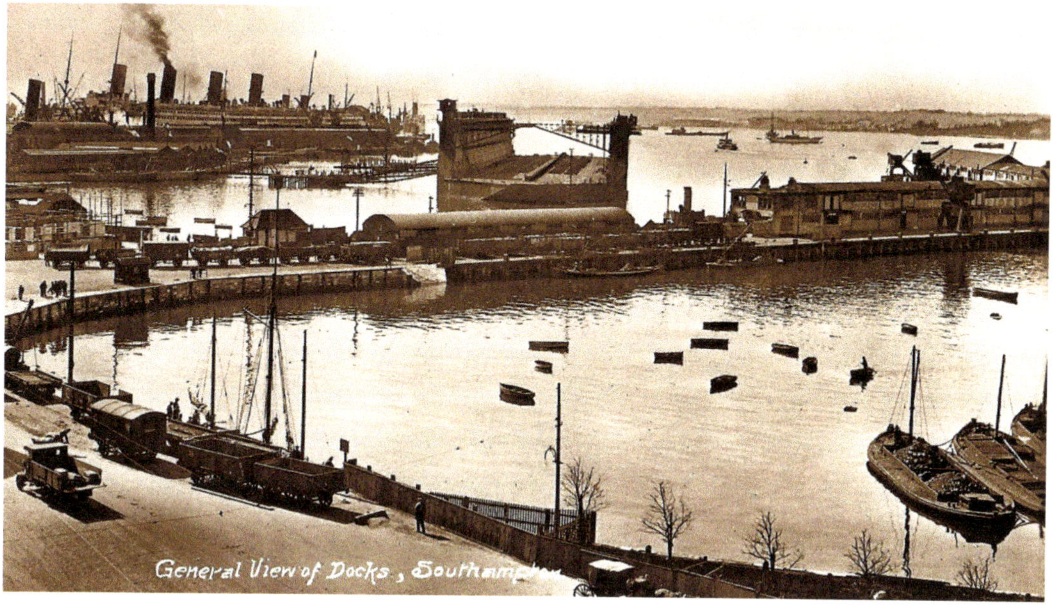

Southampton Water
This view of the docks, looking down Southampton Water, was taken from the roof of the Royal Southern Yacht Club headquarters. In the foreground are the fly cabs waiting on the rank outside the Royal Pier (out of shot). In the mid-ground the busy Town Quay that catered for local seaborne trade. Beyond, the mighty Floating Dock and a glimpse of the Eastern Docks can be seen.

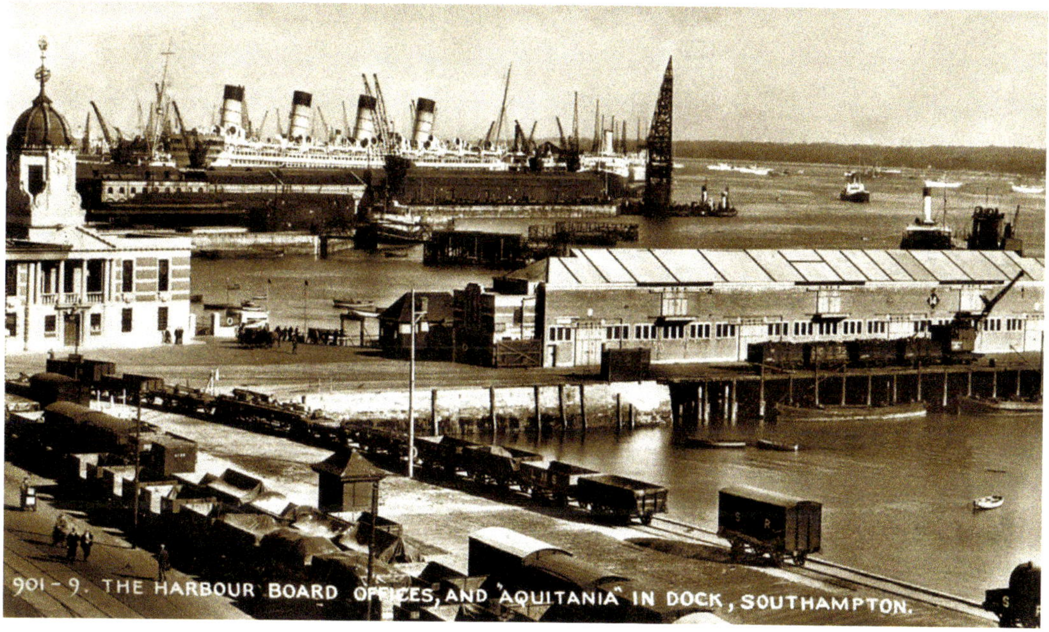

Town Quay
A view down river, taking in the Town Quay in the foreground and the Harbour Board Office on the left. In the background we see the Test side quays of the Eastern Docks, and in the background the four funnels of the *Aquitania*.

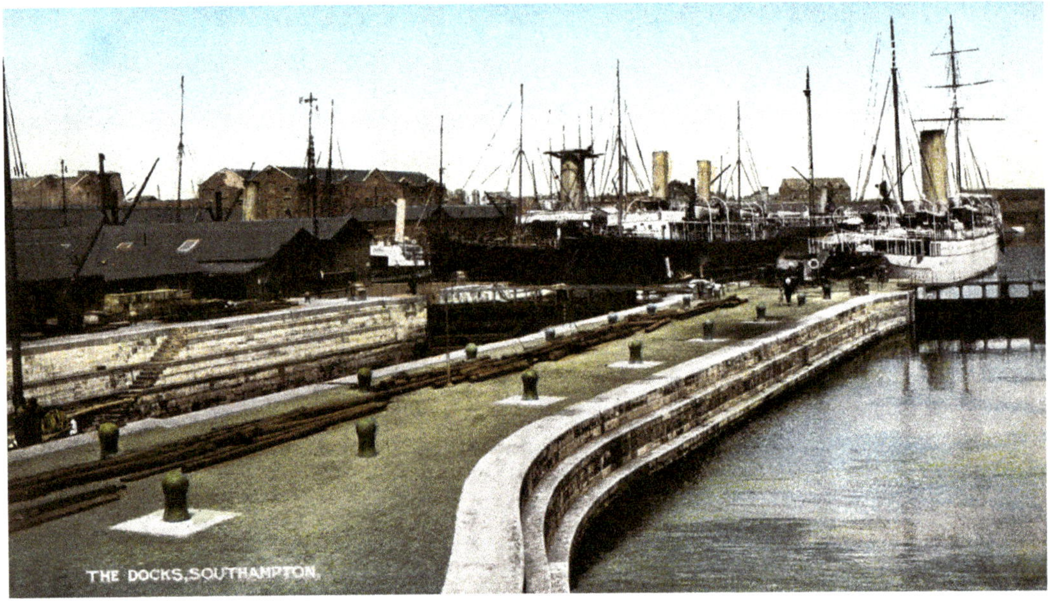

Inner Dock, *c.* 1900
The inner dock was opened in 1851 and was connected to the outer dock by locks. It was the only closed wet dock in Southampton.

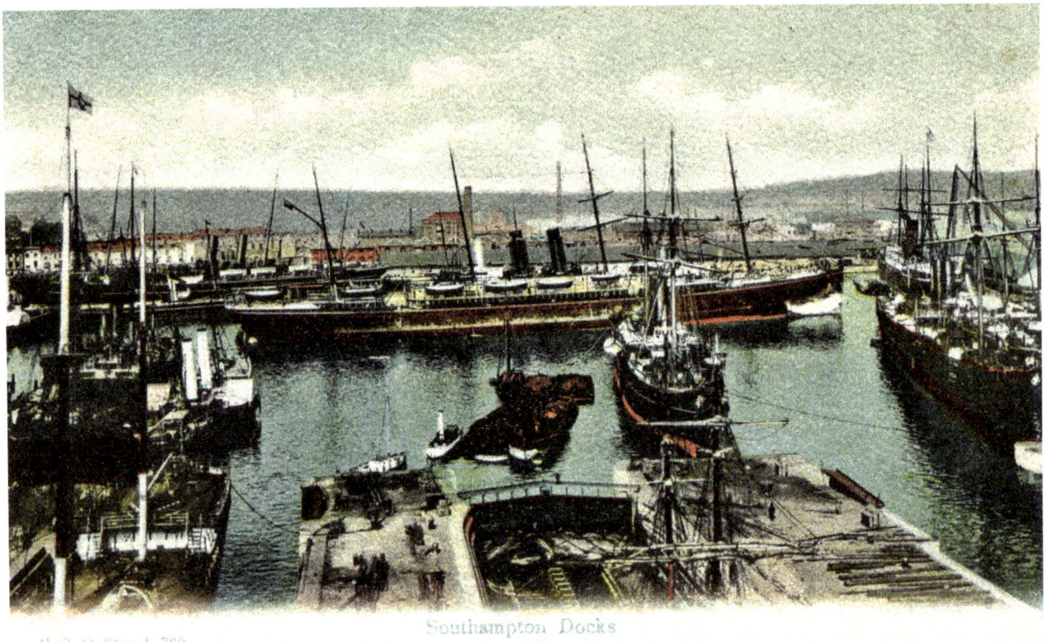

Inner Dock, *c.* 1900
Inner (closed) dock showing the locks to the outer (open) dock. The outer dock opened in 1842, the first ships to use it being the P&O liners Tagus and Liverpool. The continental steamers moved to the outer dock once the railway arrived. The first three dry docks at Southampton were built between 1846 and 1854, and were able to take the largest ships of the day.

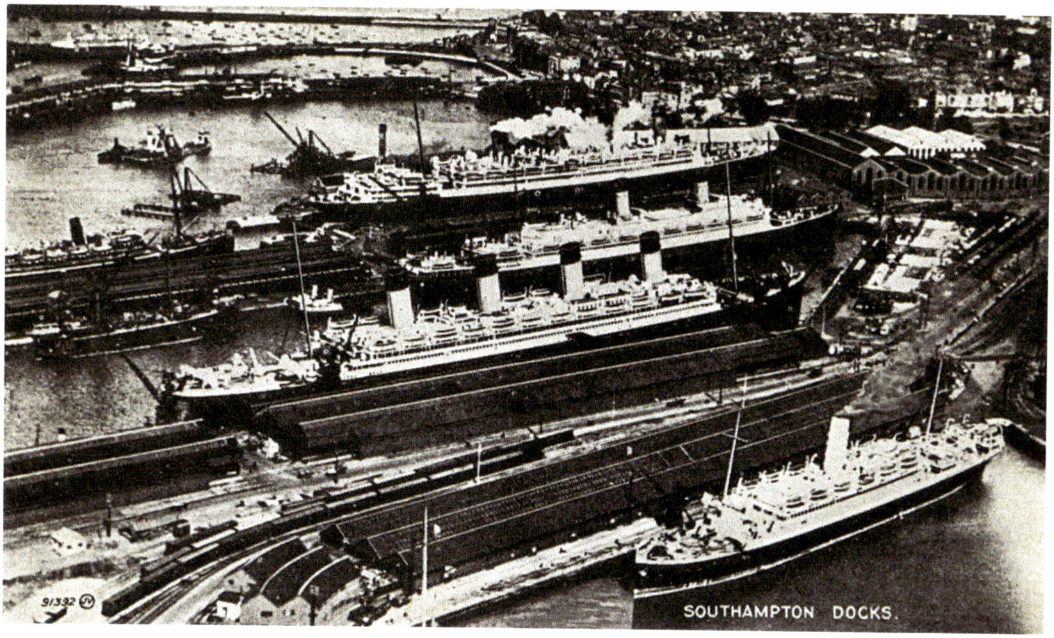

Docks, *c.* 1920

Olympic and *Homeric* in Ocean Dock, with *Aquitania* behind in the Trafalgar dry dock, then a Royal Mail liner in the Empress Dock. Views such as this aptly illustrate how important the dockside areas have been to Southampton.

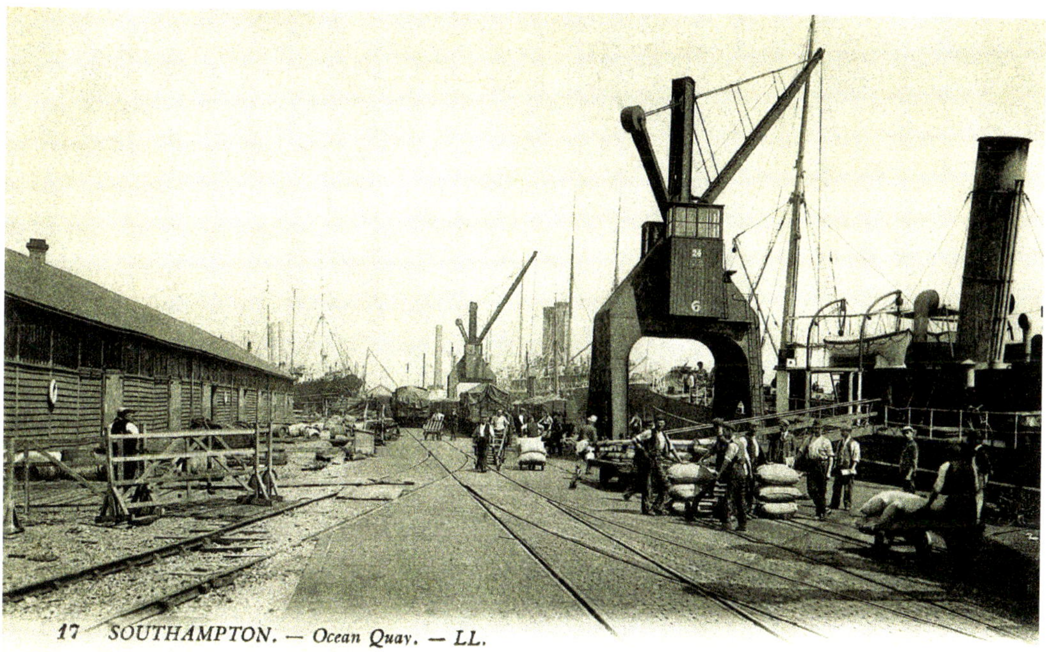

Ocean Quay

Ocean Quay showing early electric dockside portal cranes. The first electric dockside cranes in England were installed at Southampton Docks by Stothert and Pitt in 1892.

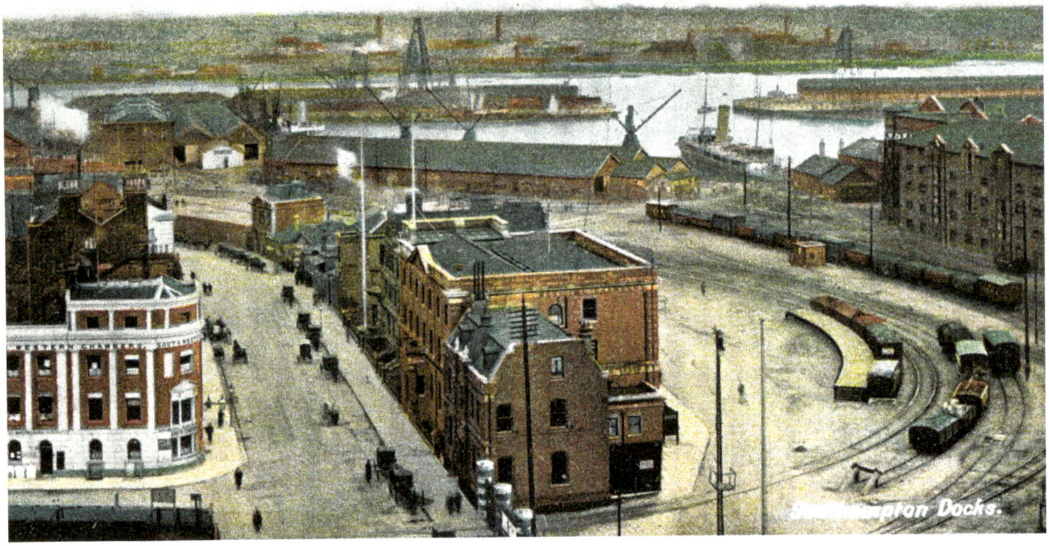

Dock Gate No. 4

Main entrance to the docks through Dock Gate No. 4 on Canute Road. South Western Chambers on the left was originally occupied by the London & South Western Railway Steam Packet Company. This later became No. 1 Canute Road.

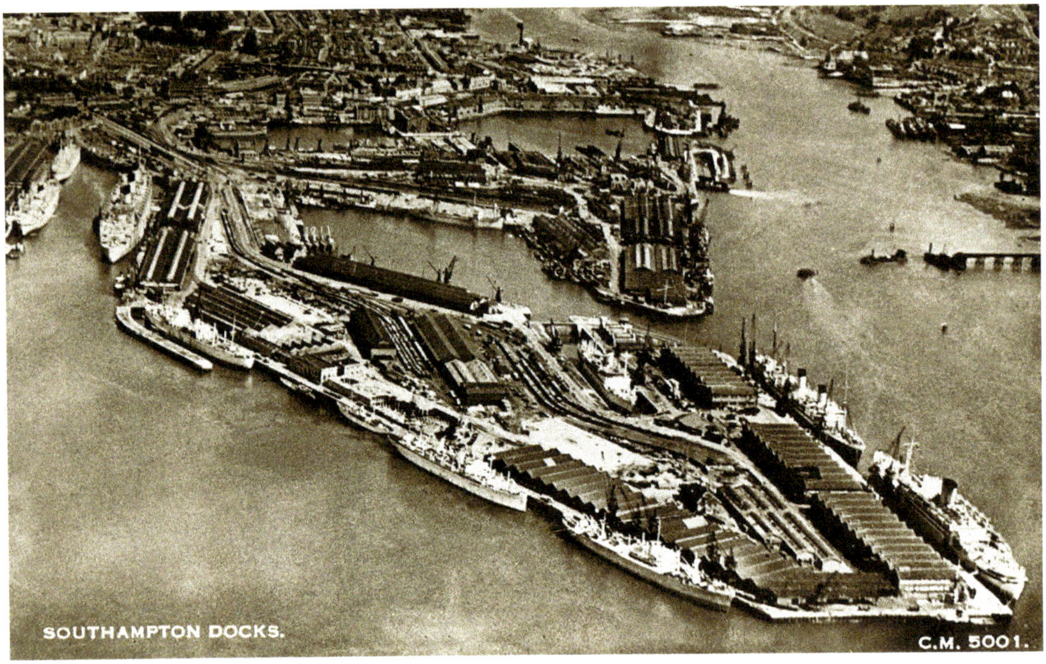

Aerial View of the Docks, 1940s

This aerial view of the docks, taken from the south, shows the impressive scale of the Empress Dock and the inner and outer docks.

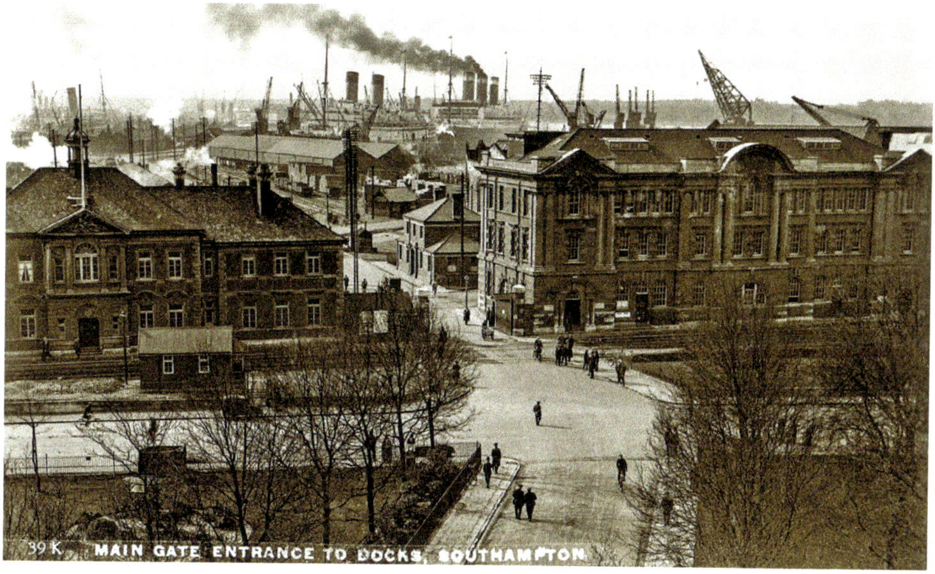

Dock Gate No. 4, *c.* 1920s

View into the docks at Dock Gate No. 4, showing the imposing old Post Office and Telegraph building on the right of the entrance. Following the road through the gate and bearing round to the left would take you around to Berth 44 in the White Star Dock, from which *Titanic* sailed on her fateful maiden voyage. The liners in the dock are RMS *Homeric* with United States line SS *Leviathan* behind.

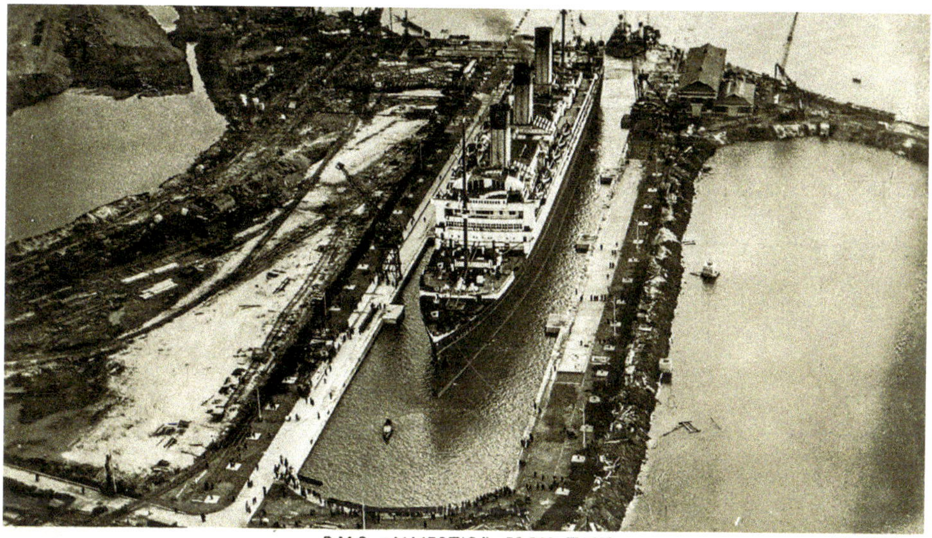

R.M.S. "MAJESTIC," 56,599 TONS,
IN THE WORLD'S LARGEST DOCK. SOUTHAMPTON

THE AERIAL PHOTOGRAPHIC CO. LONDON

RMS *Majestic*

RMS *Majestic* entering the King George V Graving Dock, the first ship to do so after it was opened in 1933. The new dry dock at the western end of the new Western Docks was opened by George V in July 1933 and named in his honour. It was the largest dry dock in the world at that time, having been built to accommodate the 1,000-feet-long passenger liners that were then being brought into service.

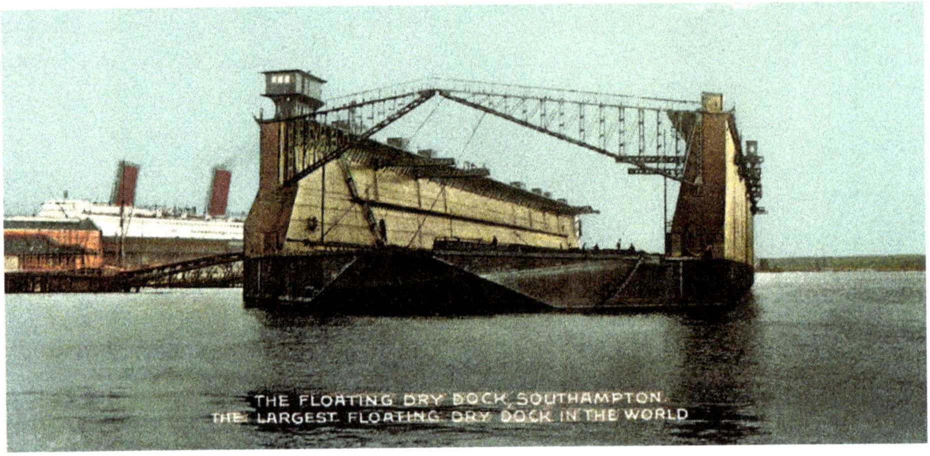

Floating Dock, late 1920s

The dock had an overall length of 960 feet, being made up of seven sections – five middle sections and two end sections, which had cantilevered platforms at their outer extremities. With a clear width inside between the side walls of 130 feet 8 inches, the total internal area of the deck was 3.5 acres. The outside walls were 70 feet high and the depth of water over the blocks when the dock was fully submersed was 38 feet. Any one of the seven sections could be disconnected from the remainder and docked. By turning the sections through ninety degrees, they could pass between the side walls of the dock. The dock weighed 18,990 tons and had a total lifting capacity of 60,000 tons.

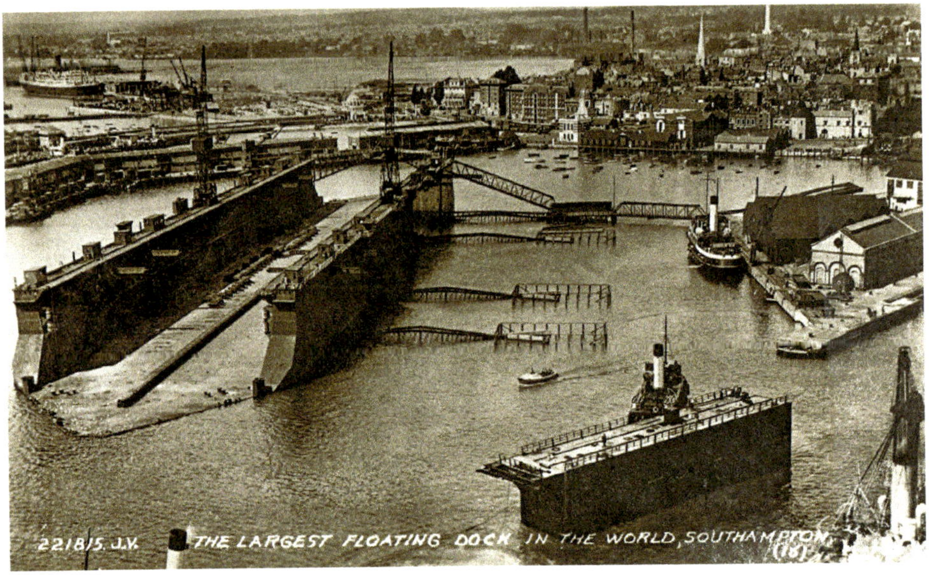

Floating Dock

The Southampton floating dry dock was built by Armstrong Whitworth in Newcastle upon Tyne and moved to Southampton in April 1924. It was opened by HRH the Prince of Wales on the 27 June 1924. It remained in regular use until 1934 when the new King George V dry dock was inaugurated in January of that year. It was the largest floating dry dock in the world at that time. On the 27 February 1940 it was moved to Portsmouth and was used by the Admiralty as 'AFD 11' during the Second World War.

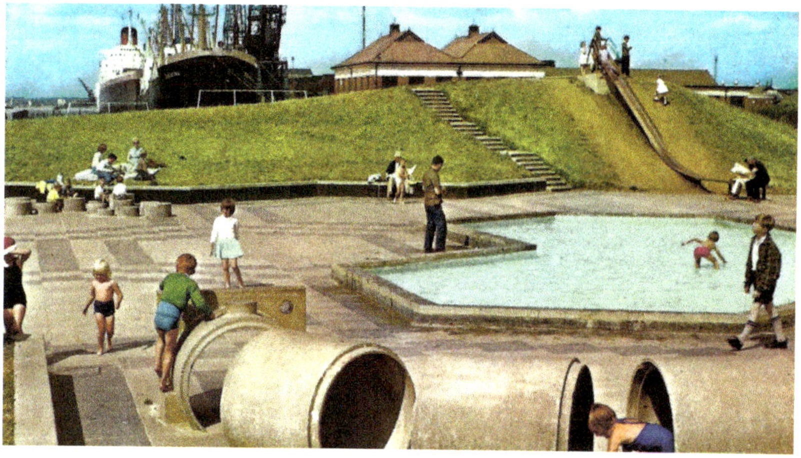

Mayflower Park, 1960s

During the construction of the Eastern Docks in Southampton in the late 1920s/early 1930s, a marshalling yard for the docks contractors was built on reclaimed land between the Royal Pier and the new Berth 101. Once the railway lines were removed after the dock's construction the park was given over to public use. Originally called by the rather grand title of the Royal Pier Recreation Ground, the open space provided access to the water side for the townspeople. In the mid-1950s the space was landscaped and a children's playground provided. Now renamed Mayflower Park, the area proved extremely popular, especially in fine weather. For over three decades the playground provided many memories for a generation of youngsters. The brutalist concrete maze, rings and paddling pool collected the skin of many a young knee.

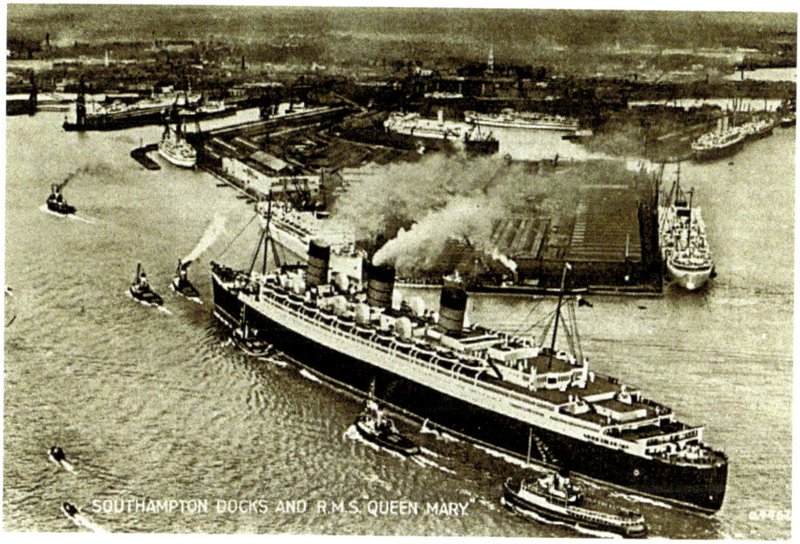

RMS *Queen Mary*

Queen Mary arrived in Southampton to cheers and whistles on the shore and from ships in port. She passed by Germany's *Bremen*, outward bound and signalling best wishes. As hundreds of craft swarmed around her, she approached the Southern Railway Dock, on which more than 12,000 people had gathered to see her in. She passed the docks amid screaming sirens and whistles from other liners docked there.

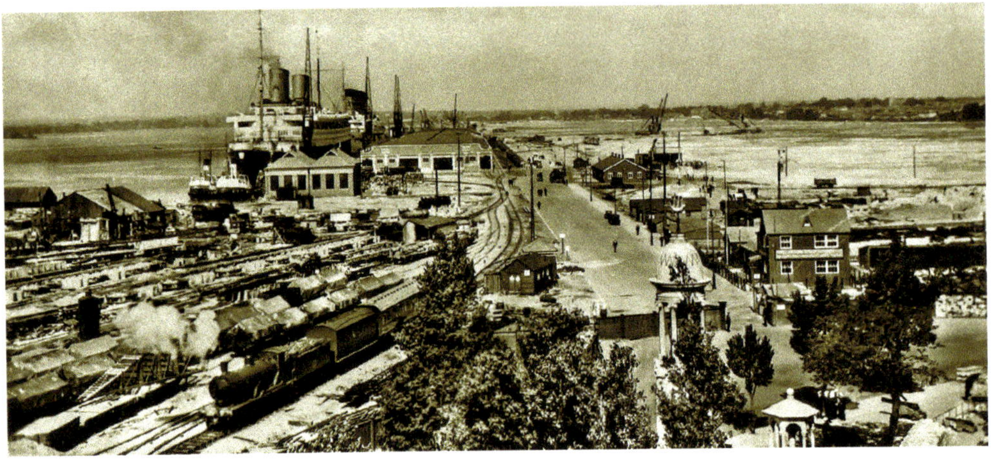

Western Docks

The building of the new Western Docks required the reclamation of 400 acres of mudflats between Western Esplanade and Millbrook shore. It was the largest reclamation scheme ever undertaken in the country at that time. A straight line of quays, measuring over 800 feet, was then constructed. The work started in 1928 and was completed by 1934. The first ship to visit was Cunard's *Mauritania* in 1932. This postcard looks towards the eastern end of Western Docks, where the Berth 101 shed can be seen. In the foreground on the left is the contractor's yard and the concrete mixing plant in use for the construction of the docks. To the right, in the foreground, we see both the Mayflower Memorial and the Stella Memorial. SS *Europa* is berthed in front of what appears to be the *Aquitania*.

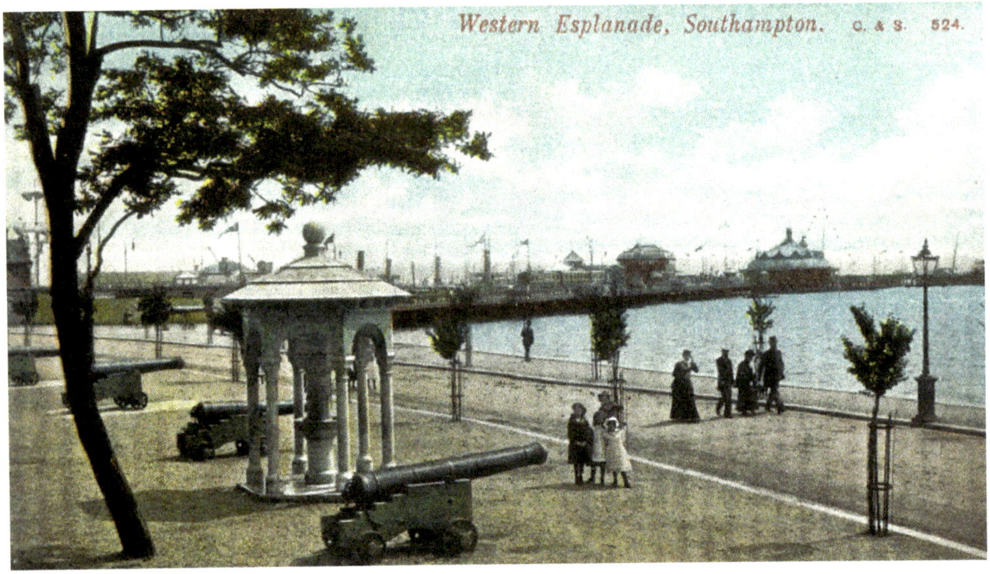

Stella Monument

Western Esplanade showing the Stella Monument with the Royal Pier and docks in the background. This landmark memorial stands in tribute to Mary Ann Rogers, who was hailed a heroine for giving up her life to save another when the SS *Stella*, en route from Southampton to Guernsey, struck the Casquets reef and sank with the loss of seventy-seven passengers and crew.

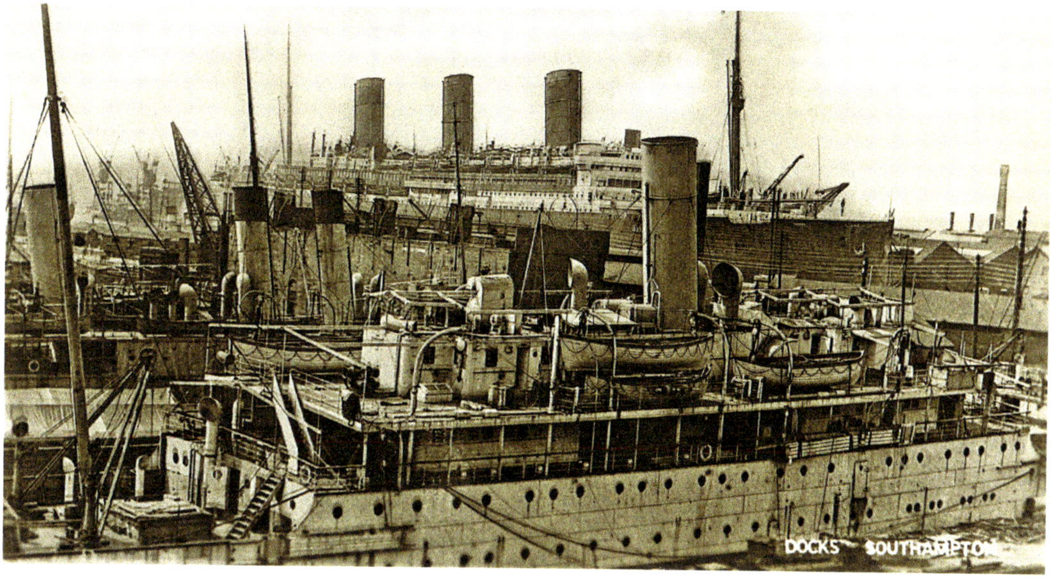

RMS *Berengaria*

The large vessel in the background is the RMS *Berengaria*. Built in the early 1900s for the Hamburg American Line, she was originally named SS *Imperator*. At the time of her launch she was the largest passenger ship in the world. Held in port during wartime hostilities, after a brief period taking American troops back to the US, she was transferred to the Cunard Line as part of the post-war reparations.

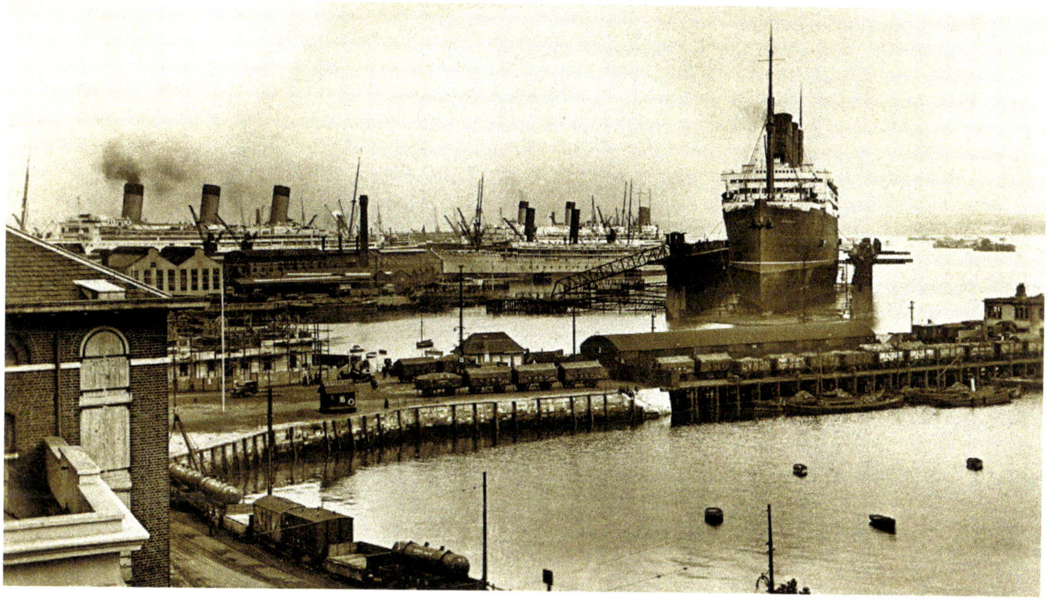

Town Quay

Town Quay with RMS *Berengaria* in the floating dock. The three-funnelled liner in the background on the left is the White Star Line RMS *Majestic*. The other White Star Line two-funnelled liner in the far background is RMS *Homeric*. The two-funnelled ship in front of Homeric is unidentified; perhaps you can identify it?

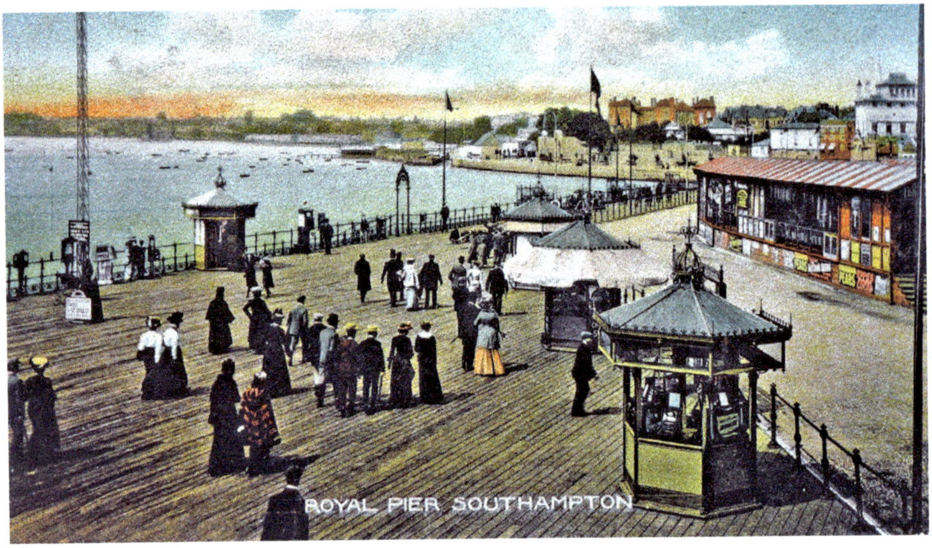

Royal Pier, late 1800s

Opened in 1833, the Royal Victoria Pier was arguably the jewel in Southampton's crown. Loved by generations of townspeople, the pier attracted crowds in good weather. It was somewhere to promenade, sit and watch the ships pass by, or perhaps catch a ferry or a pleasure steamer. One could take tea and enjoy the entertainment facilities.

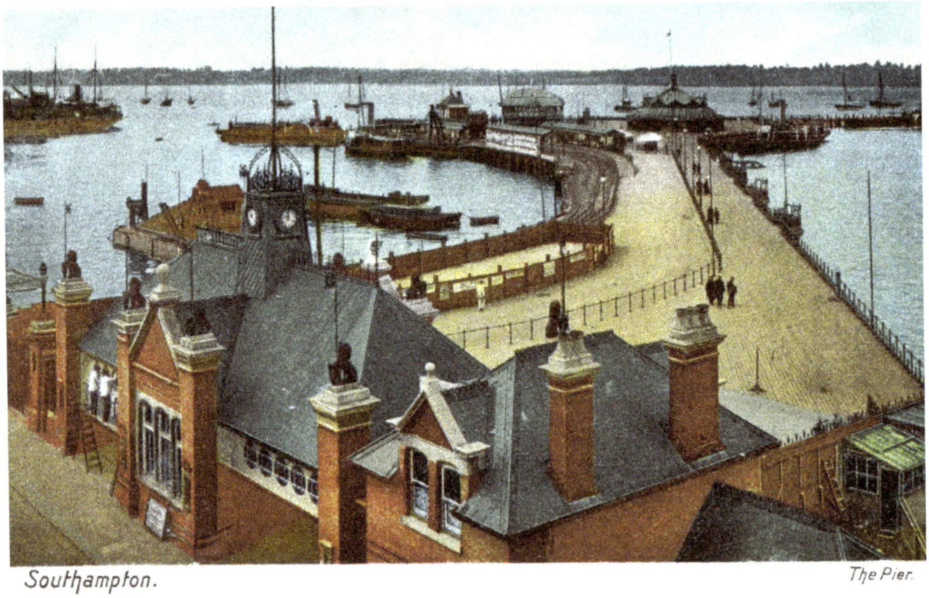

Royal Pier

After the war, the Royal Pier was a major venue for dancing and music. However, poor maintenance led to the pier falling into disrepair and it was eventually closed off to the public. During the 1980s, the pier fell victim to a disastrous fire and its useful life was over. Its remnants remain to the present day, but the structure sadly retains none of its former splendour. One redeeming feature is the gatehouse, which replaced that pictured here and is now a popular restaurant.

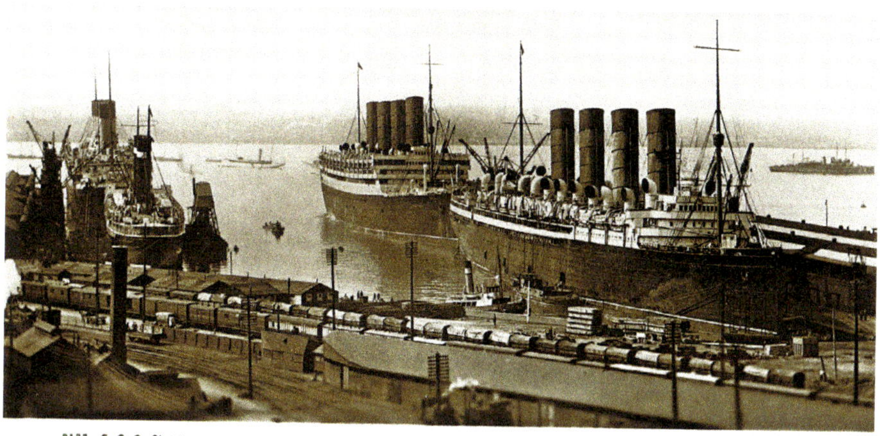

2123. F. G. O. Stuart. WHITE STAR DOCK, SOUTHAMPTON.

White Star Dock

Liners in the White Star Dock, which opened in 1911. RMS *Mauretania* is in the right foreground, behind which is RMS *Aquitania*. On the left is an unidentified Red Star liner with RMS *Olympic* behind. The White Star Dock was built to take the liners of the White Star Line when they relocated their operations from Liverpool to Southampton. It was renamed Ocean Dock after the First World War when Cunard and Canadian Pacific also relocated to Southampton.

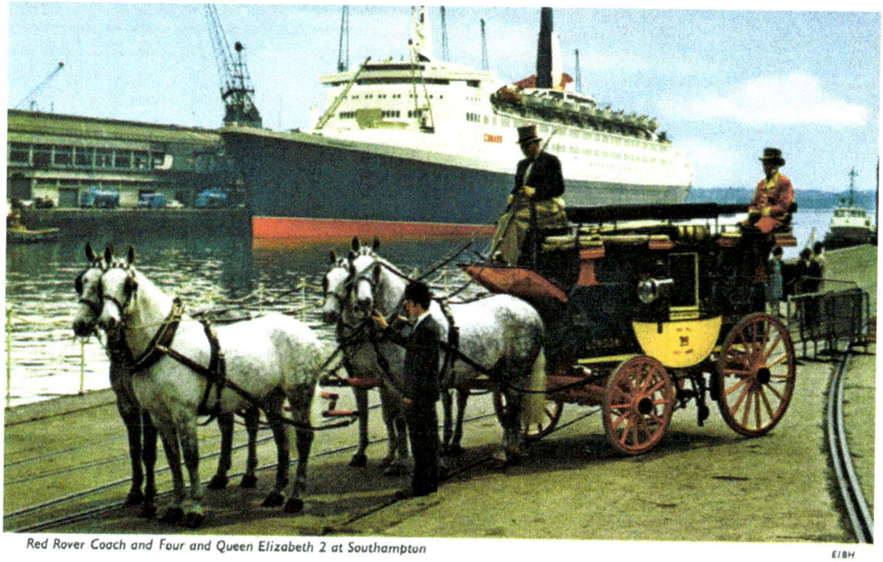

Red Rover Coach and Four and Queen Elizabeth 2 at Southampton E18H

Queen Elizabeth 2

Throughout its long service life, the *QE2* was inextricably linked with Southampton, its home port. The flagship Cunard liner of her time, in May 1982 she was requisitioned by the British government for service as a troop carrier in the Falklands War. Vosper Thorneycroft prepared the vessel for its new role, adding reinforced steel plating and two helipads. Soon afterwards she left Southampton carrying 3,000 troops plus hundreds of volunteer staff. On her return the following month, the *QE2* was met in Southampton Water by the Queen Mother onboard the Royal Yacht *Britannia*. In 2008 the *QE2* was sold and is now used as a floating hotel in Dubai.

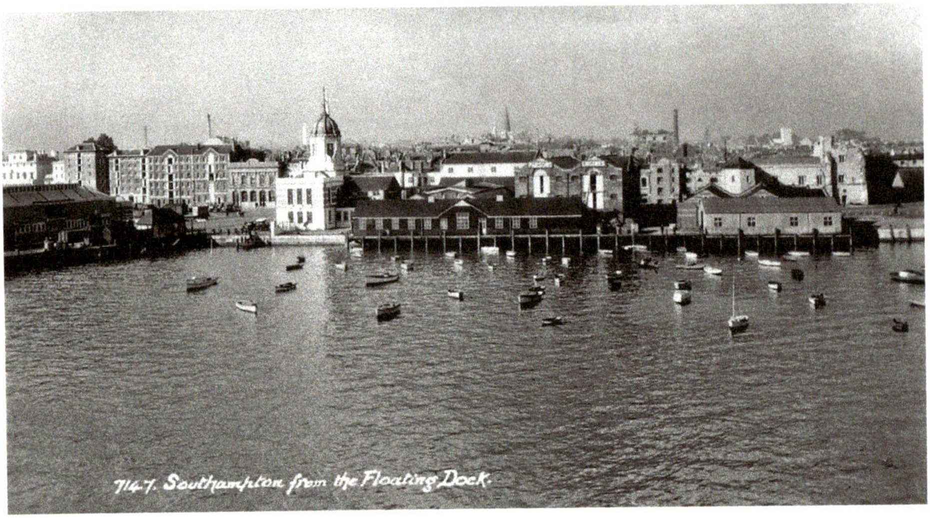

Town Quay and Harbour Board Offices

A view looking at Town Quay (left) and the Harbour Board Offices. Parsons Engine Works appears in the centre of the picture. Harry Parsons came to Southampton in 1904 where he formed the Parsons Oil Engine Company to develop the paraffin (kerosene) oil engine for marine and stationary purposes. He was the chair of Southampton Harbour Board for twenty-one years, covering the period of building the new docks and the development of an airbase.

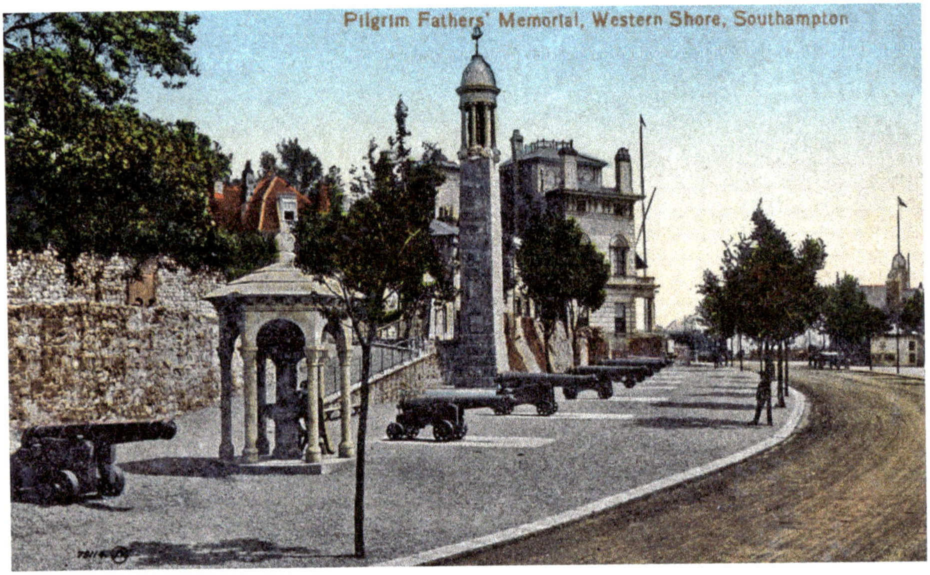

Mayflower Memorial, Western Shore

Designed by local architect R. M. Lucas and built by local stonemasons Garret and Haysom, this tall memorial commemorates the visit by the *Mayflower* in 1620. The ship containing the Pilgrim Fathers, seeking religious freedom, left Rotherhithe on the Thames bound for America. After meeting the *Speedwell* in Southampton, the two ships headed down channel bound for America. The *Speedwell* failed to stay sea worthy and only the *Mayflower* made the epic trip.

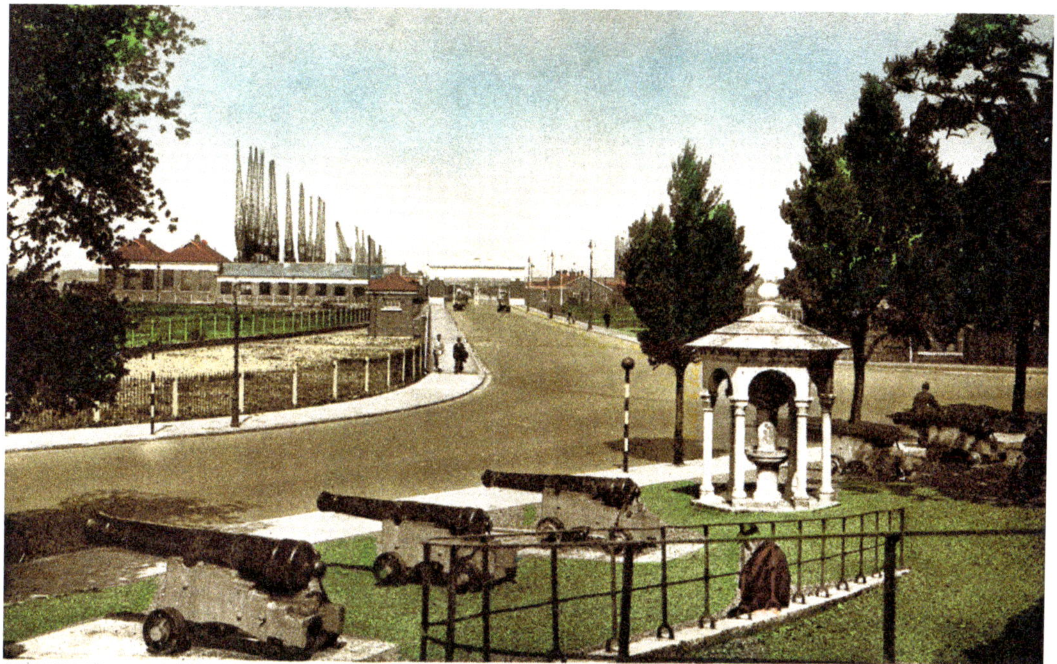

SOUTHAMPTON, ENTRANCE TO THE NEW DOCKS 7914.

Entrance to New Docks, *c.* 1935

Another view of the Stella Memorial on Western Esplanade, this time looking towards the entrance of the Western Docks at Dock Gate No. 8.

CHAPTER 2

TOWN

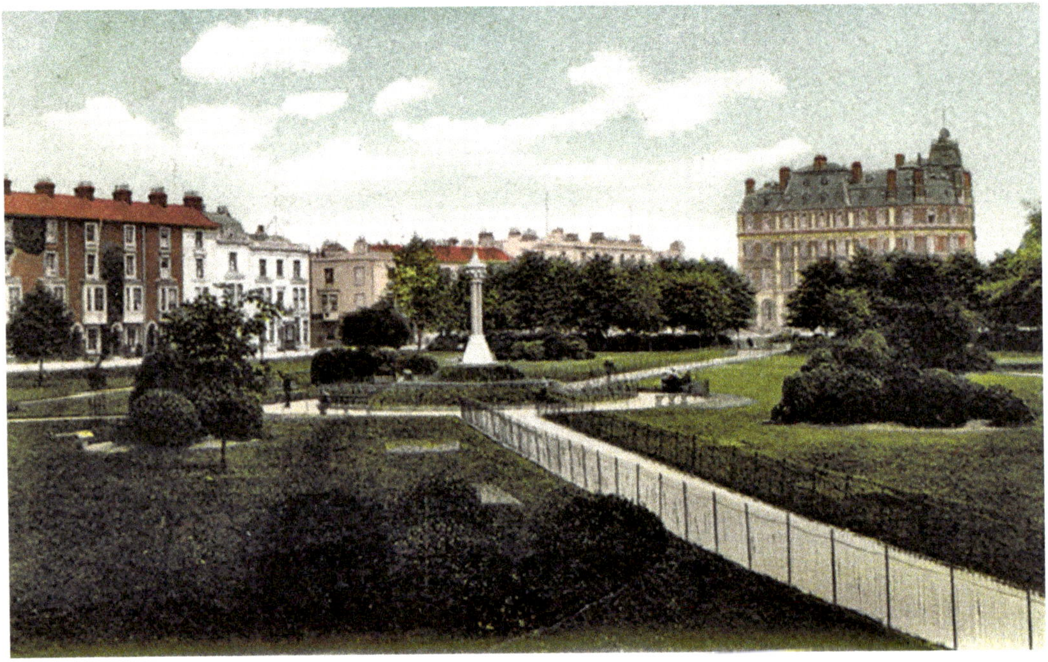

Queens Park

Originally called Porter's Meadow, this 4-acre park was once the area where the medieval porters tethered their horses. The land came under the ownership of Queens College, Oxford, as did much of the land in that area. However, it was decreed Lammas land and could be used as common land for half the year. In the 1800s the park was given over to the town and it was landscaped and renamed Queens Park. It was opened in 1885 and the memorial in the centre was dedicated to General Gordon of Khartoum, who had lived in the town.

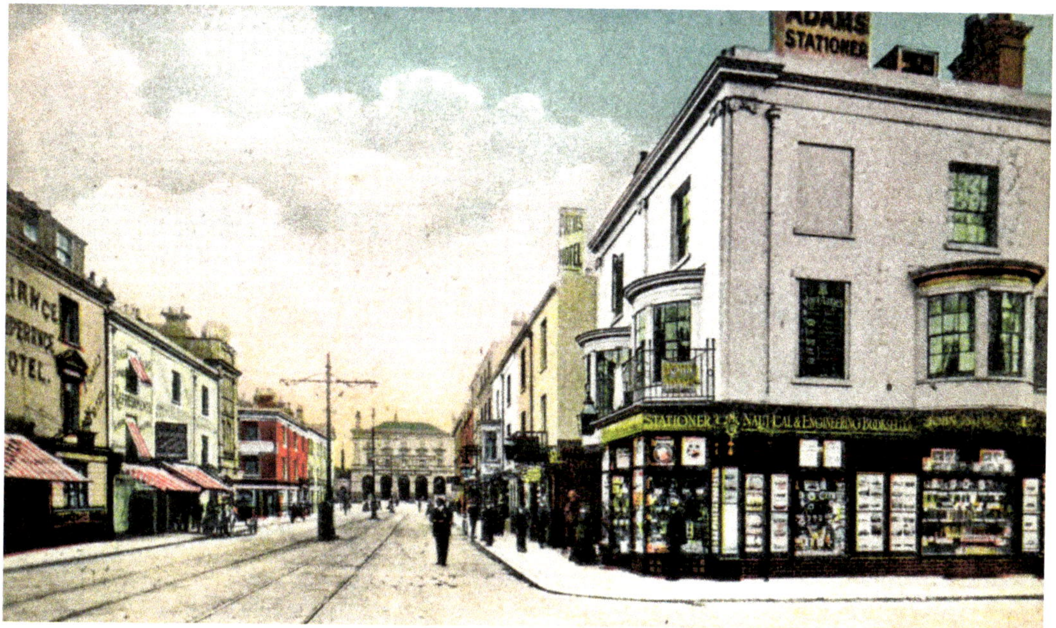

Oxford Street

Oxford Street was once one of the busiest commercial districts in the town. The vast majority of the businesses there were focused on maritime interests. There were chart suppliers, sellers of crew uniforms, shipping agents and of course busy hotels for passengers travelling to and from England. There were also the required number of public houses and bars to cater for ships crews.

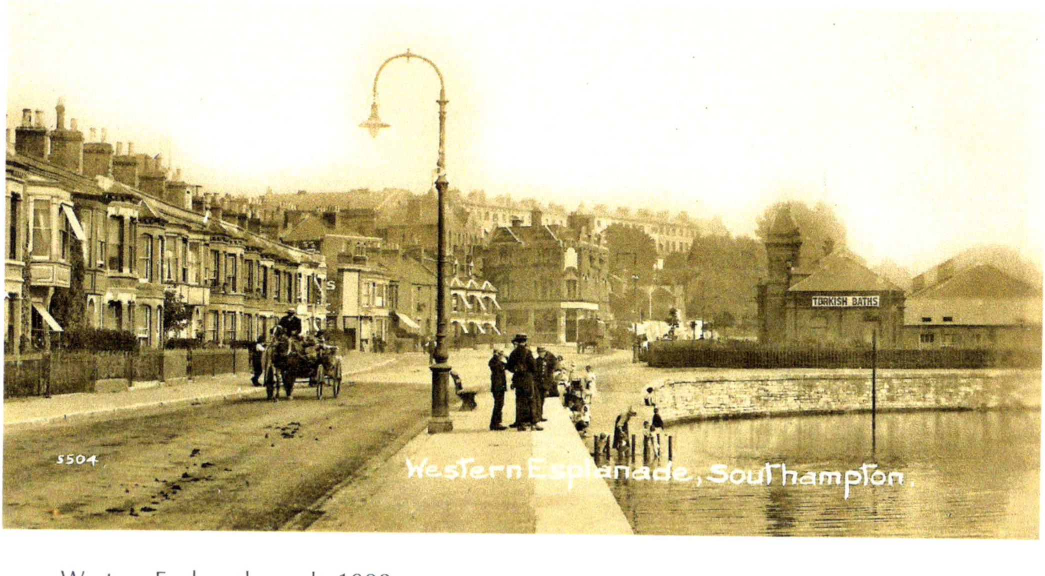

Western Esplanade, early 1900s

On the left is Weymouth Terrace, and Marina Terrace is further along the road. When first built, these desirable residences had fine views across West Bay. However, residents paid the price at very high tides when their houses were prone to flooding. On the right the Municipal Baths, built in 1892, can be seen. The indoor swimming, slipper and Turkish baths proved extremely popular. Attached to the indoor baths was the outdoor lido, a facility still much missed by local people.

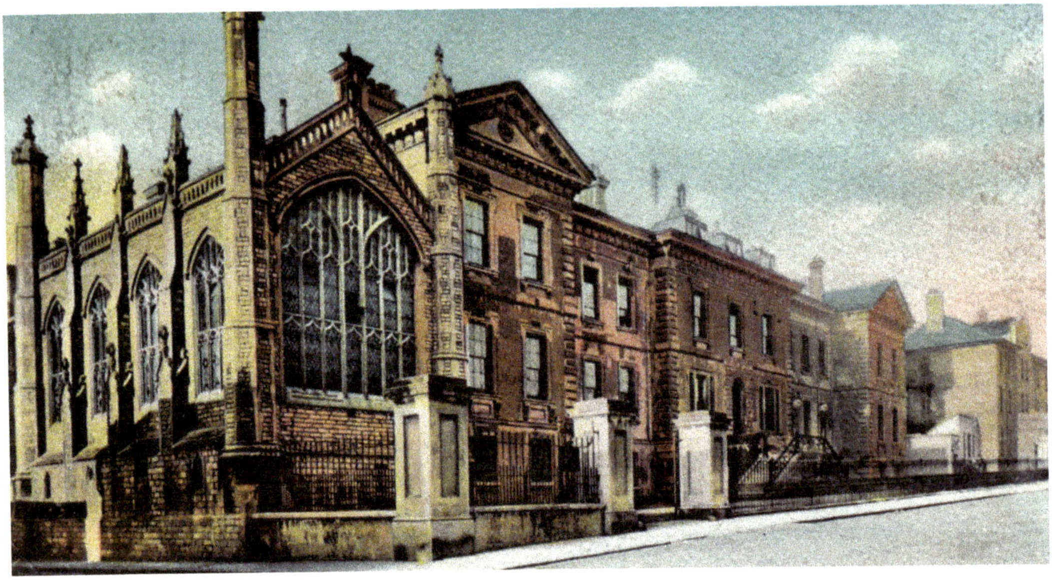

Royal South Hants Hospital, Fanshawe Street

Built in 1844 in Newtown, then a rural location, the hospital benefited from the 'clean air of the countryside'. The involvement of members of the Bullar, Fanshawe and Crabbe families in setting the hospital up ensured their names are still remembered in and around the hospital now. The chapel on the left of this picture still stands today.

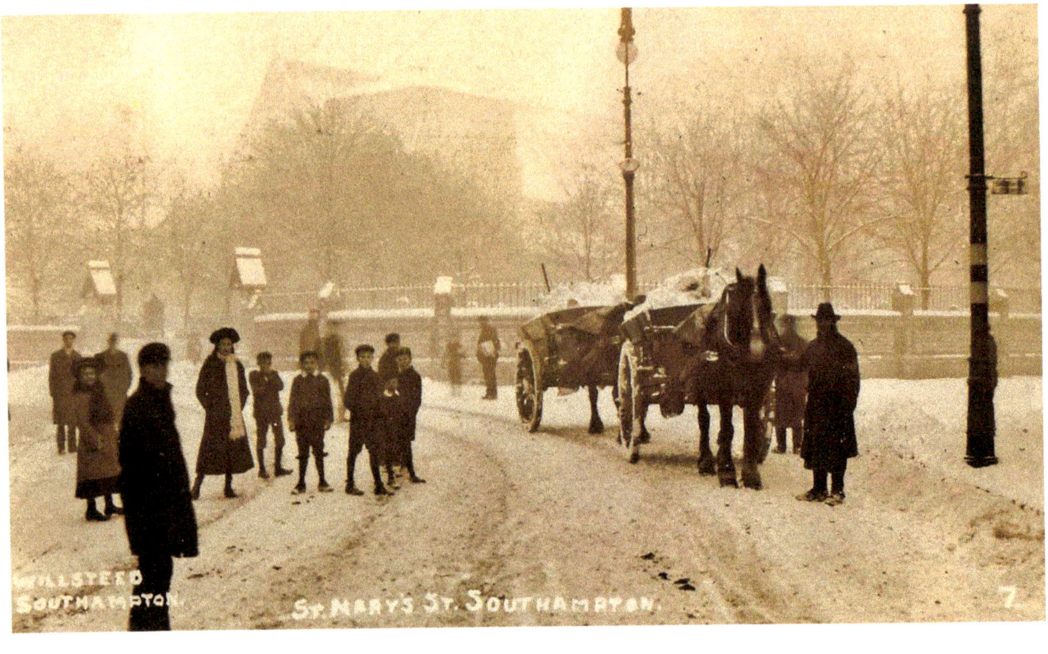

St Mary's Street

St Mary's Street and, in the background mist, the mother church of St Mary's. The heavy snowfall meant that the street cleaning crews and their horse and carts were employed to clear the main roads and pavements in the town. If the crews were close enough they took the fully laden carts to the nearest beach and dumped the snow on the tideline.

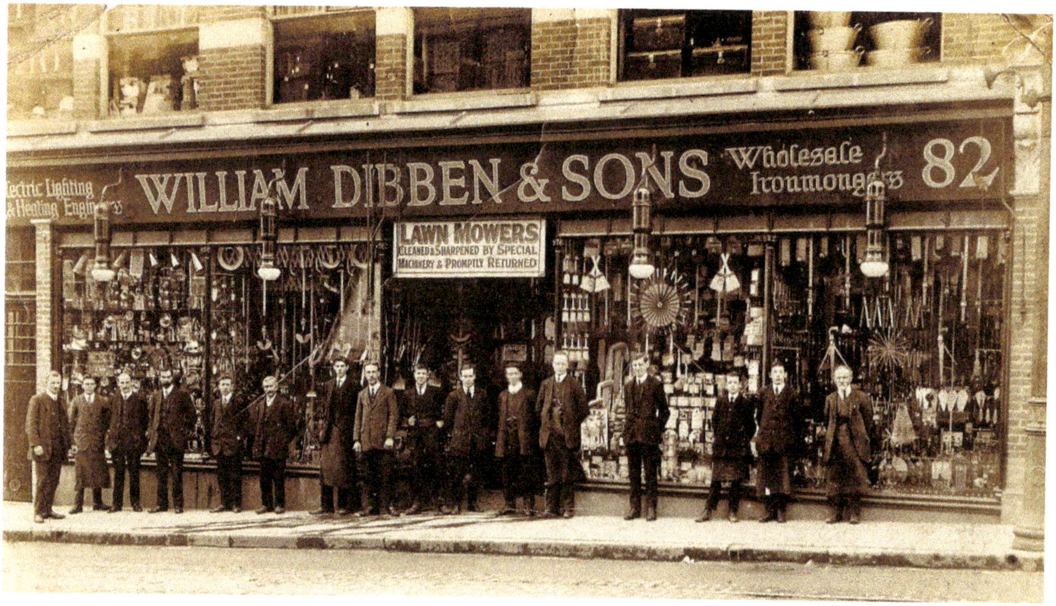

No. 82 St Mary's Road, 1912

William Dibben & Sons started in business in Southampton in 1874. Trading in all aspects of building, decorating supplies and ironmongery, the company expanded into owning brickworks in the area. Dibbens had outlets and business premises in many locations in Hampshire and even had premises in Torquay. They were a major employer, at one time having in excess of 1,100 staff.

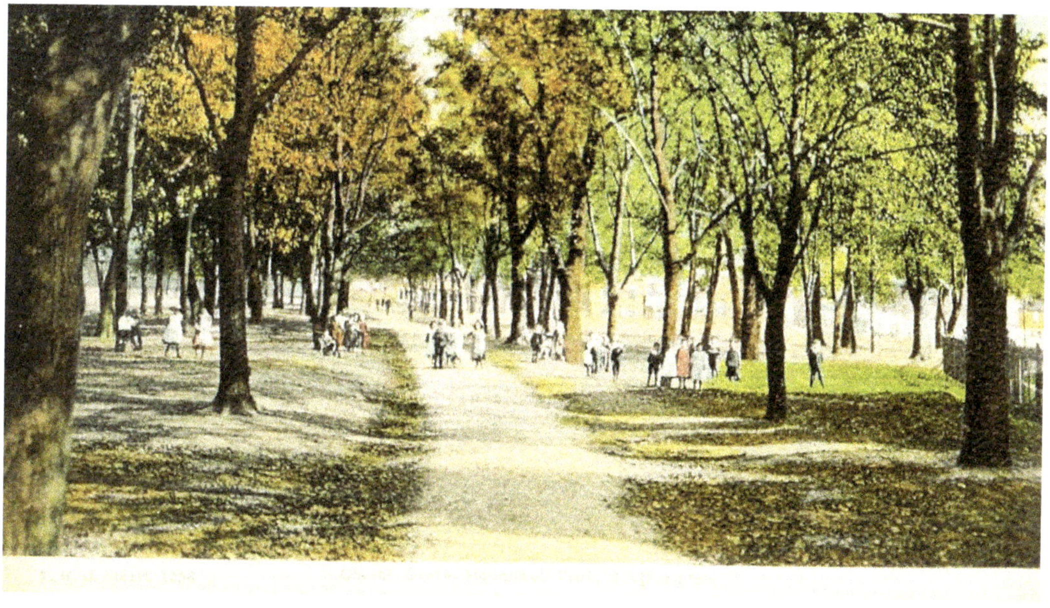

Hoglands Park

Church Grove is the old name for the avenue of trees that run from Houndwell across the park to St Mary's Church. During the Second World War it housed a US transit camp, which was later used by Southampton families whose homes had been destroyed or badly damaged during the air raids.

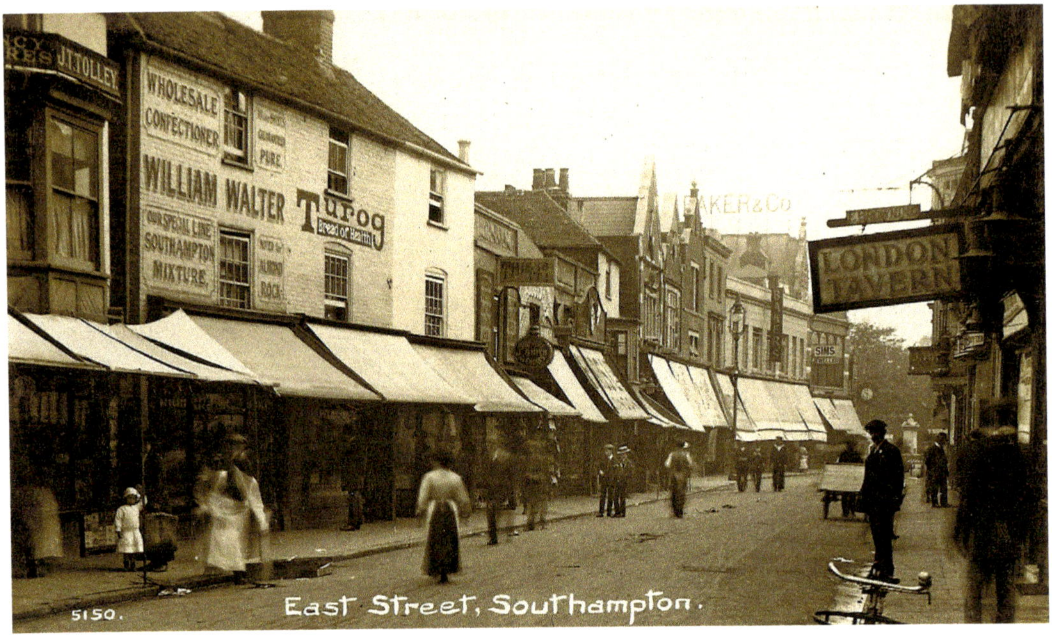

East Street, early 1900s
This animated scene shows the eastern end of East Street, which was one of the busiest shopping streets in the town, popular with townspeople seeking value for money. Everything a household needed could be found in East Street.

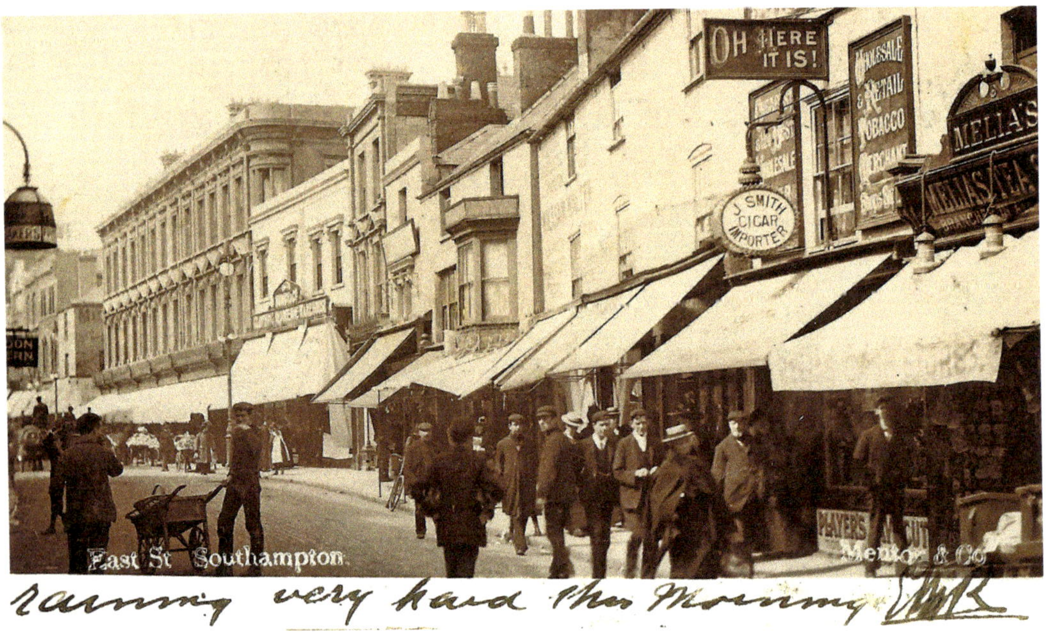

East Street, early 1900s
This very busy street ran from the High Street east to the St Mary's Church area. One of the oldest streets in the town, it had long been a popular destination for shoppers. The large building in the distance was the Edwin Jones department store, a new concept in shopping at that time.

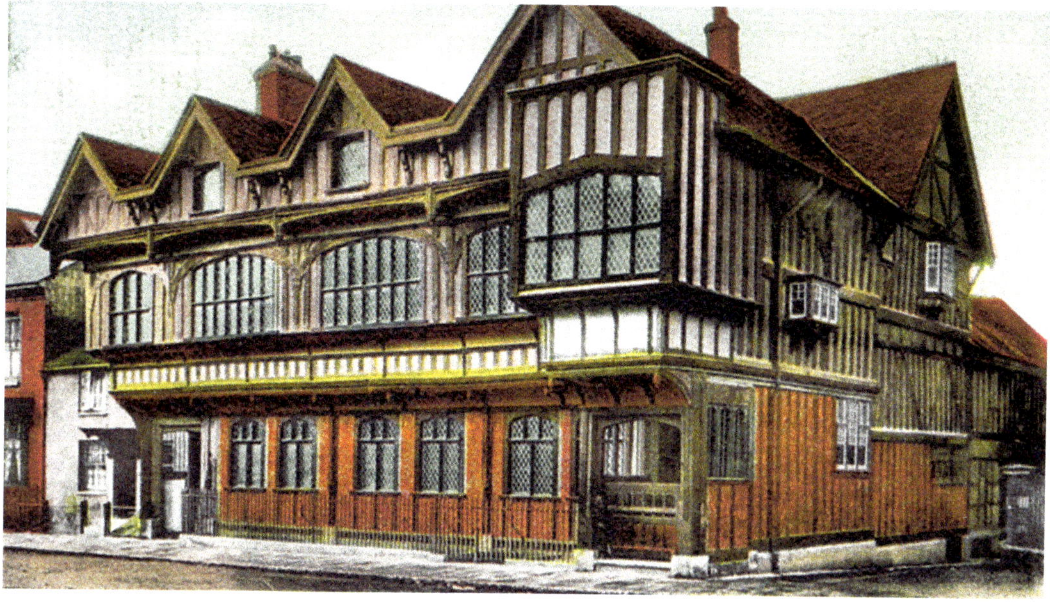

Tudor House

Tudor House is still in use today as a city museum. During its long history, spanning over 800 years, it has been a dwelling for various 'men of standing'. It has also been converted into shops and businesses, neglected, and even come close to demolition. Thankfully a local man, William Spranger, saved the house in the late 1800s, bequeathing it to the town some years later.

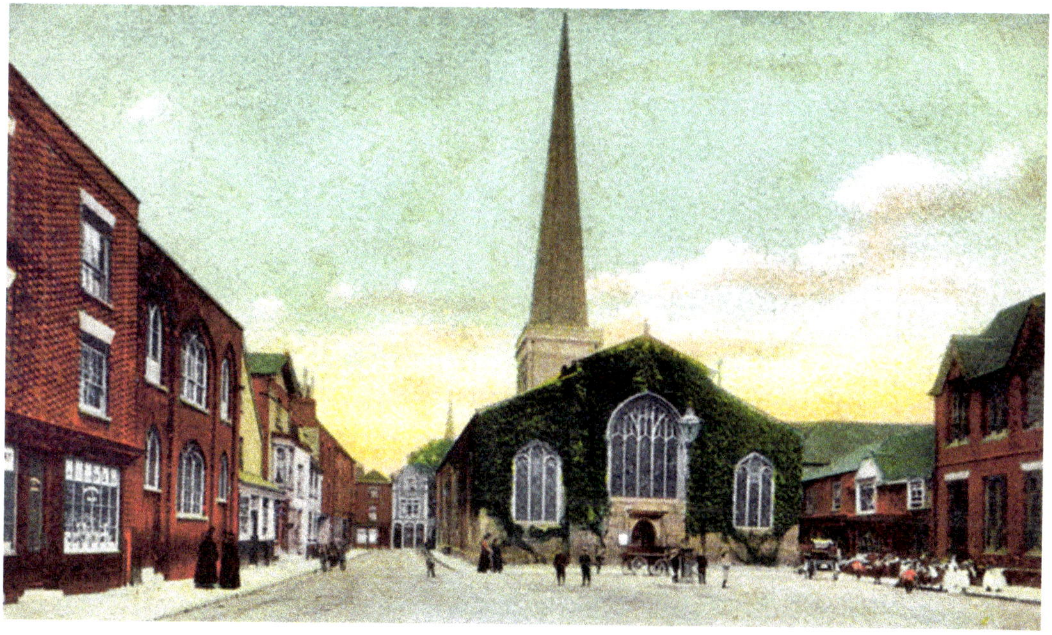

St Michael's Square and St Michael's Church

Founded in 1070, the church is claimed to be the oldest building in continuous use in Southampton. The square to the front of the church is relatively peaceful now, but in the medieval period this was a busy market square, used mainly as the fish market.

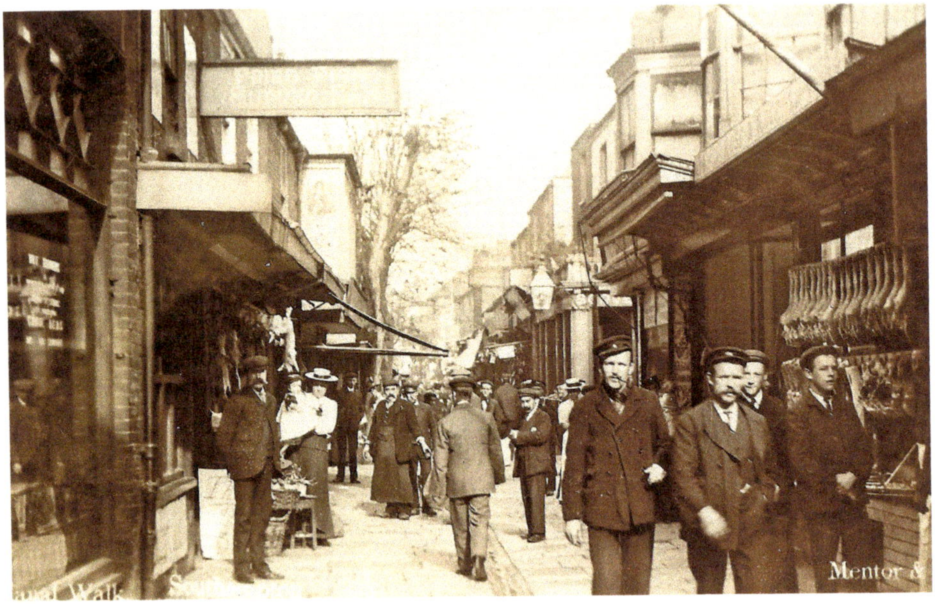

The Ditches, late 1800s

No postcard collection of Southampton would be complete without an image of The Ditches, or Canal Walk to use its designated name. It was a very narrow street that ran from East Street down to the water near God's House Tower. To say that everything you might need in life could be found there is no exaggeration. A street directory for that period would illustrate just how interesting and varied Canal Walk was.

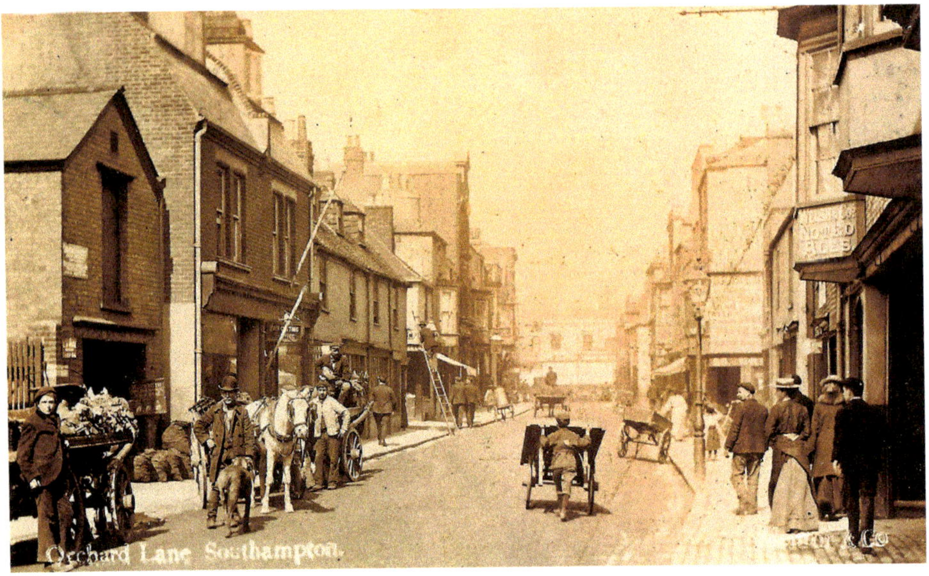

Orchard Lane, late 1800s

Orchard Lane runs from Bernard Street to East Street. Once the location of the medieval cultivated land just outside the town walls, this was where the townspeople grew their fruit trees and vegetables. The area continued to be the centre of the fruit and vegetable wholesale trade up until a few years ago.

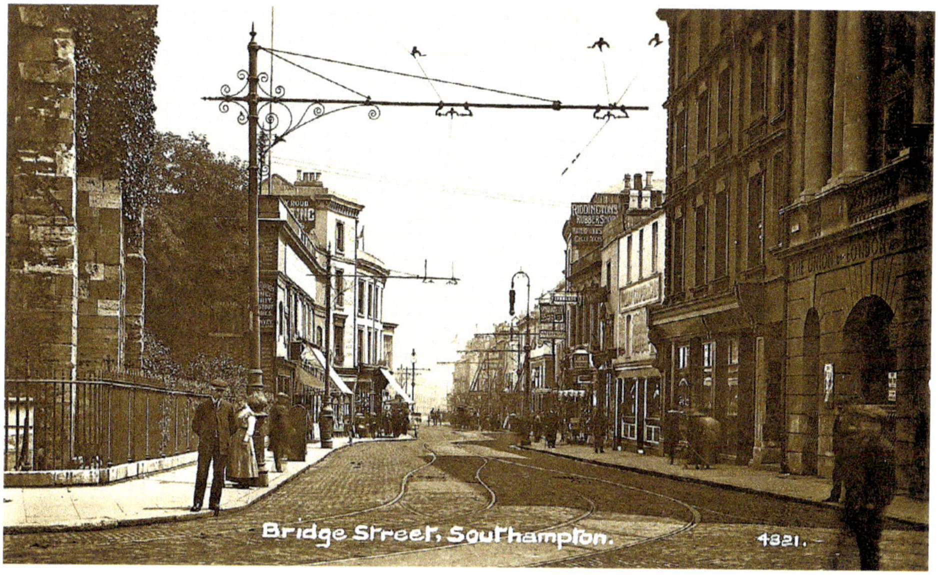

Bridge Street, late 1800s

This view shows Bridge Street at its junction with High Street. When this photograph was taken, this route east off the High Street was divided. In 1807 the narrow Pitts Lane was widened and the bridge over the town's defensive ditch removed. Eventually the whole thoroughfare was known as Bernard Street. We have often wondered why that tram rail was wavy.

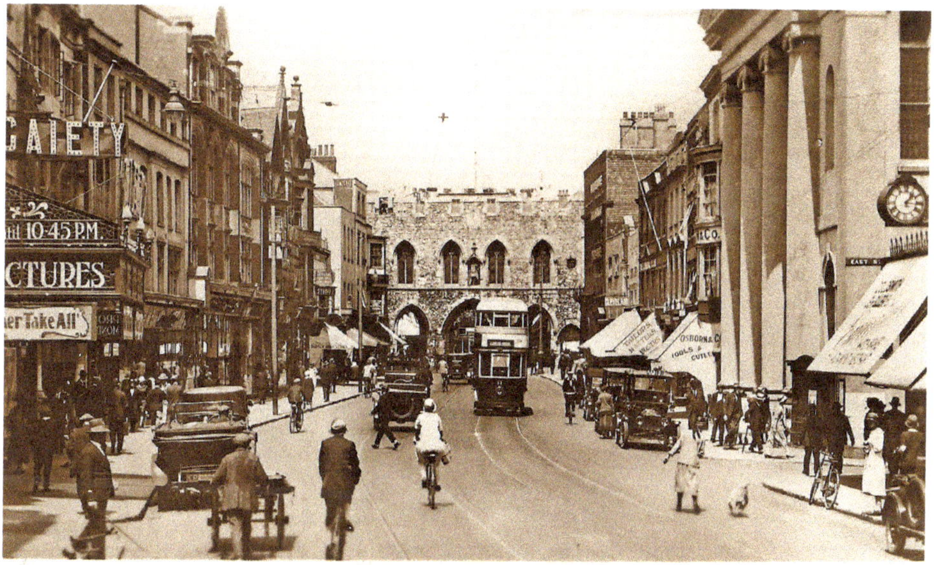

2164. F. G. O. Stuart. THE HIGH STREET, SOUTHAMPTON.

High Street/Below Bar, early 1920s or 1930s

The main street through the centre of Southampton was far more contained than it is now. It looked more intimate then, still showing its medieval origins. It was a very busy shopping area, but many found time to watch a film at the Gaiety cinema, pictured here on the left, or stand and gaze at the splendour of All Saints Church to the right.

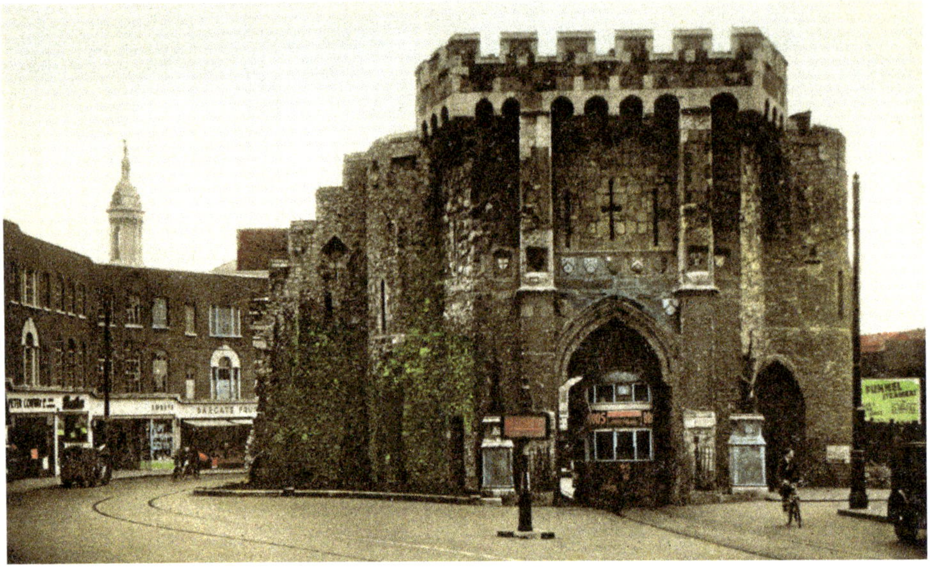

The Bargate, 1940s

The Bargate is probably the most photographed, drawn and painted building in Southampton. The north gate to the walled town, it dates back to at least the 1200s. It is pictured here between the wars, soon after it was detached from the medieval walls. The gaps were created to ease the passage of increasing traffic in the town.

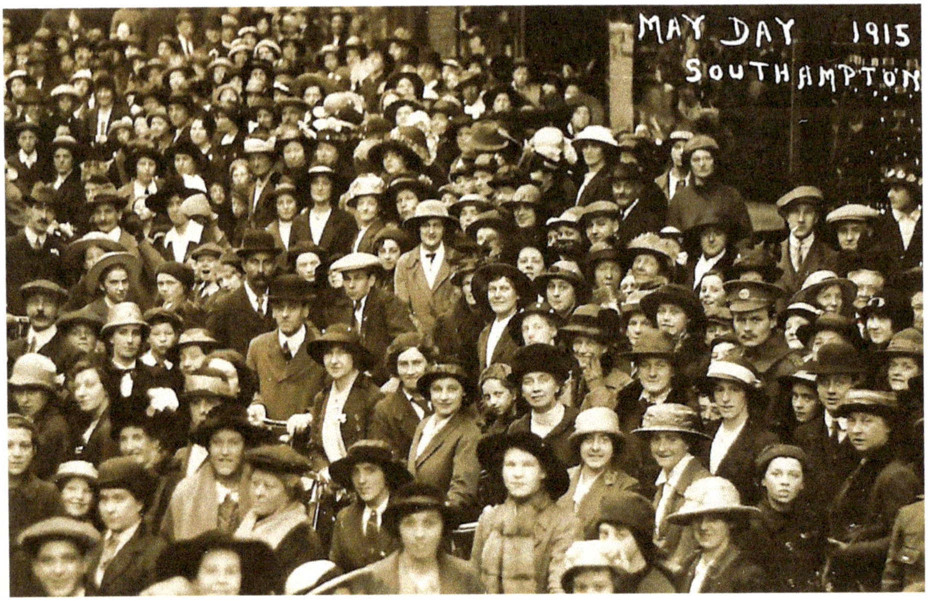

May Day Celebrations at the Bargate

It was a medieval tradition that spring was 'sung in' by choristers at dawn, on May Day, from the roof of the town's main gate. The ceremony was largely forgotten until the early 1900s when a local clergyman, Canon Neville Lovett, revived the event. As can be seen from this postcard, the ceremony proved popular with the townspeople. As with many crowd scenes from this period, the profusion of headwear is quite startling compared with today.

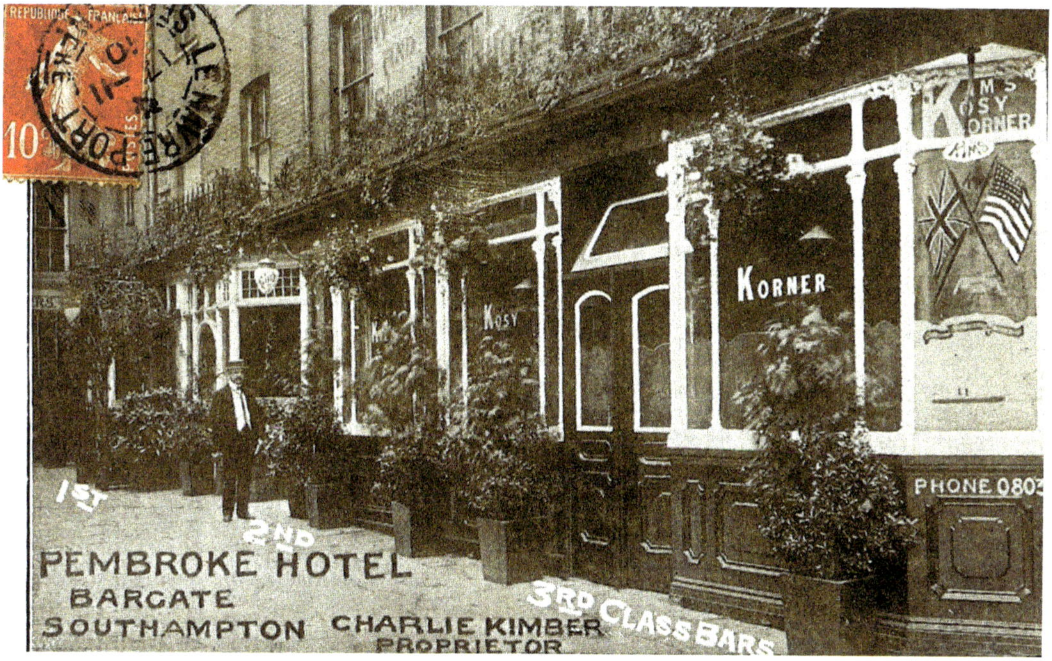

Pembroke Square, 1910

A small courtyard to the east of the Bargate, there had been a tavern on the site since the medieval period. It had various names, and at one point the tavern and the courtyard took the name Red Lion. It was a popular meeting place for local people.

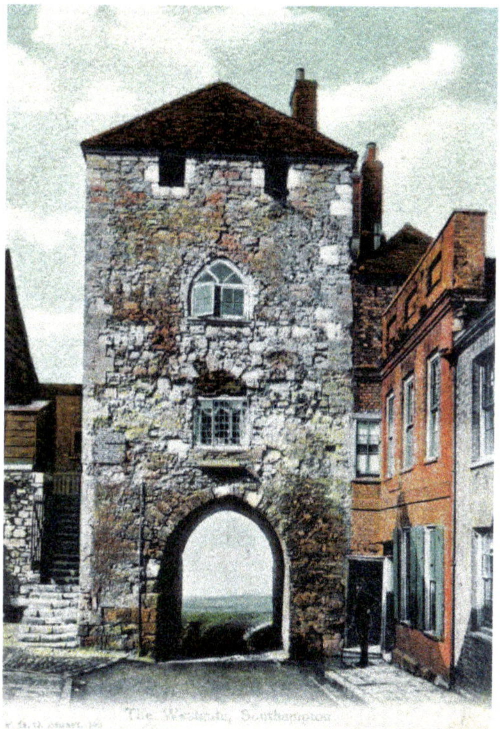

West Gate

The southern edge of the medieval town was thought secure, that is until French raiders arrived in 1338 and mounted a successful assault. In an effort to make Southampton less vulnerable to further attacks, the king decreed that the defensive town walls be extended to fully encircle the town. The West Gate, its main opening, was one of the last gates to be built along the improved defensive wall. Immediately outside the gate was the seashore and the town's west quay. Trade from around the world arrived through the West Gate. It was through this portal that the Pilgrim Fathers left for America and Henry V's army left for France.

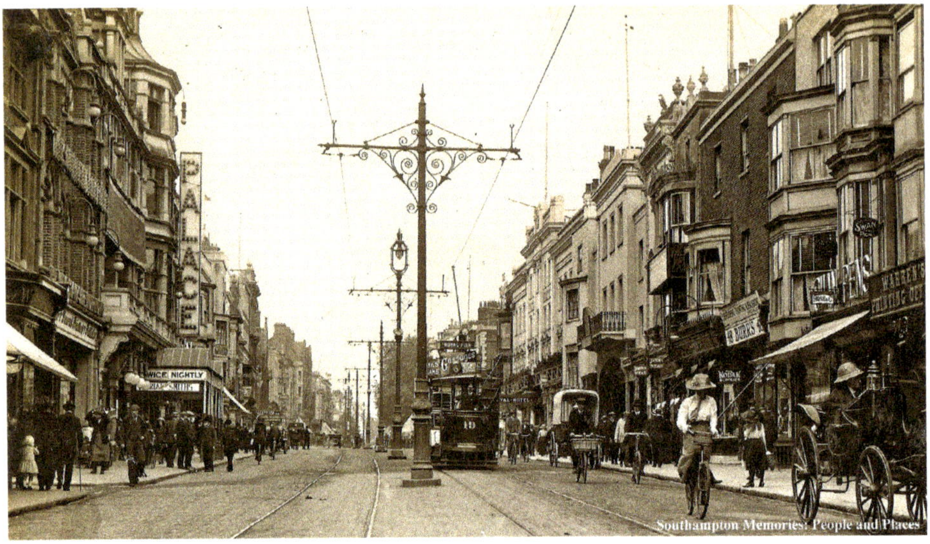

Above Bar Street, early 1900s

In effect, this road is a continuation of the High Street that runs north outside the medieval walled town. Sections of it were known by various names over the years: Boue Barre Street, Winchester Way and Hundswell Street. This much-travelled road was the main route north out of the old town.

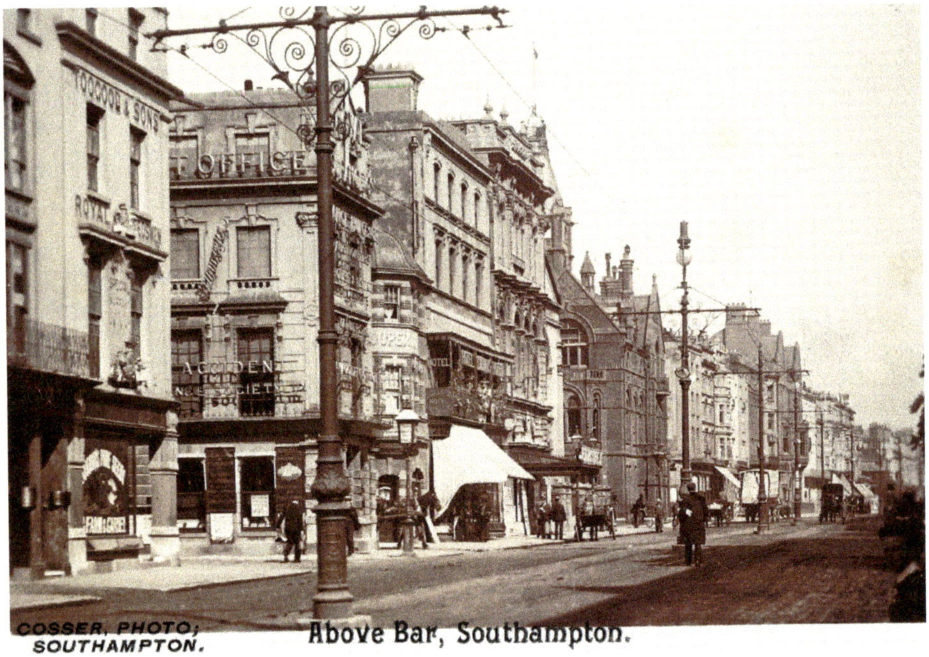

Above Bar Street, early 1900s

This postcard clearly illustrates the effect that time and armed conflict had on Southampton's main street. Only two of these buildings remain today, by coincidence both connected to the insurance industry. The General Accident Office building is shown here on the left, and in the far distance is the Prudential Assurance office.

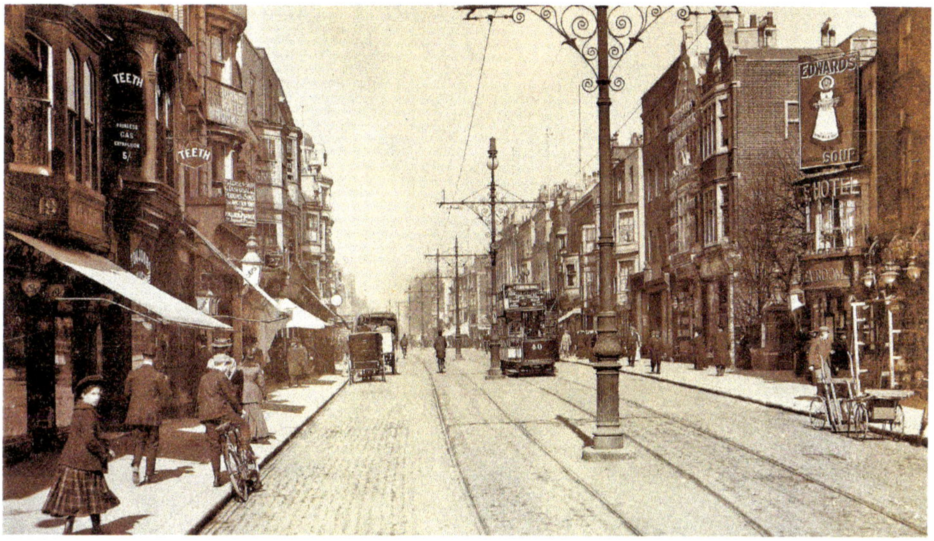

Above Bar Street, early 1900s
Postcards of street scenes never fail to provide interest. This one shows the ornate street poles that carried the electricity supply to the town's trams, the inquisitive look of passers-by and the signs above the shops advertising soup powder to buy, perhaps best enjoyed while recovering from one of those 5*s* tooth extractions.

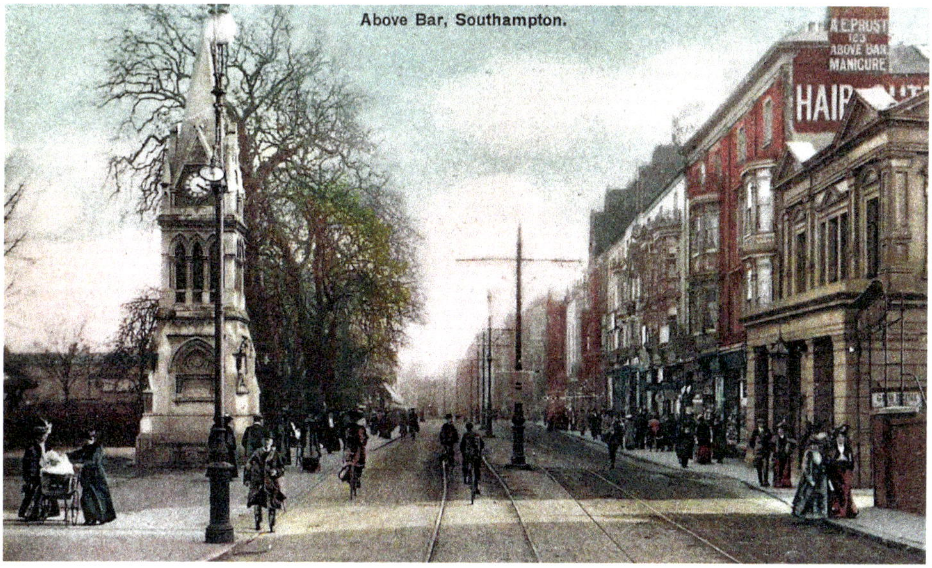

Clock Tower, Above Bar
One of the monuments bequeathed to the town by resident Henrietta Sayers, the Sayers Monument, as it was originally called, stood in the centre of the junction of Above Bar Street and New Road. It was built as a drinking fountain for horses and the passing townspeople. Eventually the monument became more popularly known as the Clock Tower, and was well used as a meeting point or simply as a place to stand and watch the world go by. In 1935 it was deemed to be impeding traffic flow, and a decision was made to move it to its present position at Bitterne Park Triangle.

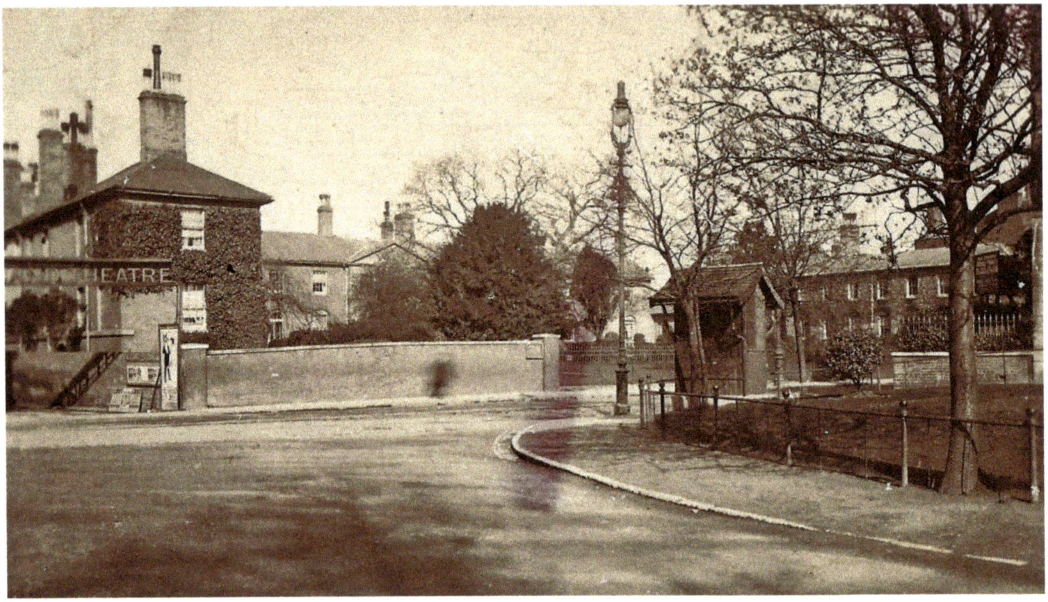

Above Bar Street and New Road, 1910s

This postcard shows the view across Above Bar Street from New Road. The ivy-clad buildings in the background were the Thorner Homes, providing sheltered housing for 'gentle-folk', which was provided by a local charity set up by a Baddesley man, Robert Thorner. The homes dated back to 1798. To the left we can just see the narrow lane that led up to the Grand Theatre.

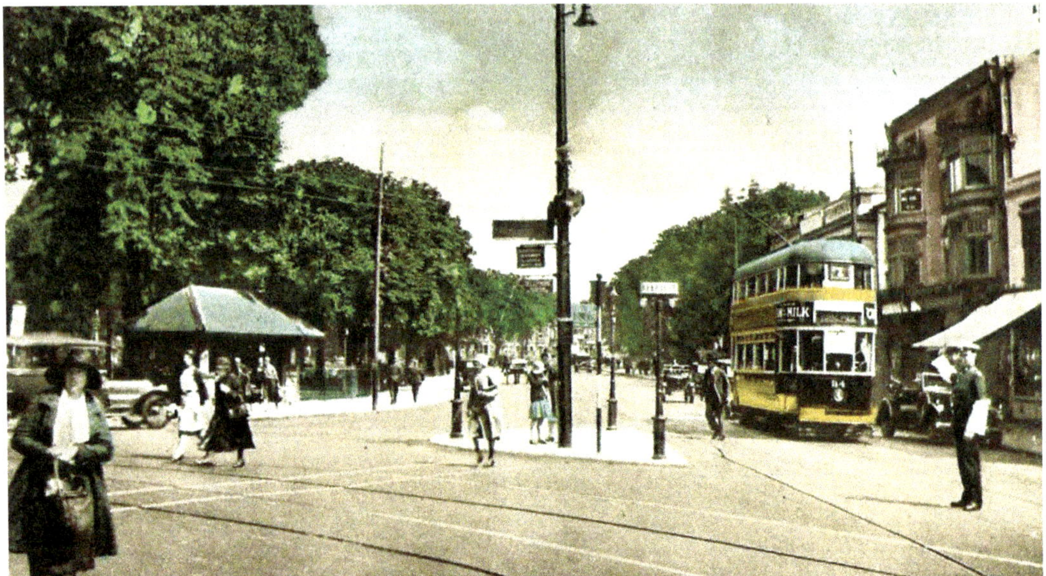

The Junction, Above Bar, early 1930s

This busy scene shows The Junction, the meeting point of Above Bar Street and Commercial Road, overshadowed by the Plummer Roddis Department Store. The store was destroyed in the Blitz, but was rebuilt and reopened in 1965, trading until its final closure in 1993.

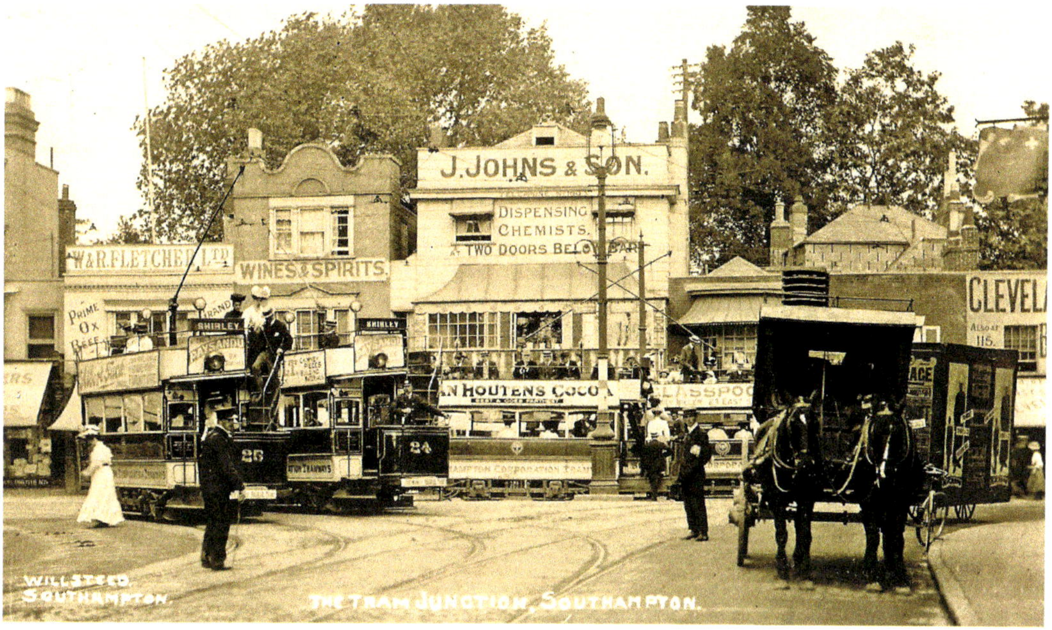

Prospect Place, late 1800s

Something of a traffic jam at Prospect Place in Above Bar Street, now known as The Junction. This postcard clearly illustrates just how popular the tram system traffic was.

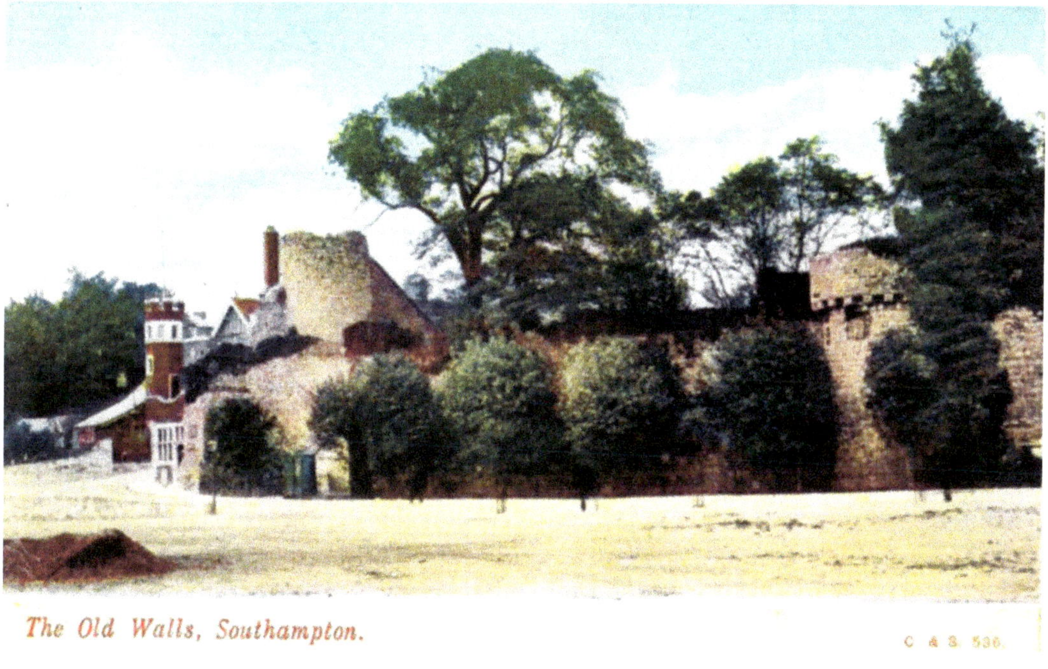

The Old Walls

The north-west corner of the town's medieval walls. The drum-tower seen here is Arundel Tower, named after a governor of Southampton Castle. Behind the tower can be seen the Arundel Towers Hotel, formerly known as the Plumbers Arms.

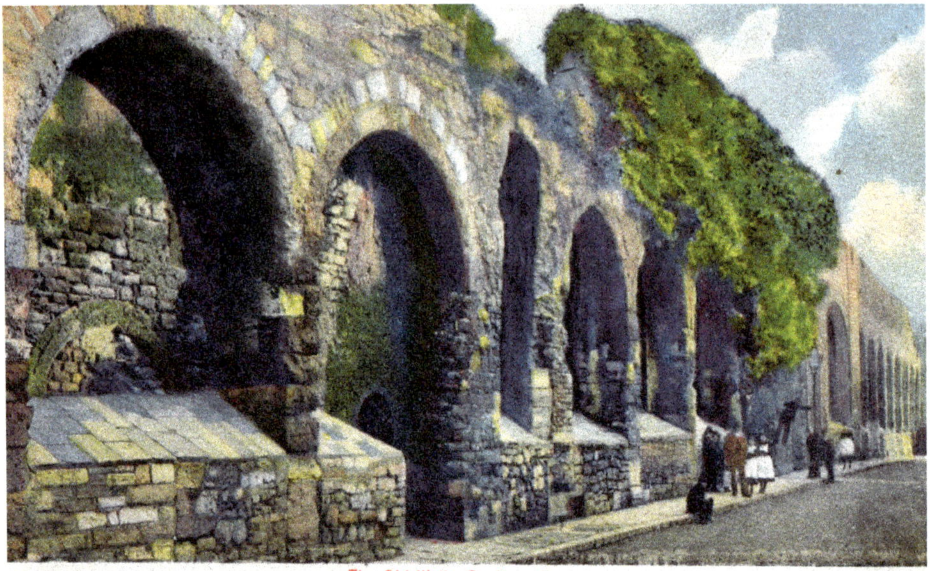

F. G. O. Stuart. 649 The Old Walls, Southampton

The Western Walls

The defensive wall around the medieval town has its own detailed history. Norman merchants built their stone houses directly onto the shore to enable the unloading of goods. Their houses provided a weak link when the walls were built. After a raid by the French in the early 1300s, the buildings were blocked off and this arcade is the result.

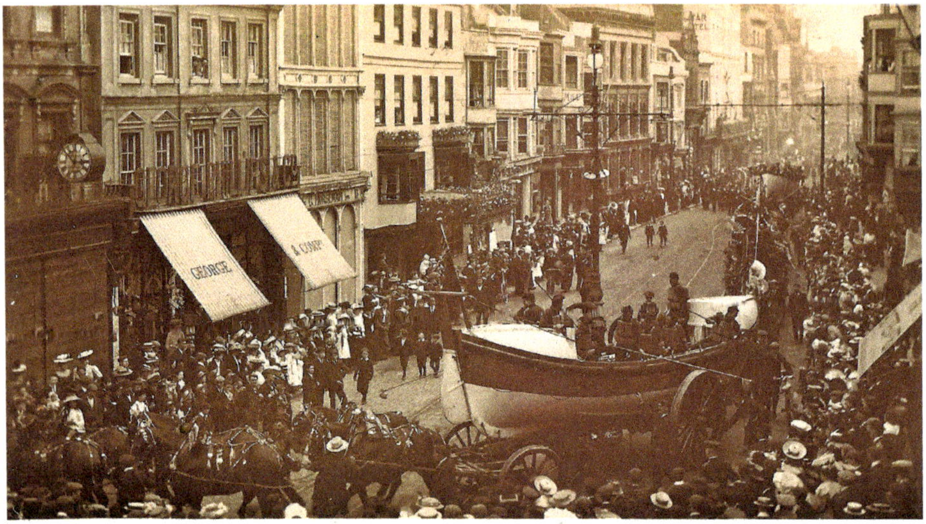

LIFEBOAT DEMONSTRATION, SOUTHAMPTON, 1906.

High Street, 1906

This lively scene shows the 1906 lifeboat demonstration and fundraising parade. Although Southampton has never had a lifeboat station in the port, its people had a good track record of generous donations to the Lifeboat Institute. Having a large population of mariners and their families living in the town, the value of this important volunteer service has long been recognised.

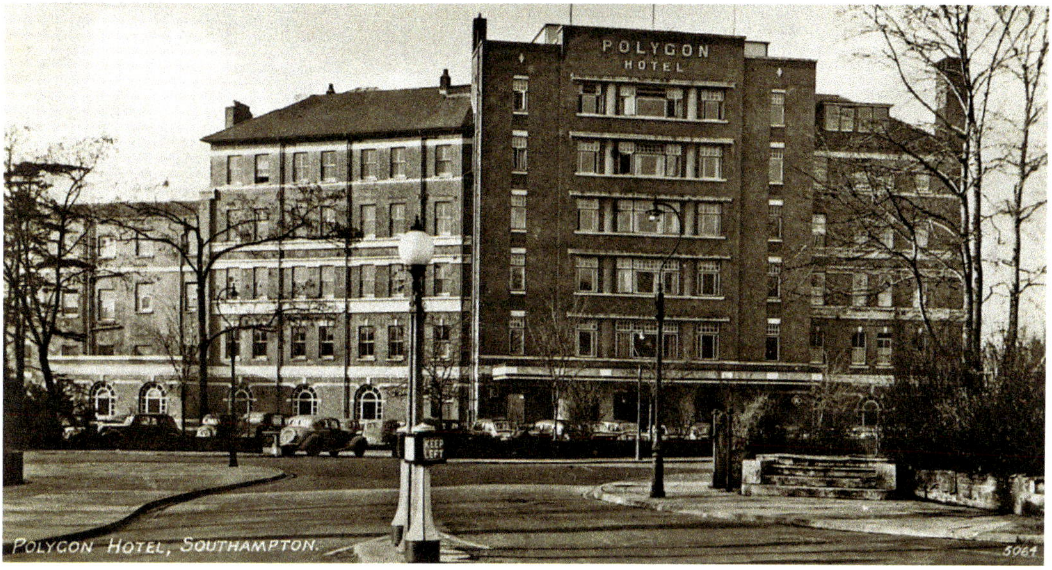

The Polygon Hotel
In its day, this was considered the top hotel in the town. Its proximity to the town's largest theatre ensured it was first choice for all the major performers. Originally built in the early 1800s, it underwent extensive redevelopment in 1870 and again in 1930. It was demolished in 1999 and a large apartment block was built on the site.

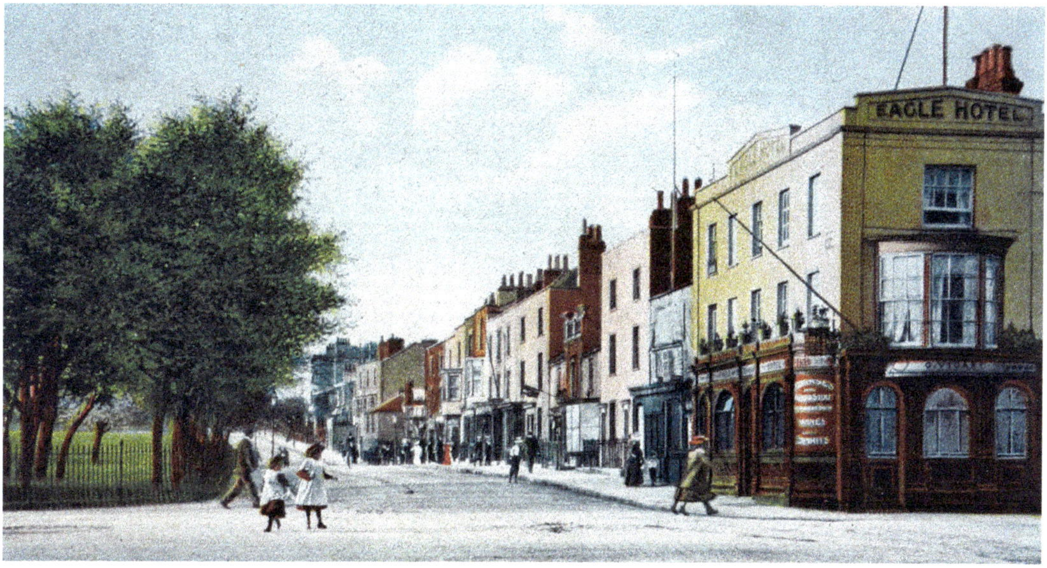

Palmerston Road
The road that connected Hoglands with New Road was named after the 3rd Viscount Palmerston, prime minister from 1859–65. Palmerston had strong connections to the area, as an MP for South Hampshire and as a burgess of the town. The Eagle Hotel was one of three hostelries in the road, but like so many pubs in the city, it recently closed and was converted into a modern mini supermarket.

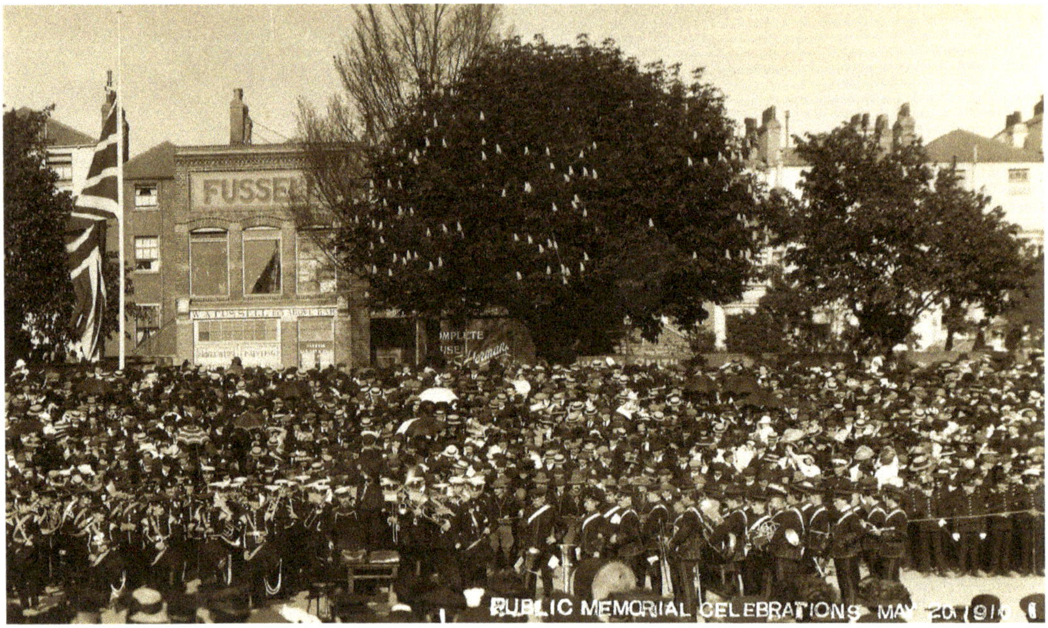

West Marlands, 1910

A huge crowd gathers on the public Lammas lands to the west of Above Bar Street. This area is now occupied by the Civic Centre, the administration offices for local government. The offices of Fussell's, the decorator and building company, can be seen in the background located in West Marlands Road.

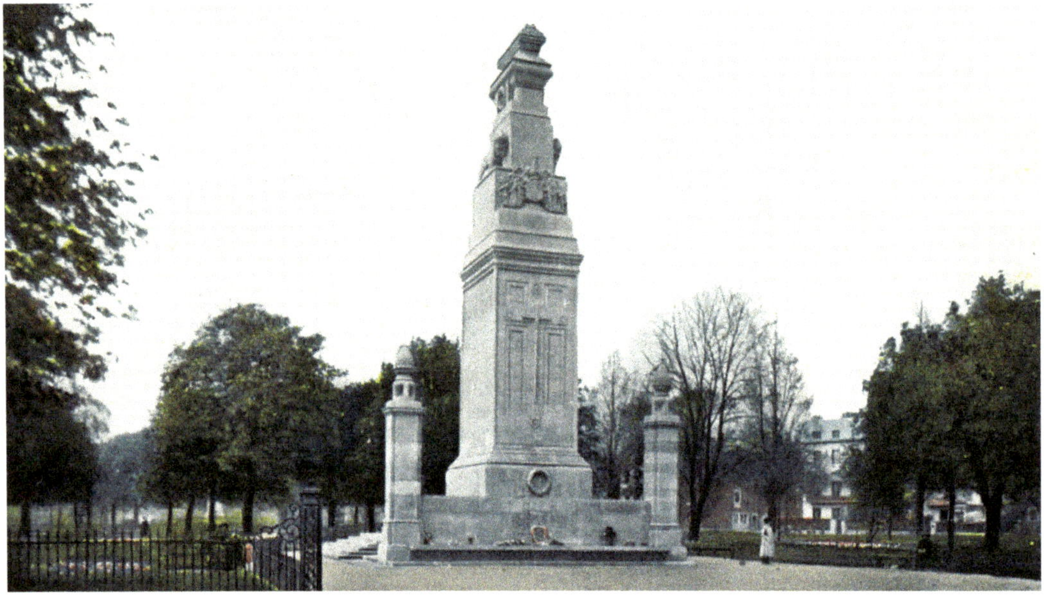

The Cenotaph, West Park

Commissioned by Sir Sidney Kimber after the end of the First World War, the memorial was designed by Edwin Lutyens. Built with a cast-iron internal framework and clad in Portland stone, the Grade II-listed edifice was unveiled in November 1920 as a lasting memorial to those who fought and died for their country.

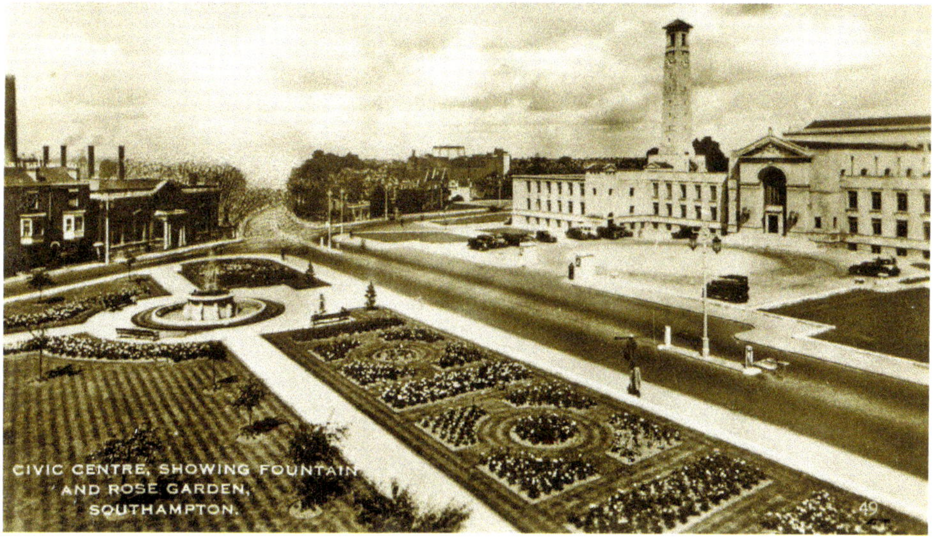

Civic Centre, late 1930s

After year of discussion, the town council decided that there should be a purpose-built seat of local government. The area known as West Marlands (common land) was chosen, and over a period of years in the 1930s the magnificent Civic Centre was built. The area to the front of the centre was laid out as a rose garden, complete with a fountain. The new road seen in this postcard was extended down towards the main railway station. It couldn't have been completed when this picture was taken as a crude attempt at drawing it in can be seen.

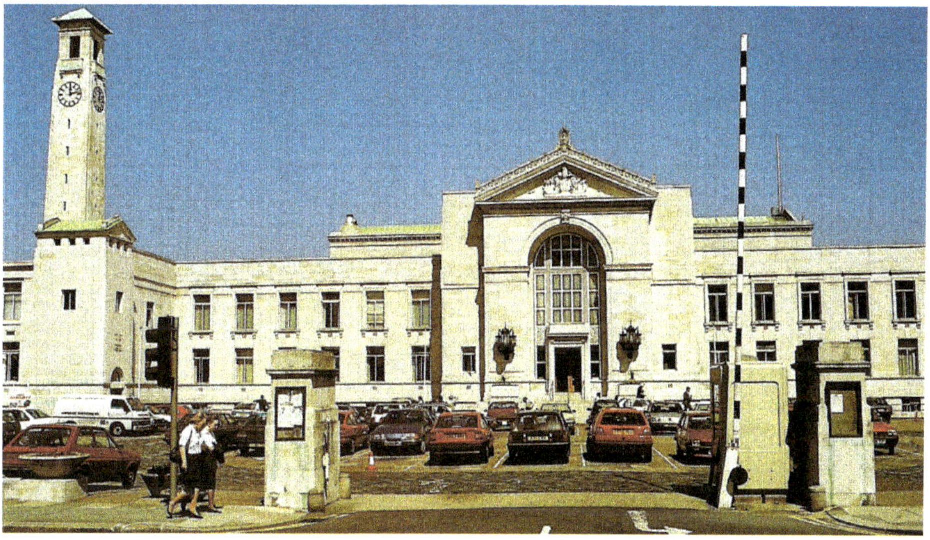

Civic Centre, 1990s

This unremarkable 1990s scene gives few clues as to the history associated with the city's administrative offices. Built in four separate stages in 1932, 1933, 1937, 1939, its construction was largely thanks to the energy of local politician Sir Sidney Kimber. Completed just prior to the commencement of the Second World War, the building was bombed once during a daylight raid. The art school in the northern block was hit and there were thirty-five fatalities, fourteen of which were schoolchildren.

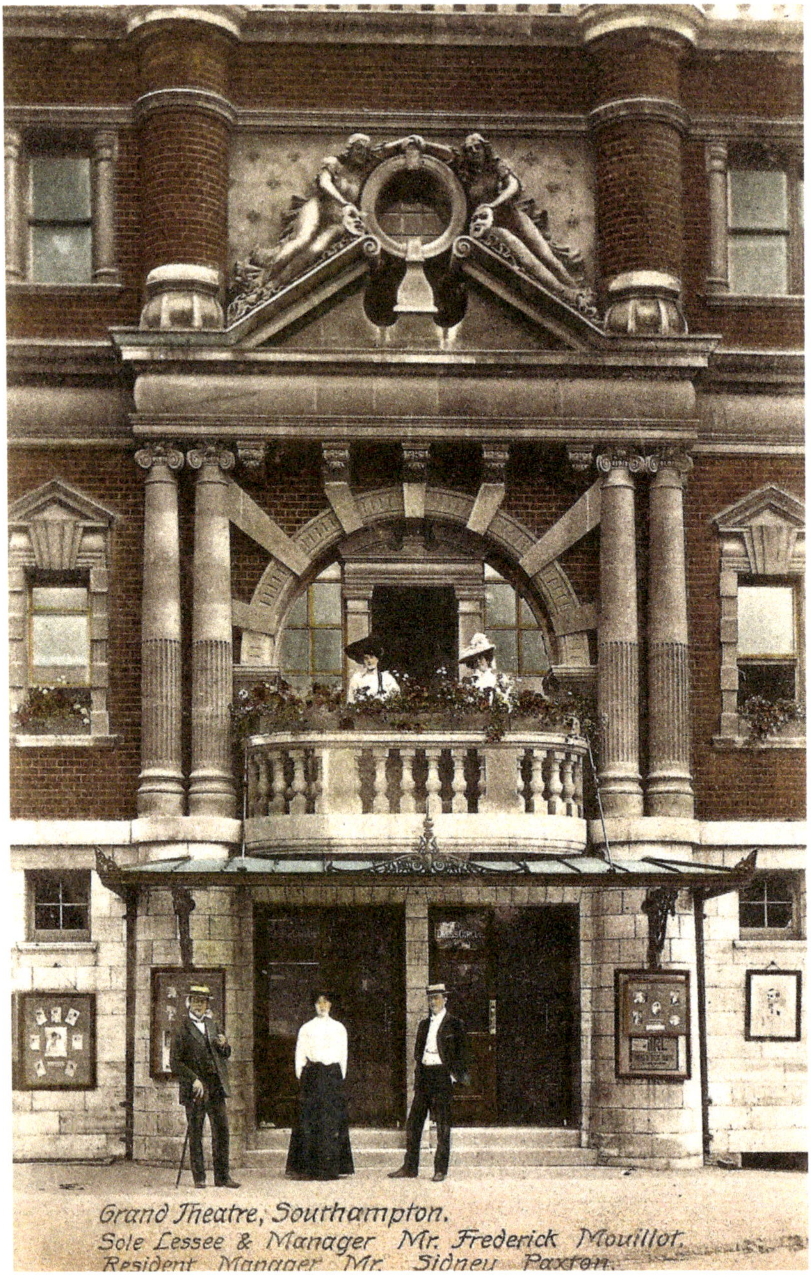

The Grand Theatre, *c.* 1905

The magnificent and ornate Grand Theatre, the most popular of Southampton's theatres. Built facing the West Marlands, the Lammas land that became the location for the Civic Centre, the Grand Theatre played host to such famous names as Sir Henry Irving and Sarah Bernhardt. In its heyday it was difficult to get a ticket to any show at the theatre. It survived the Blitz of the Second World War, and during that conflict it housed troops. A post-war refurbishment programme boosted business for a few years, but its audiences gradually declined as television gained its hold. The Grand Theatre closed in 1959 and was demolished a year later.

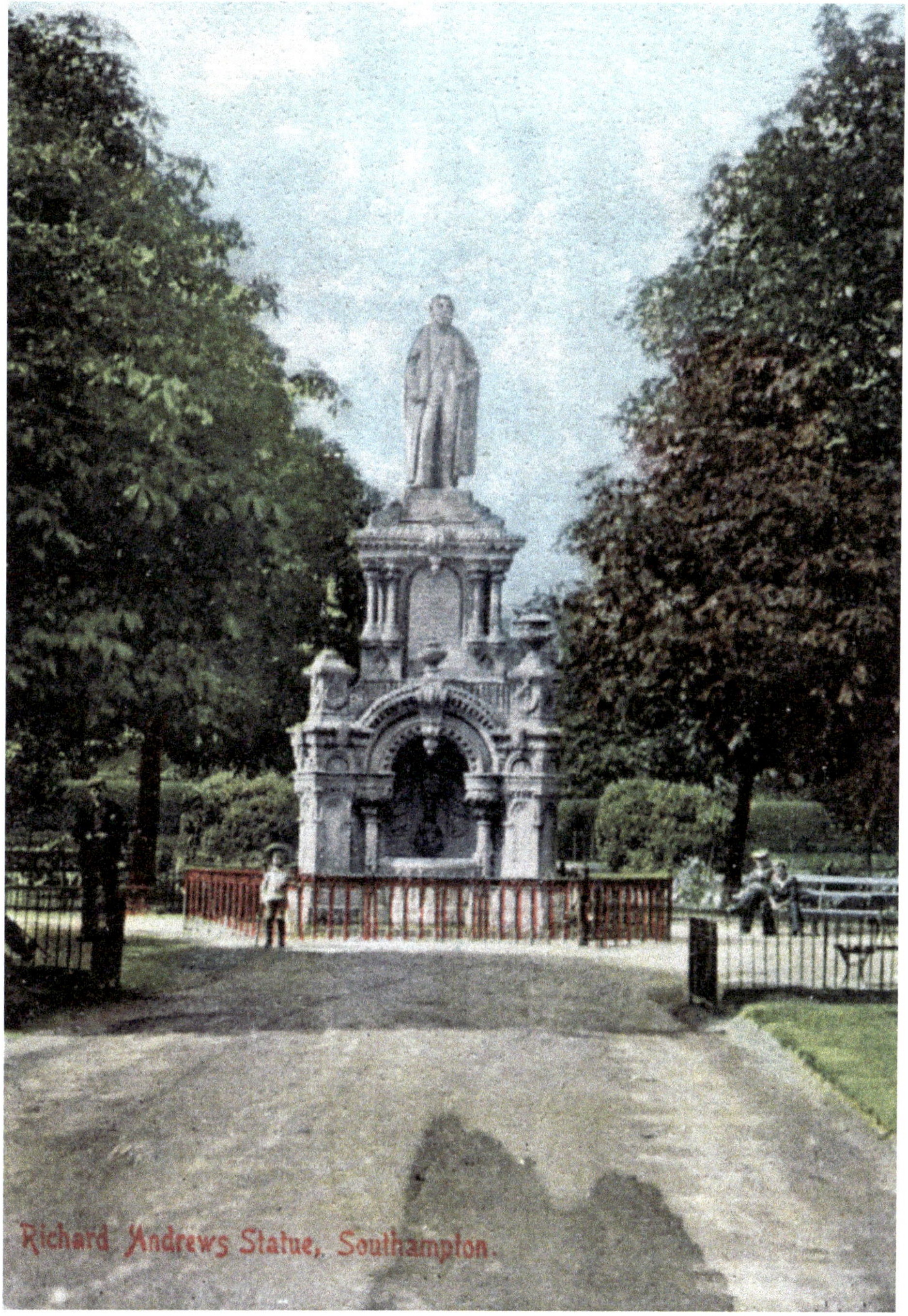

Richard Andrews Statue, East Park

Renowned the world over as a coachbuilder, Richard Andrews was a popular employer whose premises stood in Above Bar Street. By the time of his death in 1859, Andrews had served as mayor of Southampton five times. He is commemorated by this monument, which stands in East Park, now also known as Andrews Park. It is reported that some 4,000 people were present to witness the laying of its foundation stone.

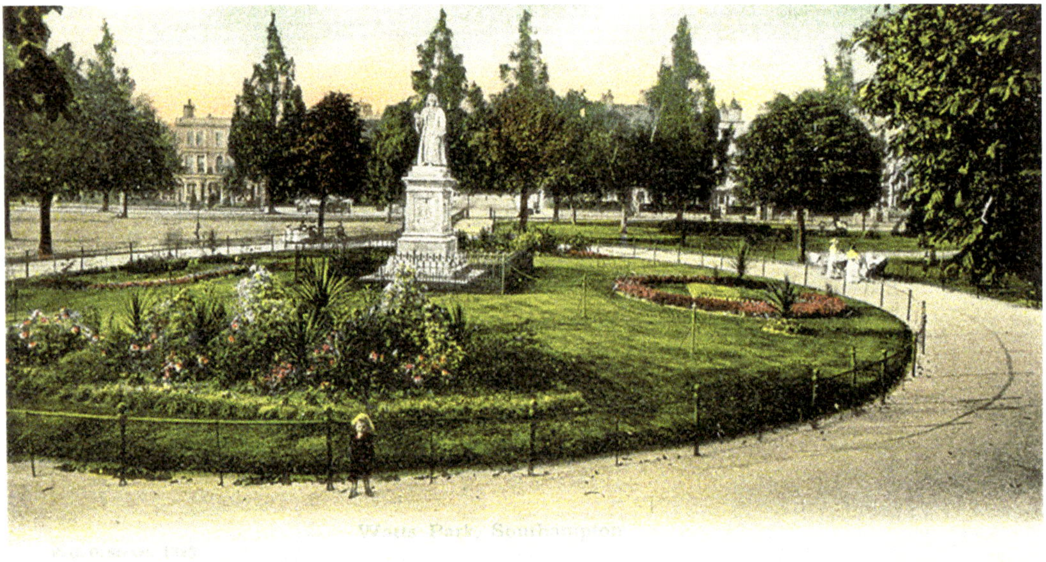

The West Park

The West Park showing the memorial to Isaac Watts, with the elegant Cumberland Place in the background. The statue was designed by local artist Richard Cockle Lucas. The tribute to Watts – teacher, poet and hymn writer – was unveiled in 1861.

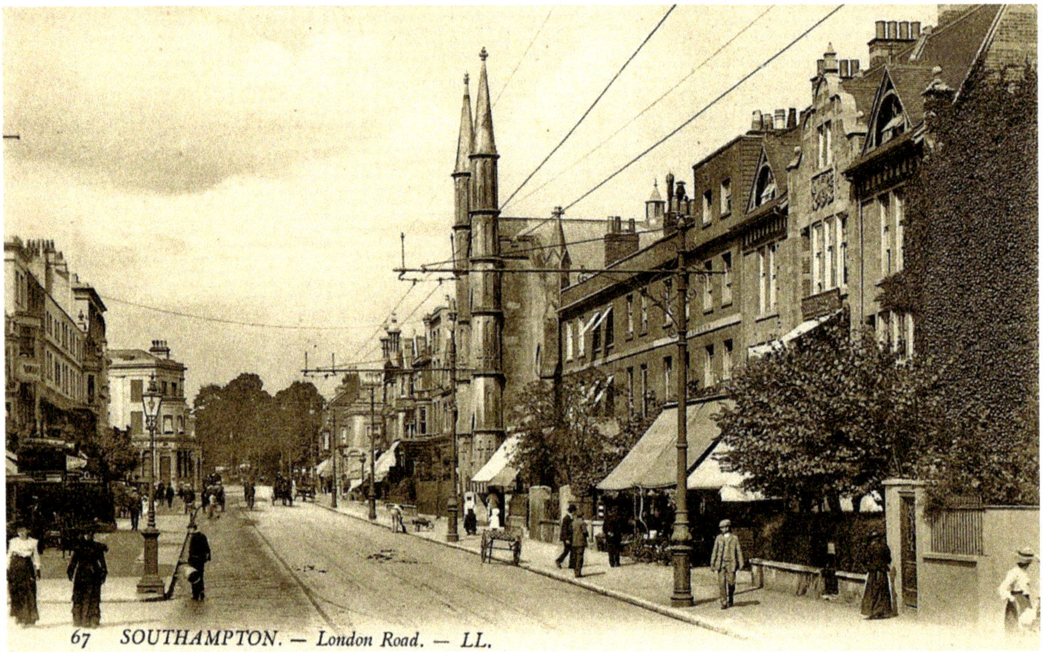

London Road, early 1900s

The story of Southampton is one of expansion as the old walled town became too crowded for the increasing population. London Road was a continuation of Above Bar Street, the main route north out of the town. In the 1900s it lay between two areas of the town that contained housing for the middle and upper classes. The shops along London Road reflected that fact.

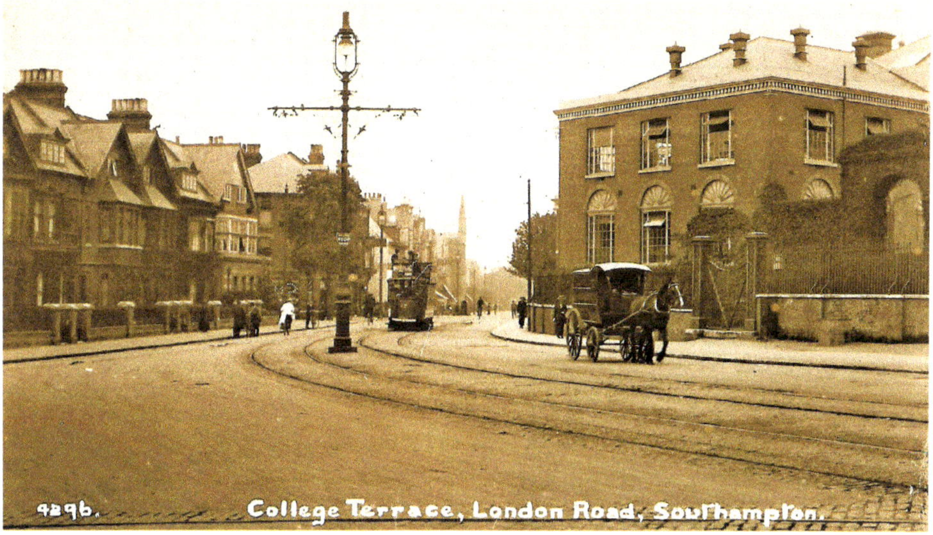

College Terrace

This postcard shows College Terrace at the north end of London Road where it joins the lower avenue at Asylum Green. On the right, part of the original Ordnance Survey Headquarters can be seen.

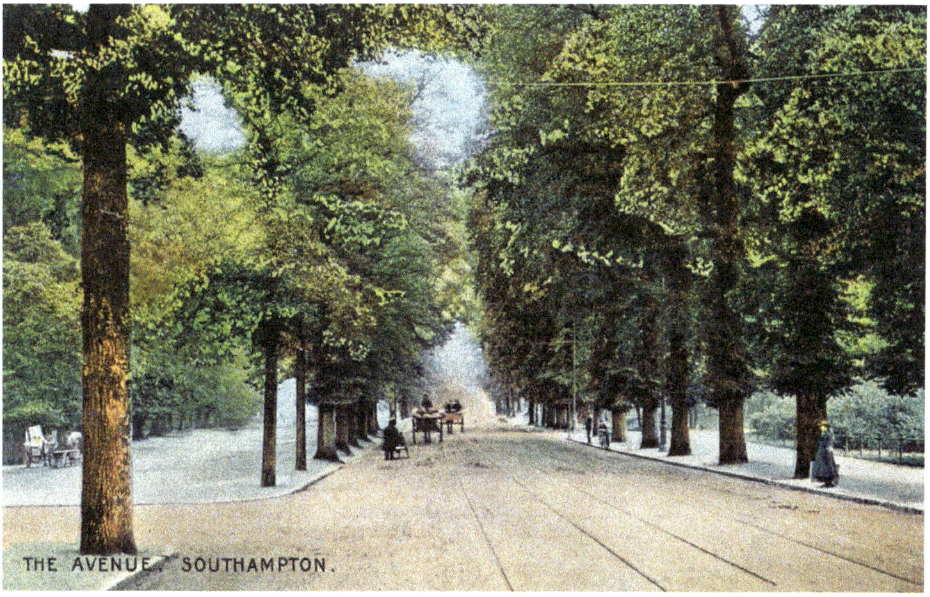

The Avenue, late 1800s

Originally no more than a cattle track in the medieval period, the Avenue slowly became the main route into the town from the north, carrying horse-ridden and drawn traffic in and out of Southampton. When the town became a fashionable spa destination, the decision was taken to plant the entire length from London Road to the north end of the Common with a grand avenue of trees. In the 1800s and early 1900s, during clement weather, the genteel townspeople enjoyed promenading up and down the Avenue under the shade of the trees.

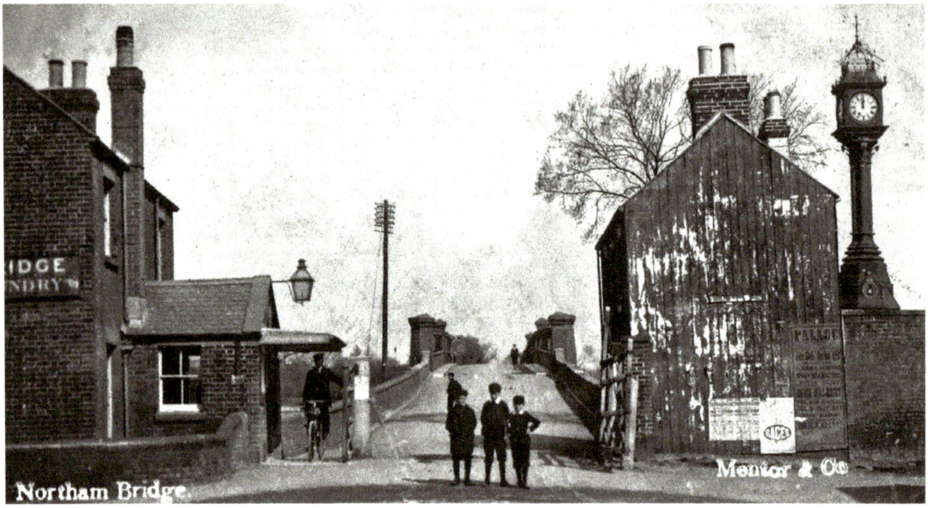

Northam Toll Bridge, late 1800s

The first bridge across the River Itchen within the town boundary was a wooden construction built in 1799. Ninety years later, that was replaced by an iron bridge. The bridge was run by a turnpike company, which collected tolls from those crossing the river. In 1929 the town council took over the bridge and rendered it toll free. The clock seen on the right in this postcard was donated by a member of the Chamberlayne family and stood near a small open-air seawater bathing pool known as the Chamberlayne Baths.

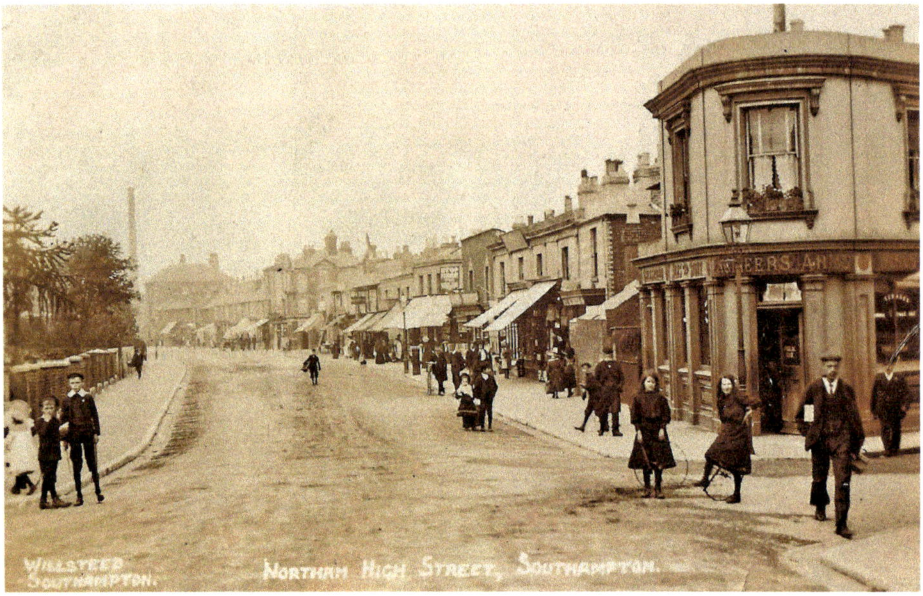

Northam, late 1800s

An early example of retail ribbon development. As the suburbs expanded during the late Victorian and into the Edwardian period, retail shops soon followed to supply the growing number of households. The main Northam Road, heading east out to the bridge crossing of the River Itchen, had a varied selection of shops, not to mention those all-important public houses.

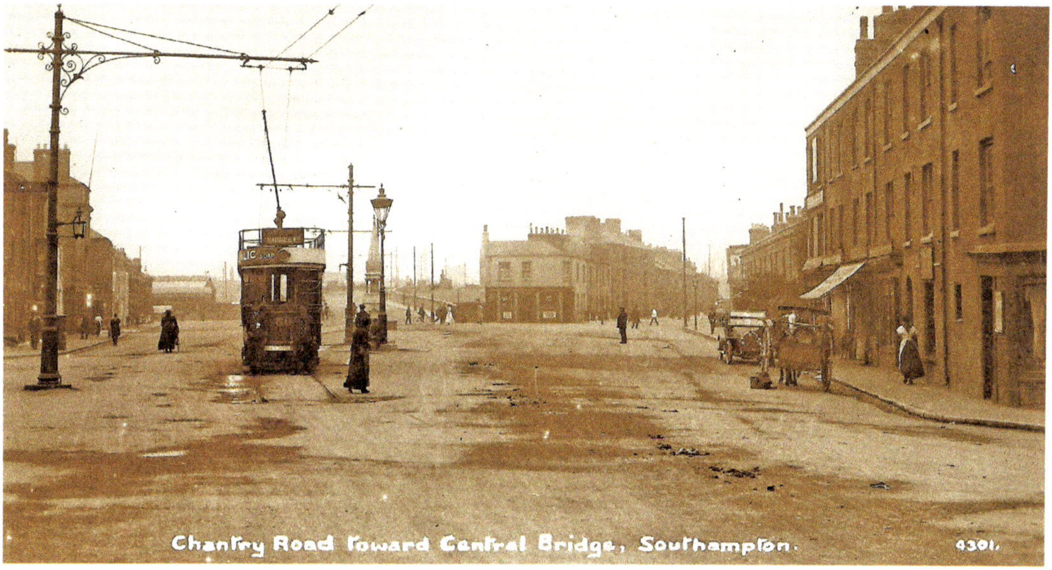

Chantry Road, Chapel, late 1800s
The broad expanse of Chantry Road, this time showing the view that awaited passengers walking towards town from the direction of the Floating Bridge across the River Itchen. The large enclave of Chapel to the right consisted of streets of Victorian terraced houses, built for those working in the riverside quays and Southampton docks. To the left of the camera lay the Eastern Docks, while the road bridge in the distance took the traveller up over the railway line and into the town itself.

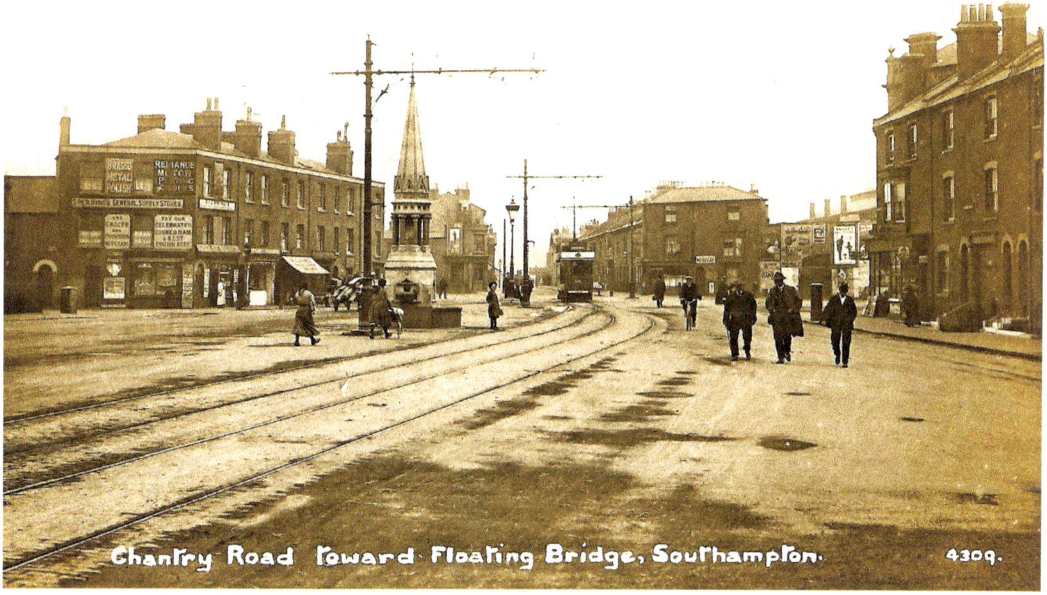

Chantry Road, Chapel, late 1800s
Another view of this wide expanse of road, which led down towards the River Itchen and the Floating Bridge to the east side of the town. The monumental fountain in the centre of the road was donated by Mrs Henrietta Sayers. Its fate remains unknown following its removal from this location.

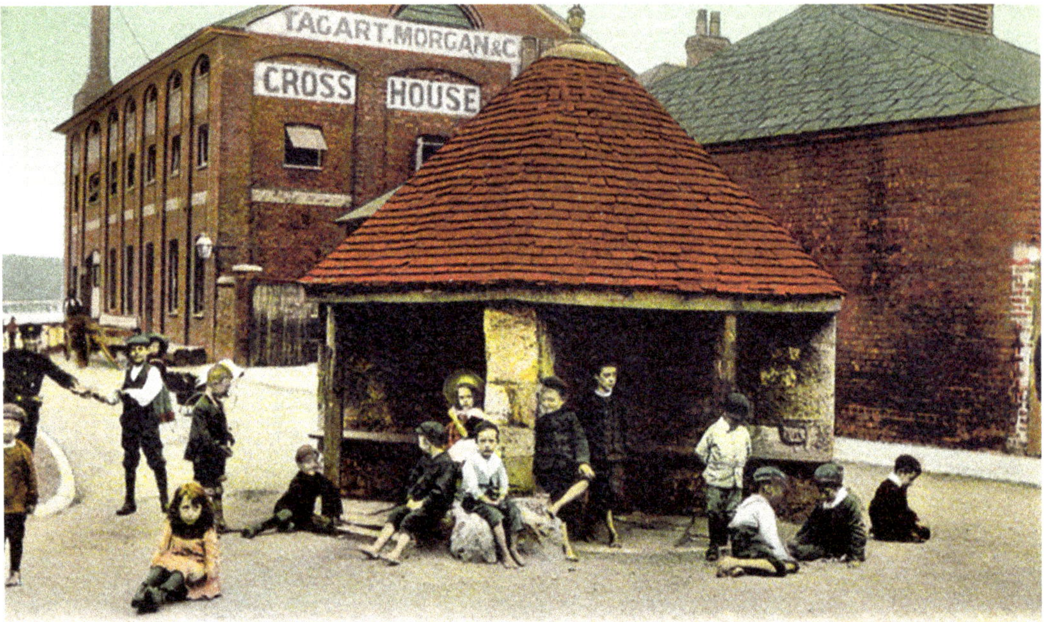

Cross House

The Cross House, used as a shelter for passengers waiting to be rowed over the river by ferry from Cross House Hard to the Royal Oak Hard on the opposite bank. It is believed that the Cross House could have originally been a medieval boundary marker for the area, then known as Itchenworth.

CHAPTER 3

EAST OF THE ITCHEN

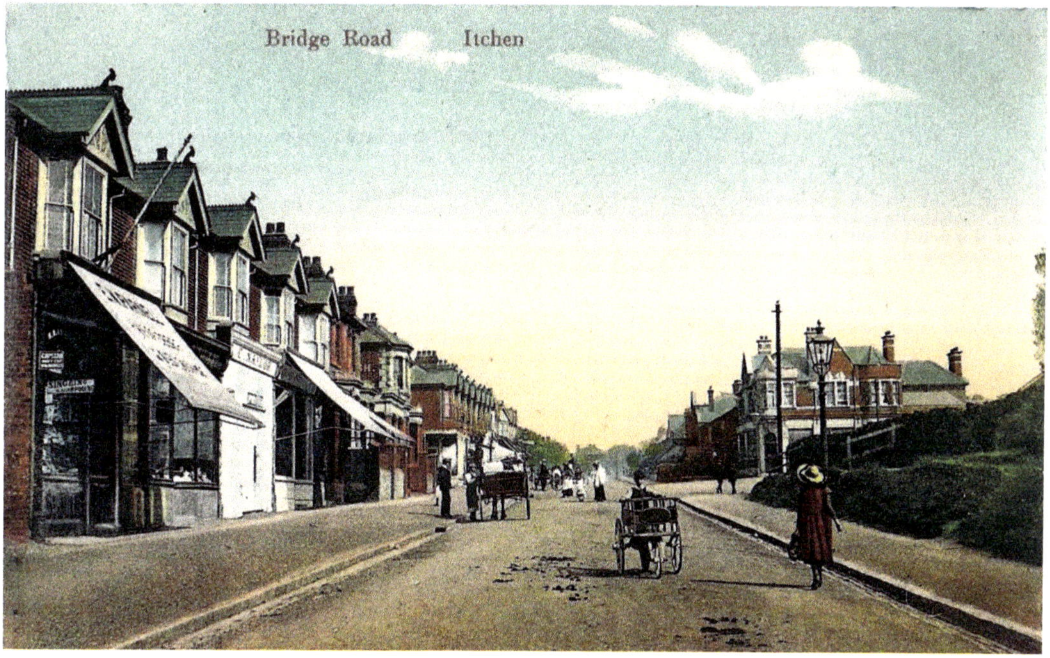

Bridge Road, Itchen

Bridge Road ran out of Woolston, through Itchen, and up to Peartree Green. As the Victorian and Edwardian suburbs spread out, the boundaries between the old parishes began to blur.

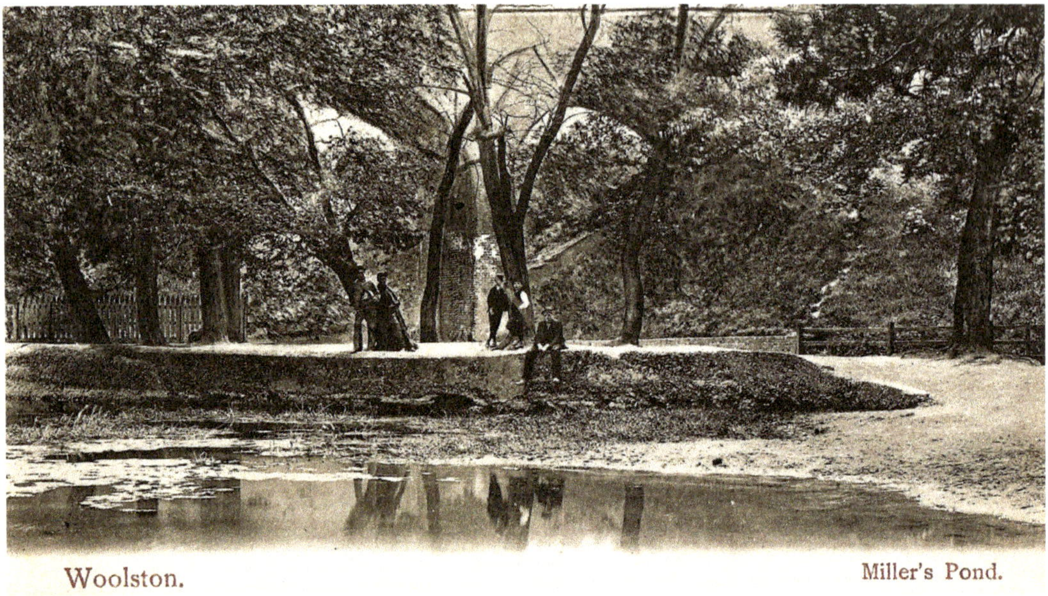

Miller's Pond, 1905

Many a resident of Sholing will be keen to point out that this postcard of Miller's Pond incorrectly identifies its location as Woolston. The pond is dear to the hearts of Sholing people, having been very much a playground for generations of local children. The pond, once much larger than it is now, was created as a power source for a mill further down stream.

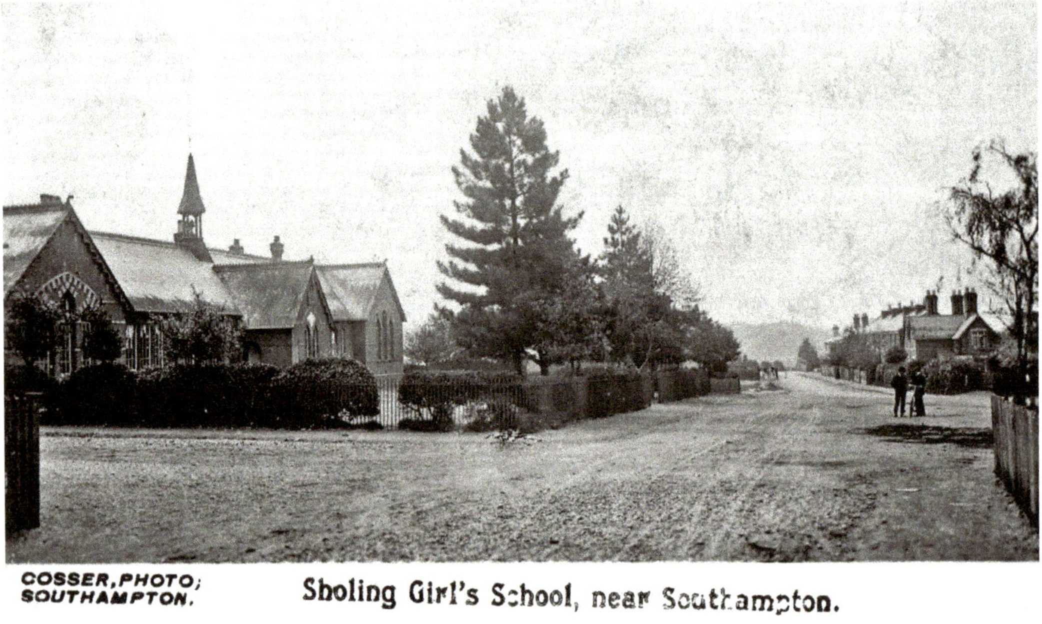

St Monica Road School, 1800s

The original school for children was in North East Road. This building on the corner of Bay Road and Church Road (later St Monica Road) was opened in stages during the mid-1800s. The girls moved in first, followed a few years later by the boys.

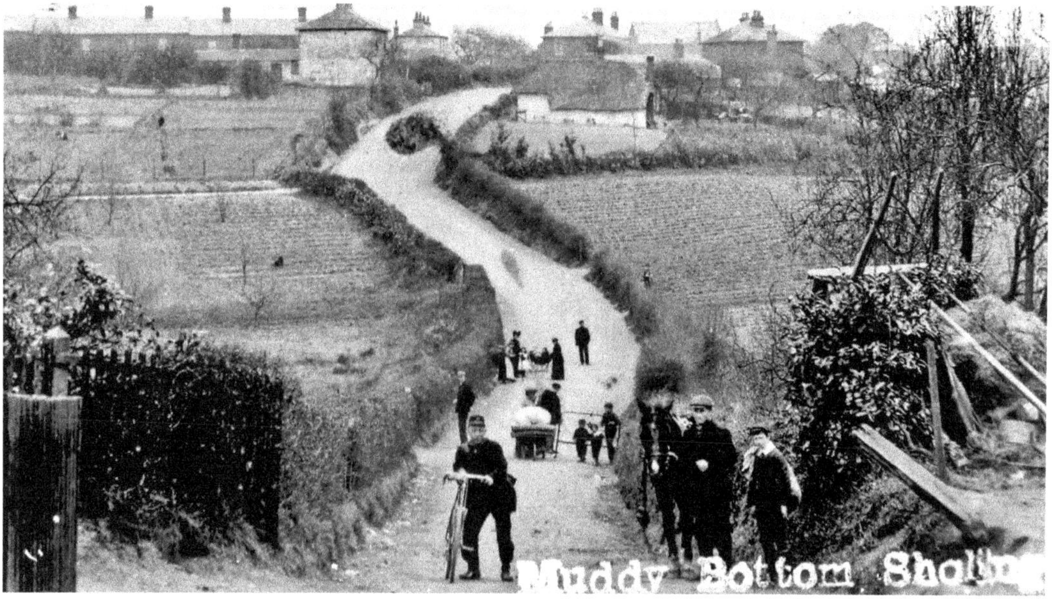

South East Road, late 1800s

South East Road, taken from Middle Road and looking in the direction of North East Road. On the immediate right was a smallholding that contained farm animals, which enthralled passing children.

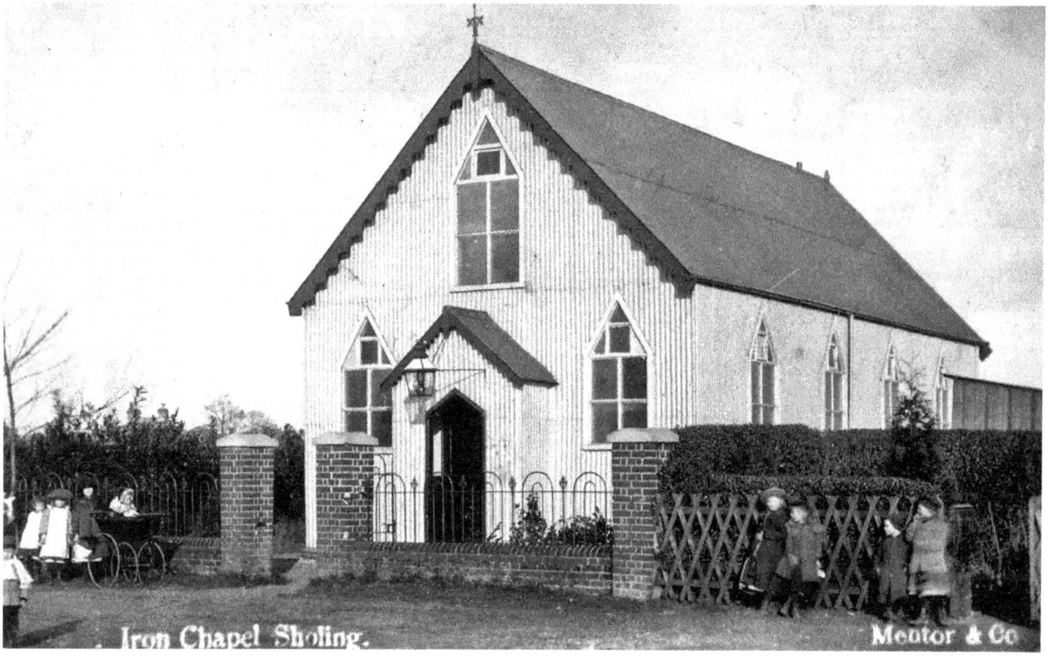

Iron Chapel, late 1800s

Nonconformist chapels sprang up in every town, city and village around the country. This fine example was erected in Sholing in what eventually became Chapel Crescent. Although not as expensive to build as a brick or stone church, the cost of an 'iron' chapel like this was borne by the mainly working-class congregation.

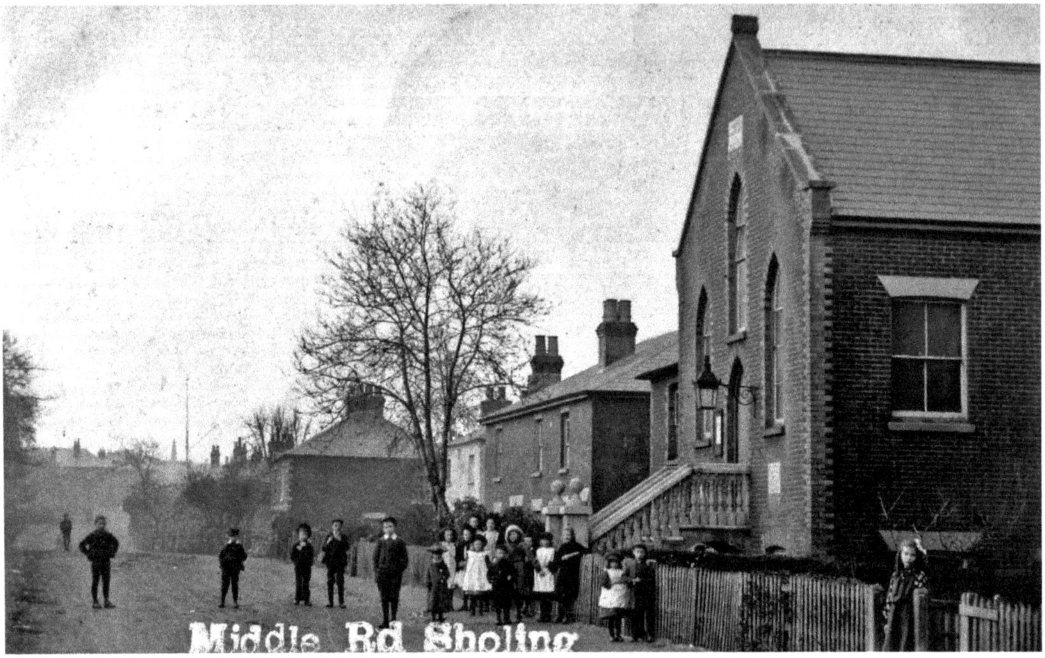

Middle Road, late 1800s
This Sholing view shows another Nonconformist chapel, this time the Baptist chapel on Middle Road. The appearance of a photographer, as usual, ensured an audience of well-dressed youngsters.

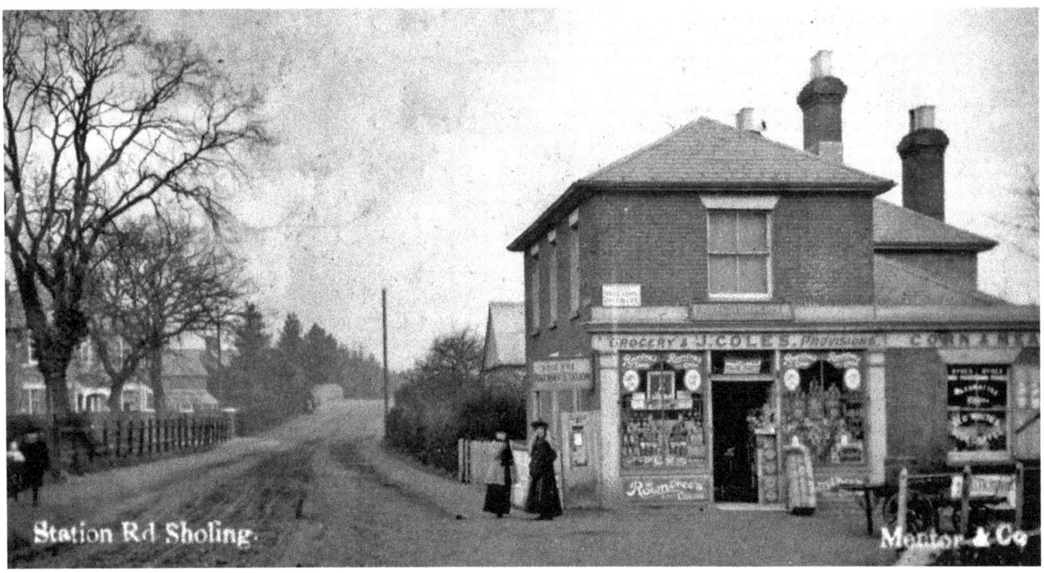

Station Road, late 1800s
This road junction marked the boundary of the parish of Sholing and its neighbouring parish of Woolston. The corner shop stood on Portsmouth Road and no doubt benefitted from plenty of passing trade. In the distance along the road to the left the bridge over the railway line east towards Portsmouth can be seen. The line originally opened in 1866 to create a rail connection from Southampton to the military hospital at Netley.

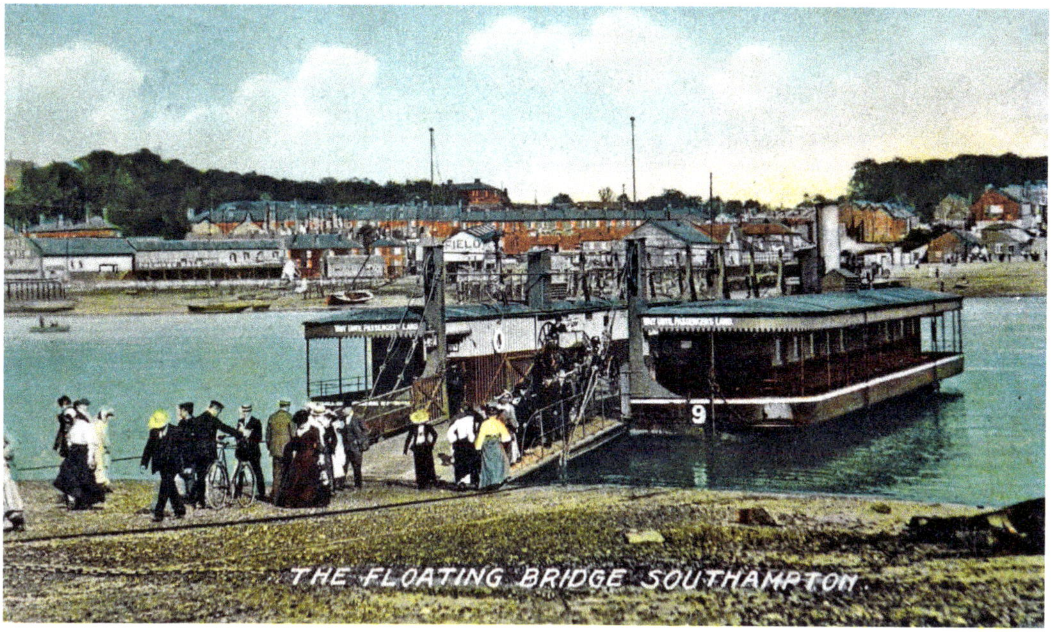

The Floating Bridge
In 1836, the first steam-powered vessel began transporting passengers and goods across the river, quickly putting the Itchen Ferry villagers out of business. Vessels were updated periodically and in 1934 the town's Corporation took over the service. In 1977 the imposing concrete Itchen Bridge finally opened, rendering the Floating Bridges redundant after many years of reliable service.

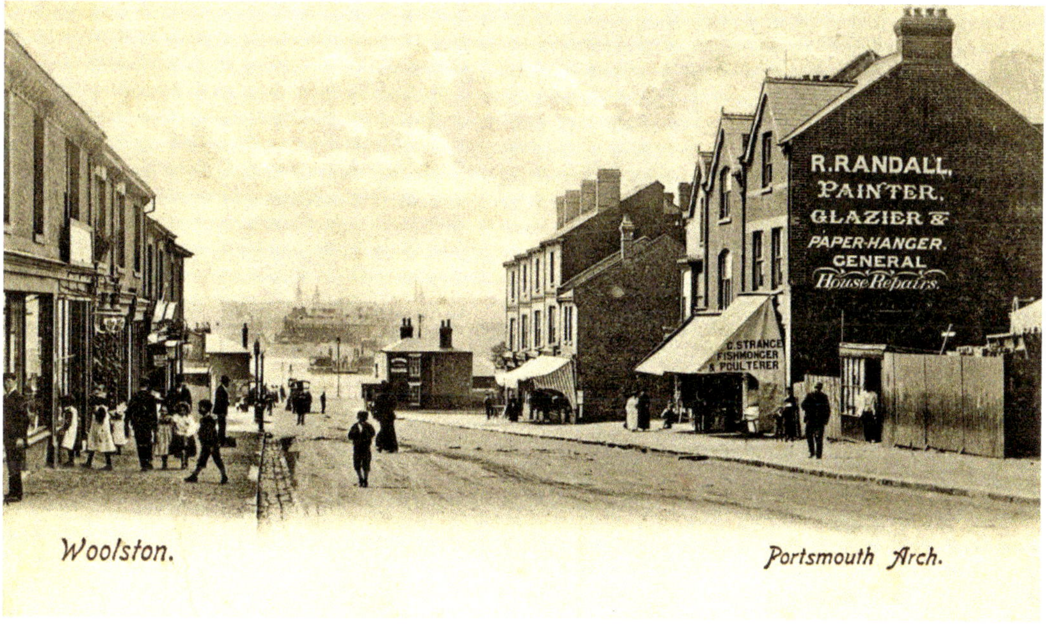

Woolston, late 1800s
Here is the road down to the River Itchen and the Floating Bridge, a busy crossing point from the east of Southampton into town. The ferry trip was always enjoyed by children and adults alike.

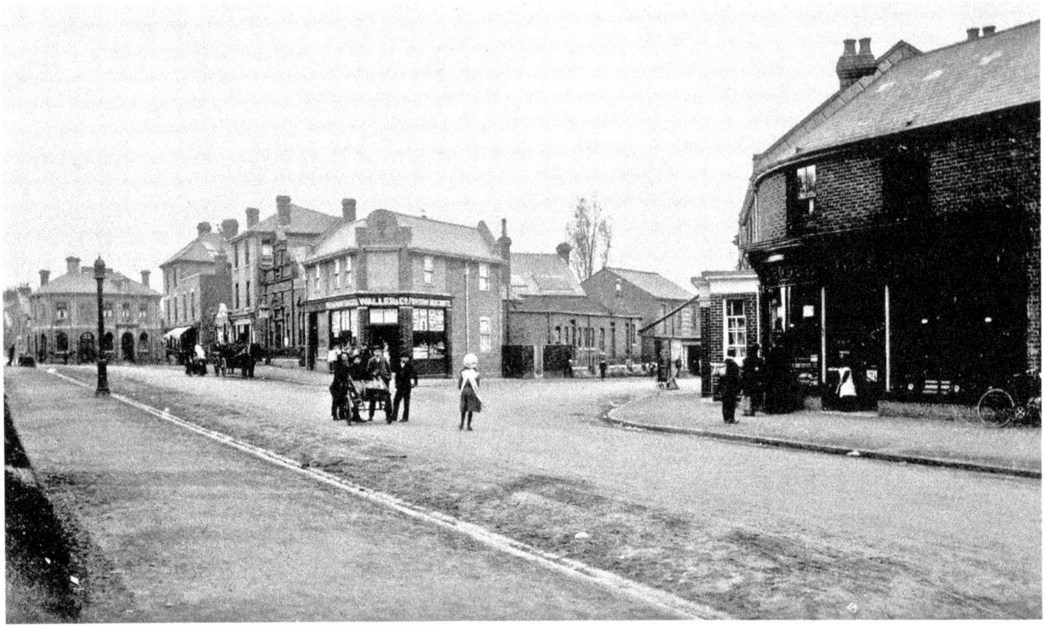

Bridge Road, late 1800s
Bridge Road led out of Woolston under the railway line and up towards Bitterne, passing Peartree Green. In this postcard, the volume of traffic – or lack of it – is easily judged by the nonchalant way in which the young people stand in the road.

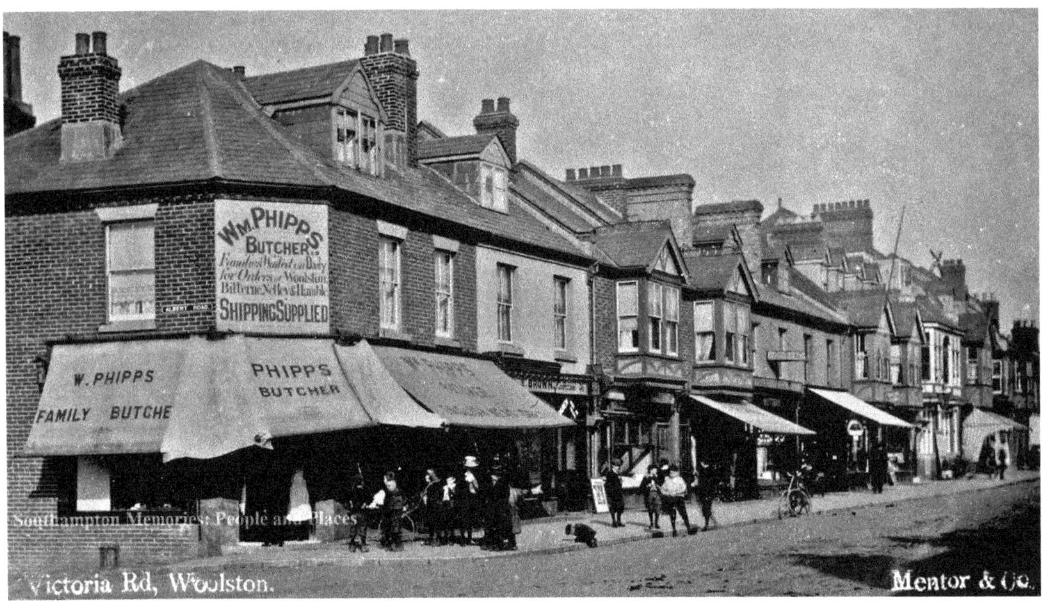

Victoria Road, Woolston
In the 1800s the port of Southampton expanded and consequently the rural suburbs became a landscape of new housing and roads. People living there relied heavily on their local shops, only venturing into the town centre for specific items. Shops like these in Victoria Road catered for everyone's daily needs.

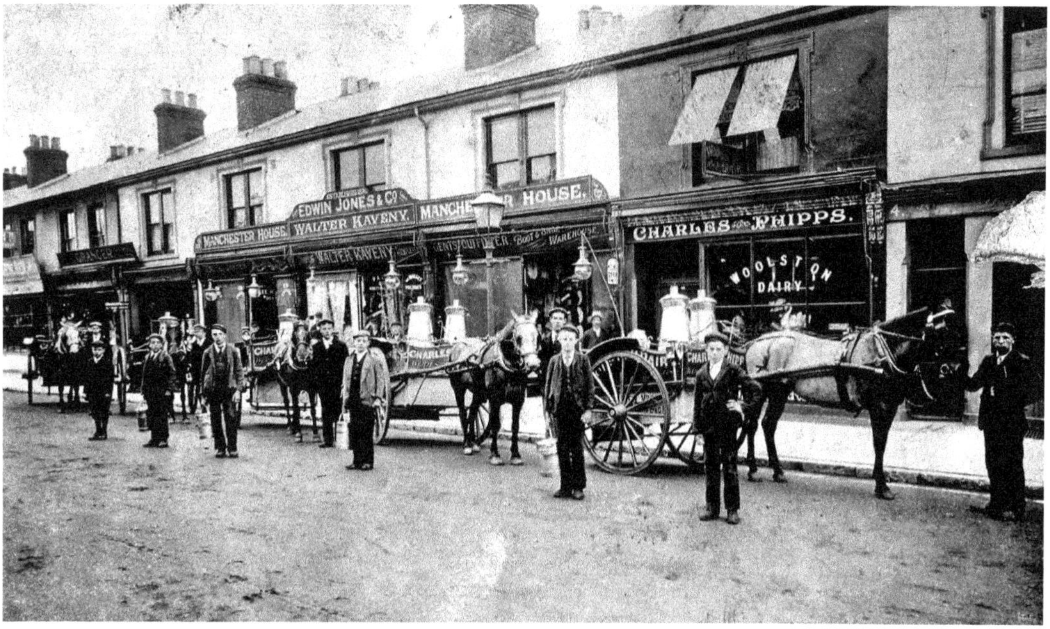

Phipps Dairy, Victoria Road
Five milk delivery carts and accompanying milkmen parade for the camera outside of Phipps Dairy. Of further retail interest, Walter Kaveny's shop next door to Phipps Dairy indicates its amalgamation with Edwin Jones, the large department store in Southampton's town centre.

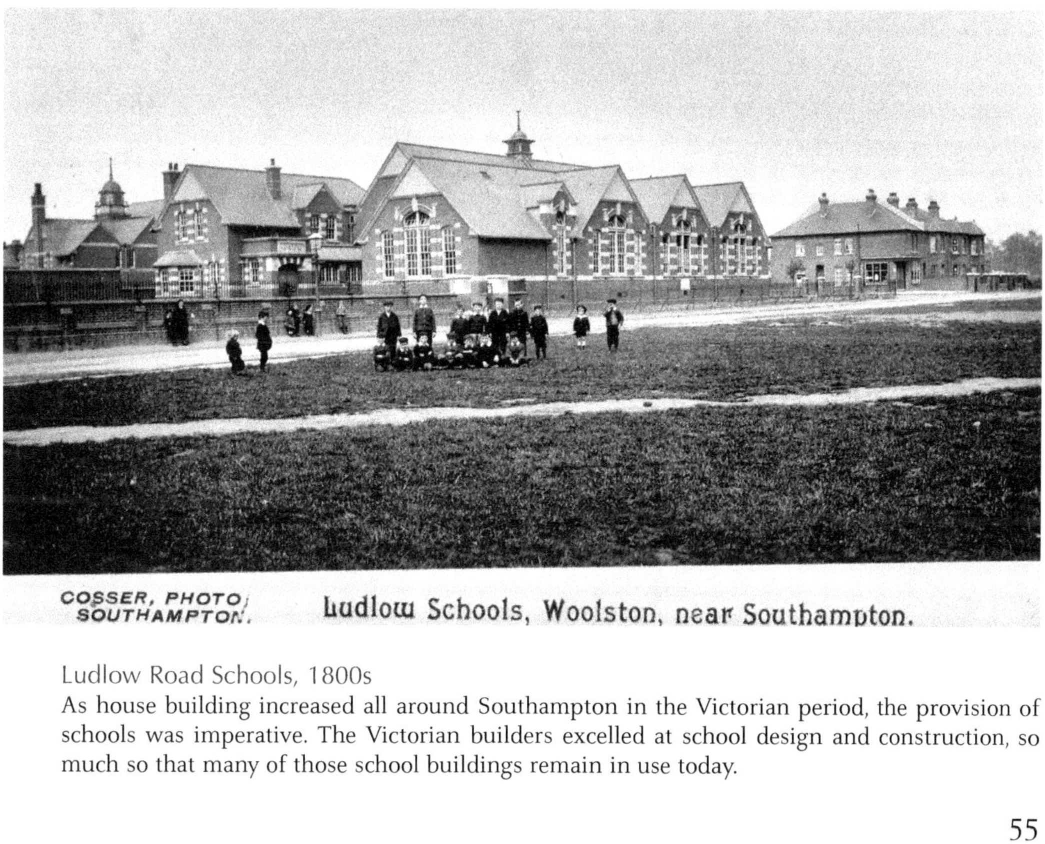

Ludlow Road Schools, 1800s
As house building increased all around Southampton in the Victorian period, the provision of schools was imperative. The Victorian builders excelled at school design and construction, so much so that many of those school buildings remain in use today.

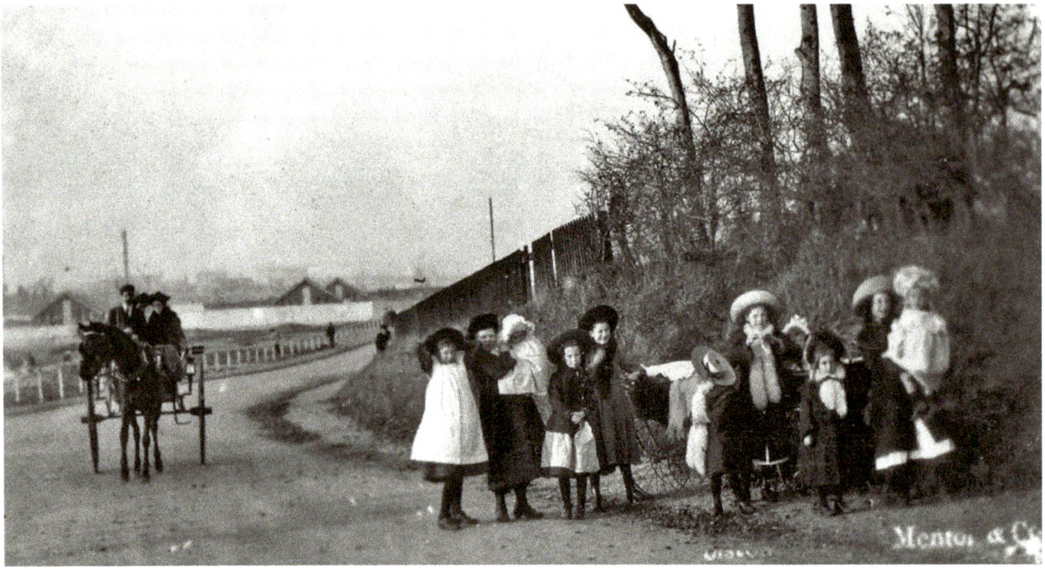

Weston Shore, late 1800s

The shore road from Weston to Netley has always been a popular place to walk, take in the sea air and get some exercise. This group of children appear to be dressed for a Sunday stroll.

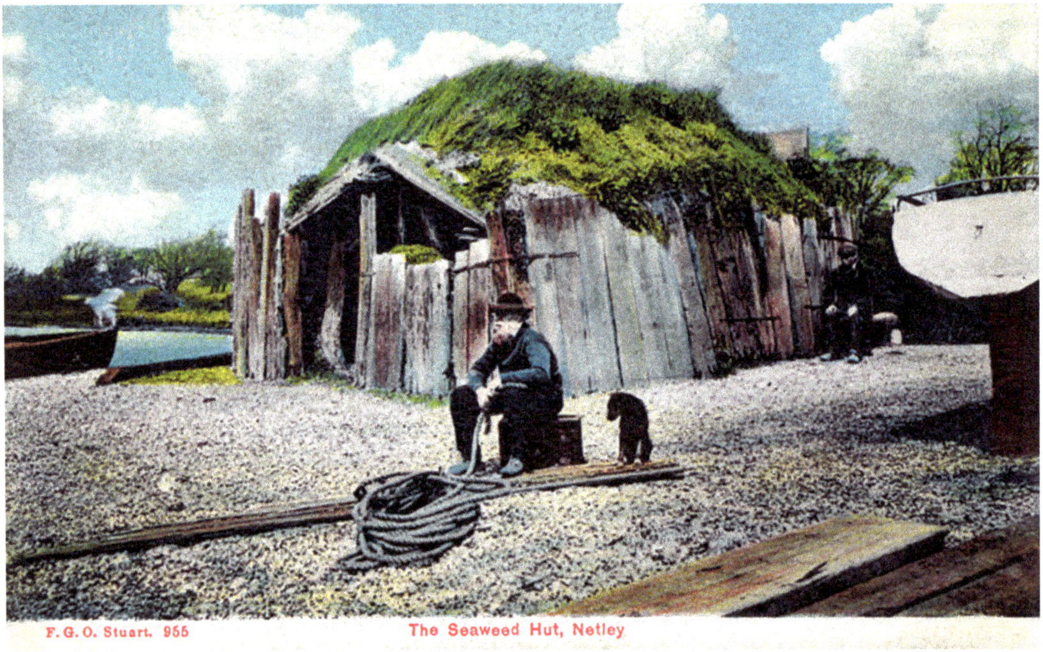

The Seaweed Hut

The seaweed hut was a curious ramshackle building on the shore at Weston. Marked on admiralty charts since the 1700s, it is thought the shelter was much older still. Built as a store for nets, sails and oars, the shelter was used and maintained by the fishermen of the nearby hamlet of Weston. Built with old oak spars and a seaweed roof, it served not only as a store but also a meeting place for the fishermen. Eventually it fell into disuse and was demolished by the local council in 1967.

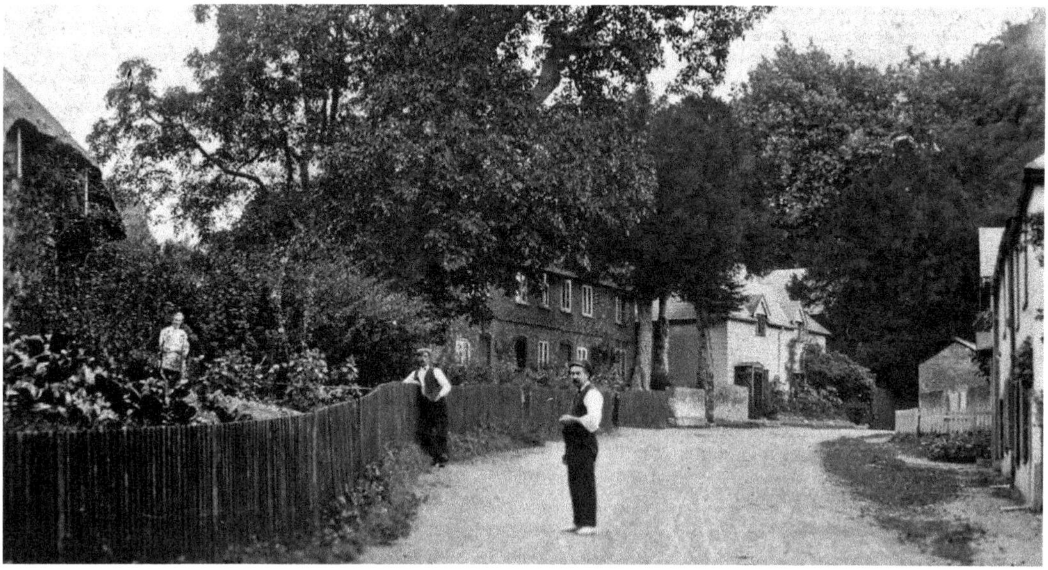

Weston Village
In common with many other Southampton suburbs, Weston had humble rural beginnings. Originally a small fishing hamlet, the land passed into the ownership of the Dummer family during the 1400s. It became the extensive Weston Grove estate, control of which was later transferred into the Chamberlayne family by marriage. The estate land, at one time, reached the neighbouring village of Netley.

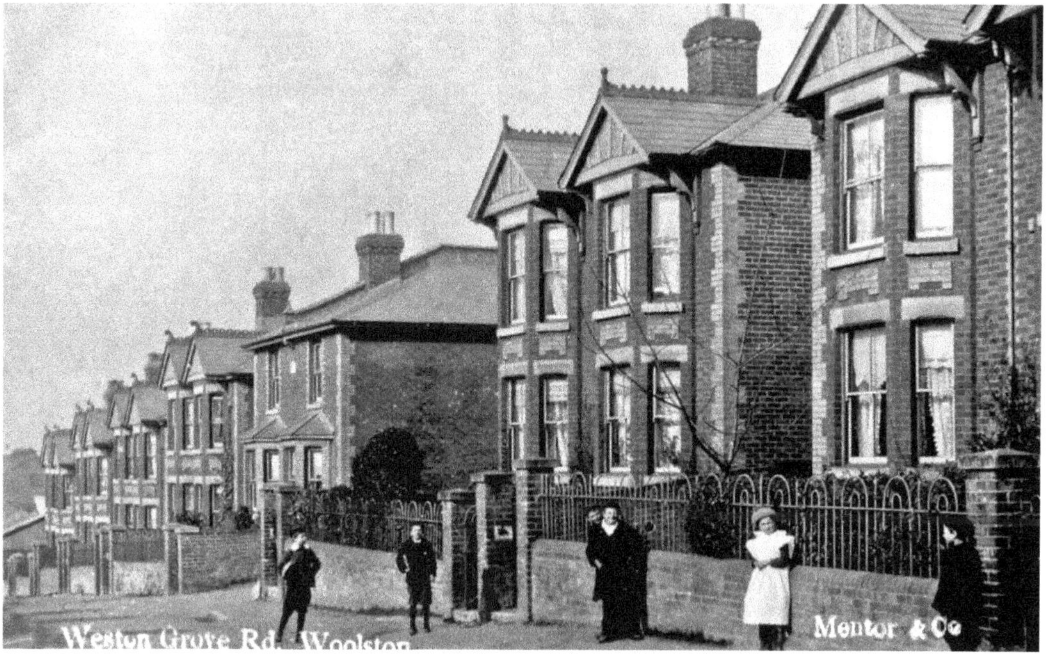

Weston Grove Road
This eastern suburb expanded rapidly in the 1800s. Close to the River Itchen shipyards and the Eastern Docks, homes were needed for the ever-increasing work force and their families.

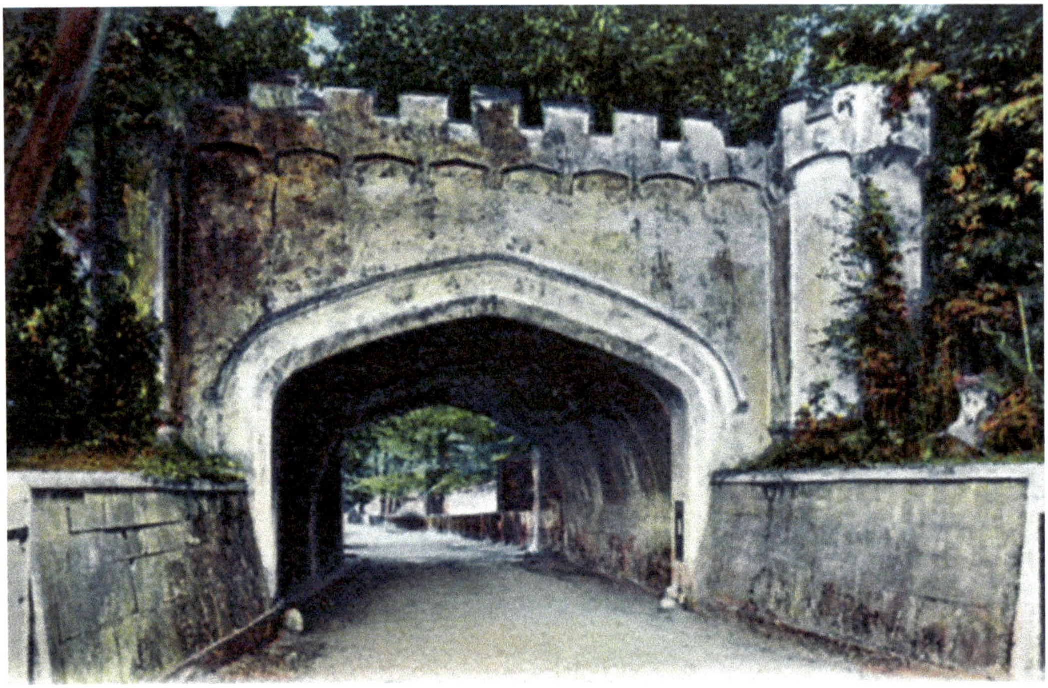

Arches on Weston Lane

There were, at one time, two ornate arches spanning the rural Weston Lane. Both were carriage roads that served the Weston Grove estate, built for William Chamberlayne in the very early 1800s. Mr Chamberlayne had the arches built to provide him and his guests a route round the rest of his estate. One arch was demolished in the 1930s, while the second came down in the 1940s.

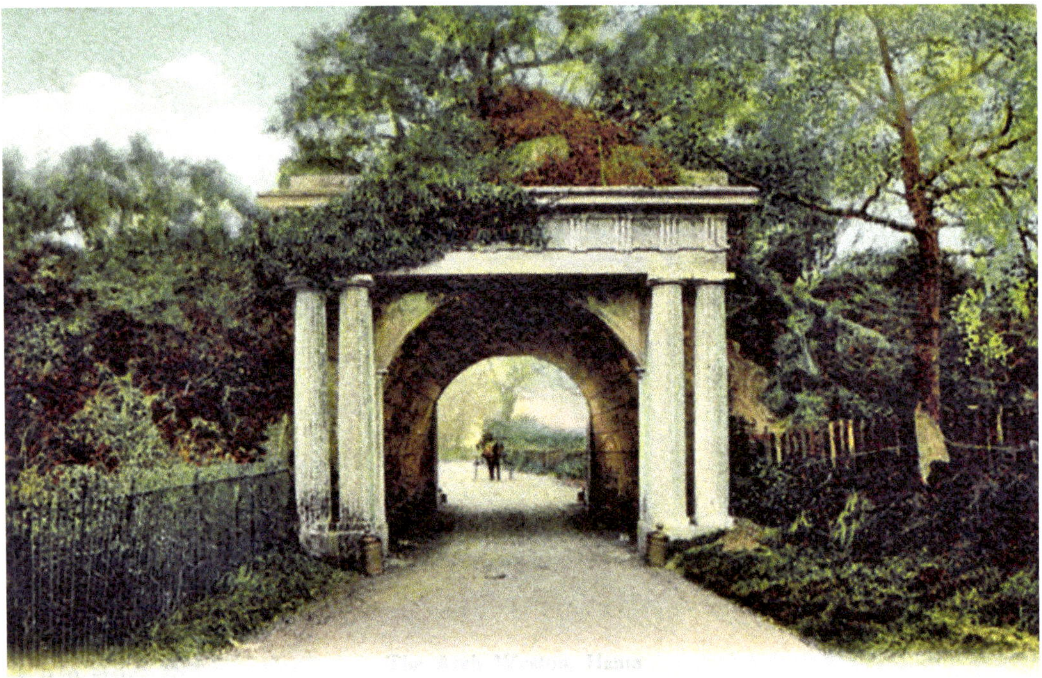

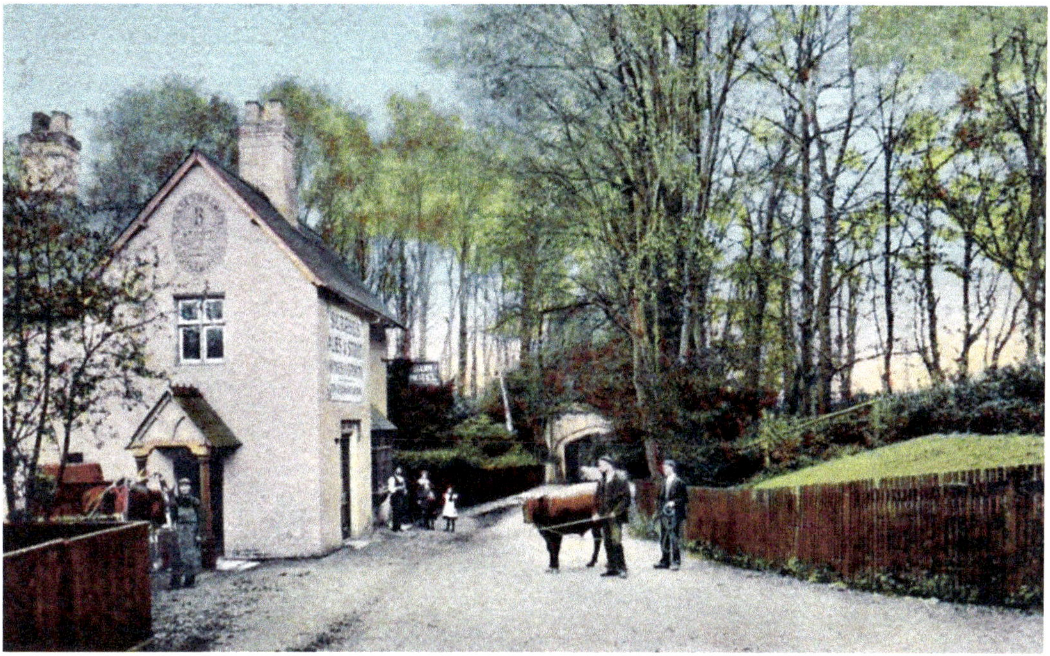

The Sun Public House, Weston

At one time, The Sun was Weston's only public house. It dates back to the very early 1800s, and was then a relatively isolated pub on a very quiet country lane.

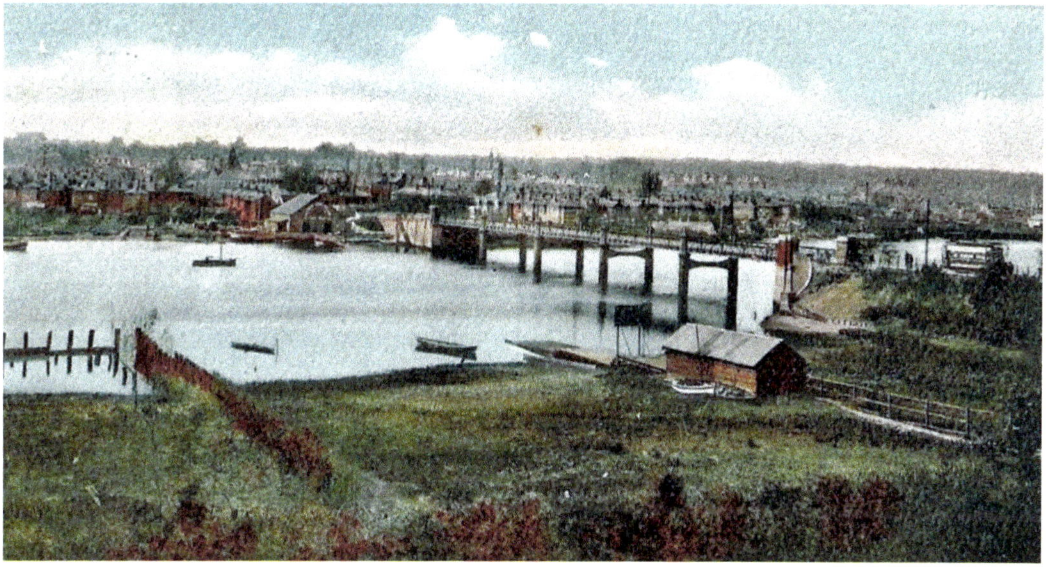

Cobden Bridge

This postcard shows the first bridge built at this point on the River Itchen, which was constructed in 1883 by the National Liberal Land Company, the developers of the suburb of Bitterne Park.

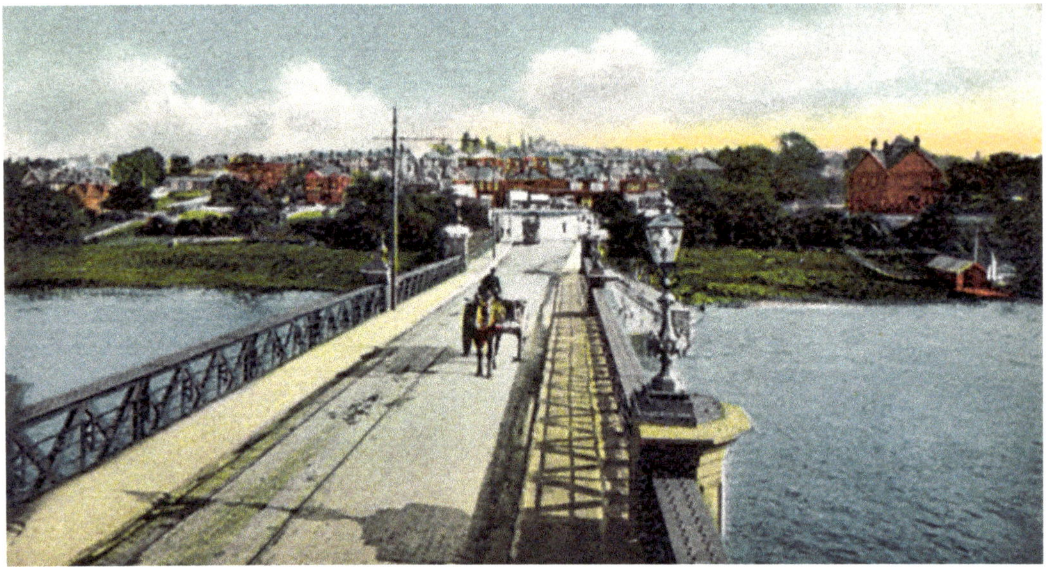

Cobden Bridge
The bridge proved immediately popular as it was toll-free. Named after the liberal campaigner Richard Cobden, this iron girder bridge was replaced by one made of concrete in the mid-1920s.

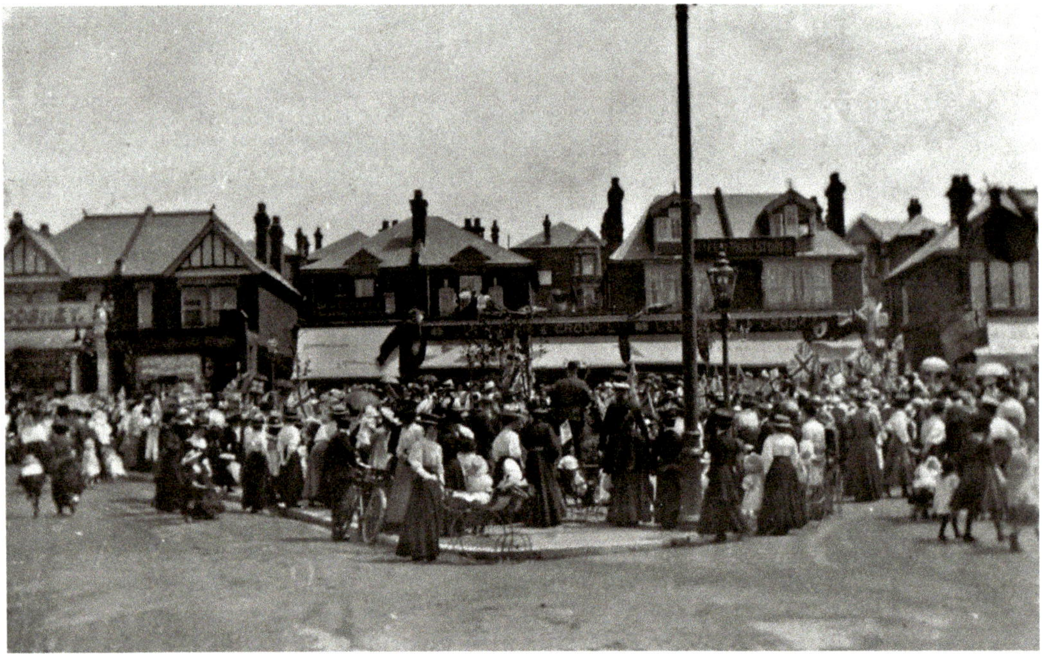

Bitterne Park Triangle, 1909
Up until 1882, the area now known as Bitterne Park was mainly farmland that sloped down towards the River Itchen. The land was part of the estate of Bitterne Manor. In 1882 the land was sold to developers, and within a few years Bitterne Park became a suburb of Southampton and a popular place to live. The triangle of land created where two main roads met to cross the river became a focal point for the area, in effect its village green.

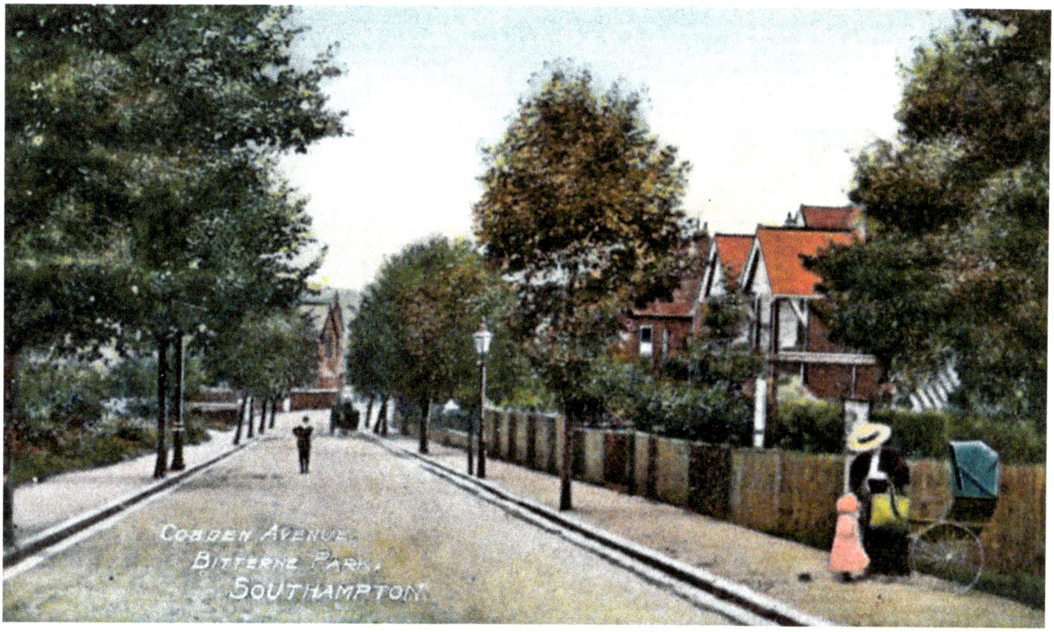

Cobden Avenue, early 1900s
This idyllic scene, looking downhill in the direction of Bitterne Park Triangle, bears little resemblance to the busy road Cobden Avenue has become in modern times. The church in the distance is nowadays sandwiched between a supermarket and a plumbing warehouse.

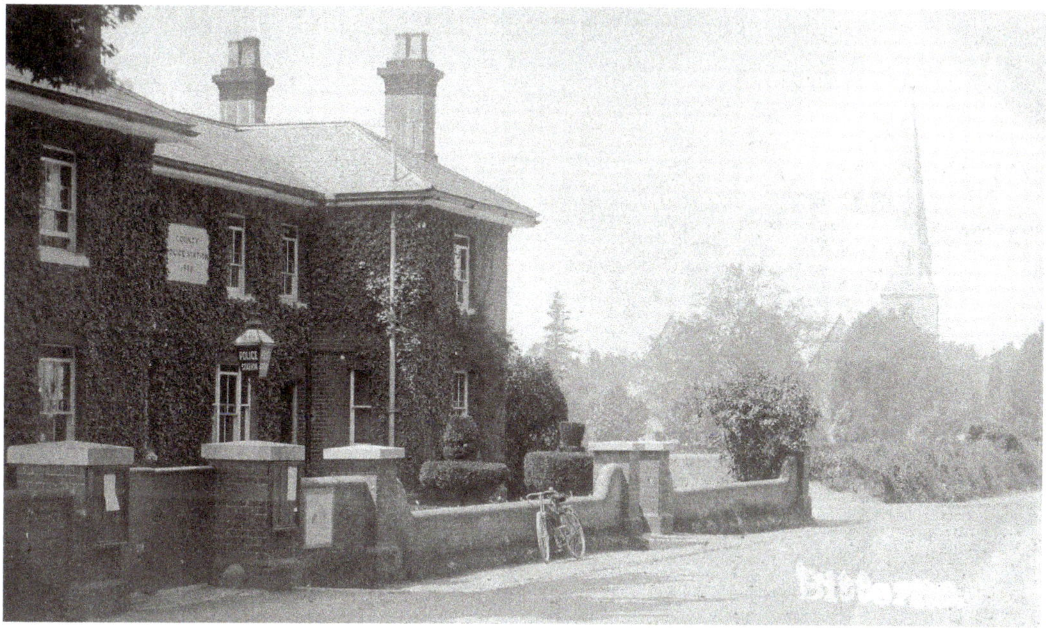

Bitterne Police Station, early 1900s
Bitterne Police Station was built in the mid-1800s, to help ensure law and order was maintained in Bitterne and the surrounding areas. The station stood on the corner of Bursledon Road and Whites Road until it was demolished in 1963.

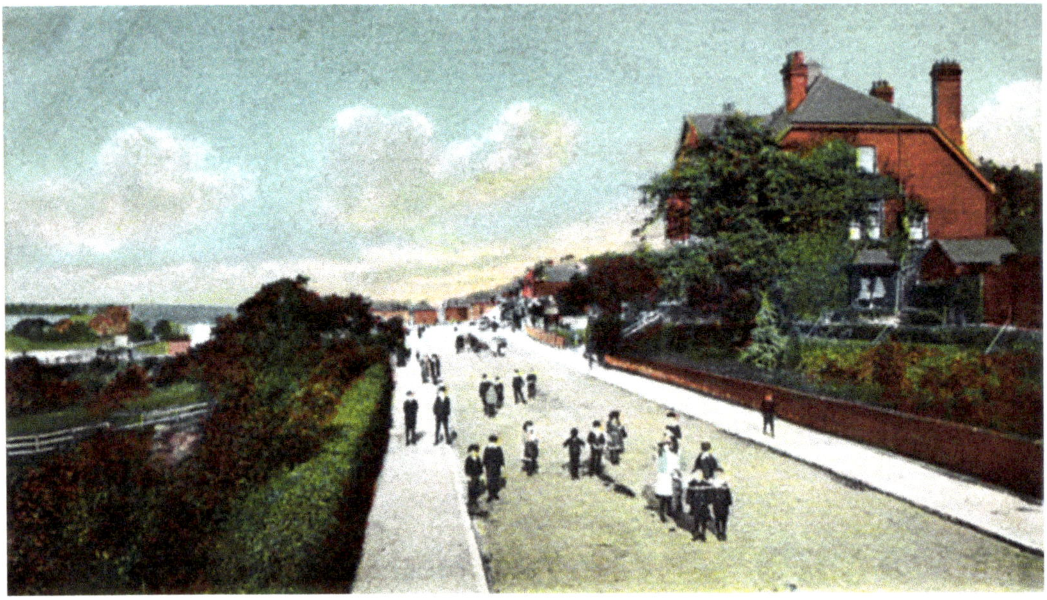

Whitworth Road

Whitworth Crescent and Road were laid out in the late 1800s during the development of the suburb of Bitterne Park. Running up alongside the river from Bitterne railway station to Bitterne Park Triangle, the large house built here must have had a fine aspect. The area could certainly draw a large audience of children to watch the photographer at work.

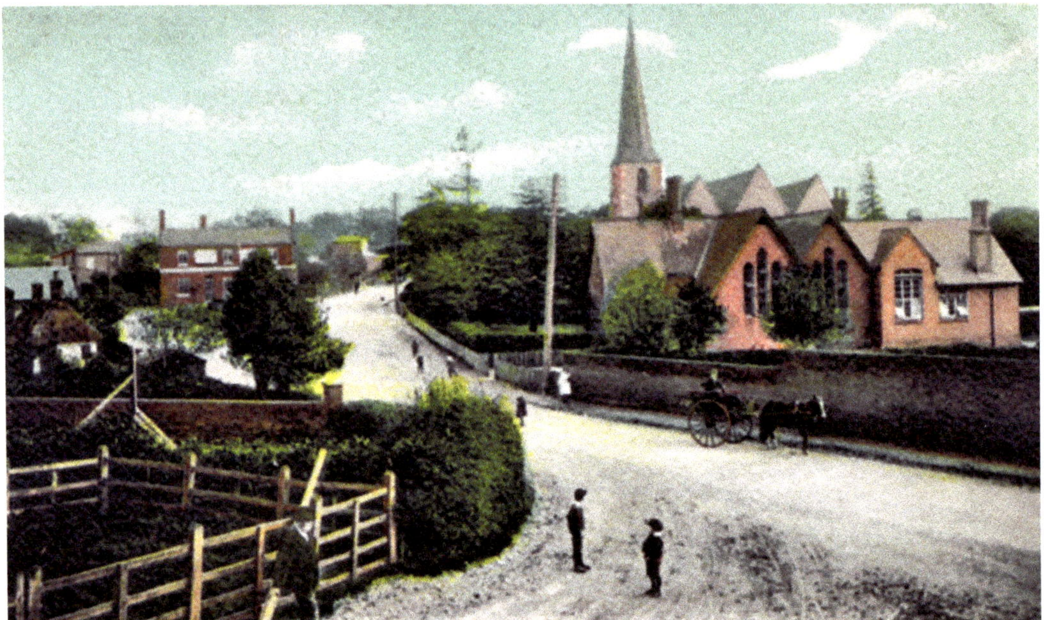

Bitterne, late 1800s

This scene shows most of the essentials for village life in one shot: the church, the school and the pub, with the pound and a thatched cottage in view.

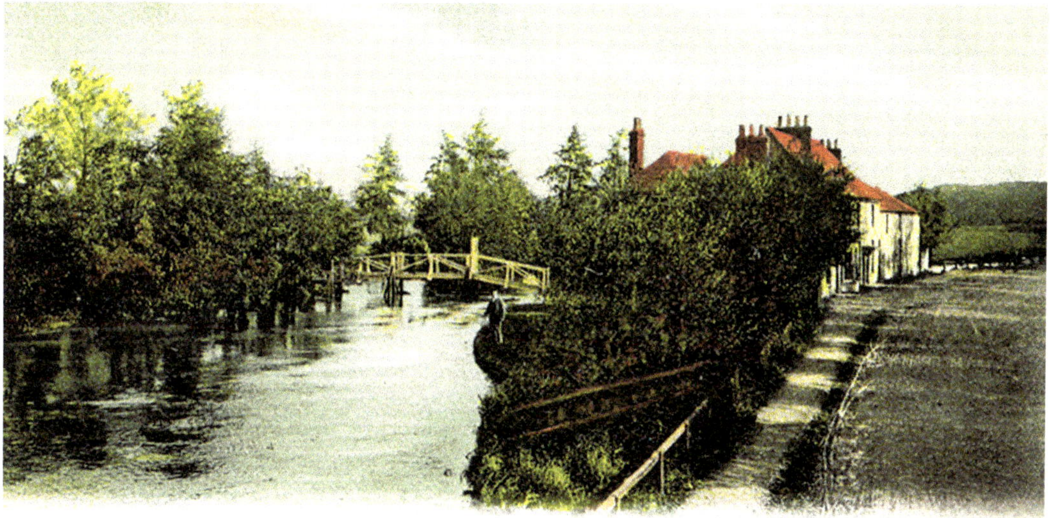

The White Swan, Mansbridge

Opened in the early 1800s, this riverside inn was called the Middleton Arms after the family who owned the nearby Townhill Park estate. By 1870 it had been renamed The White Swan and boasted fine gardens, which were accessed by the footbridge over the river. The venue also offered excellent trout fishing along the banks of the Itchen.

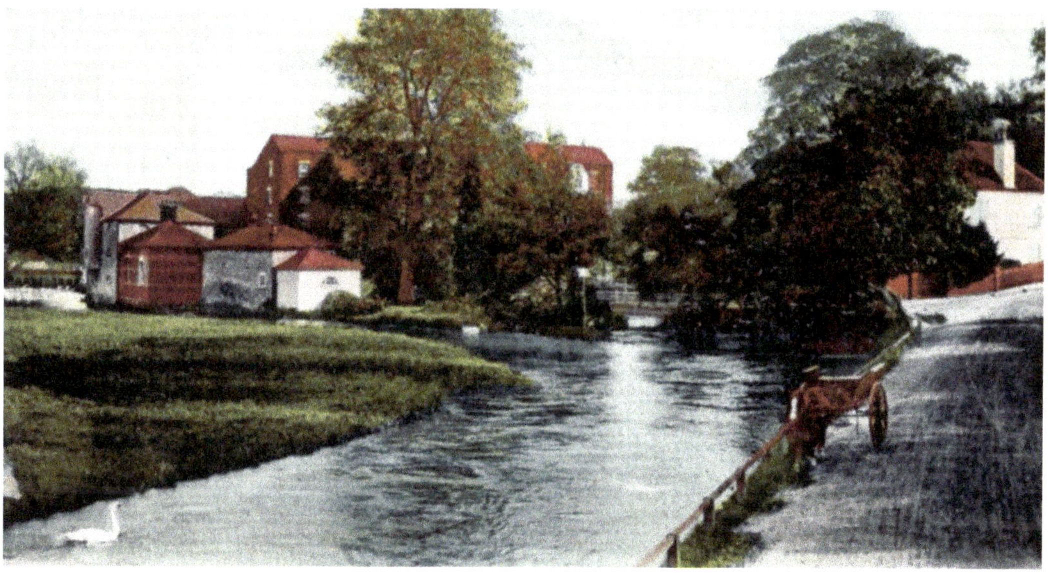

Gaters Mill

Gaters Mill, or West End Mill, occupies a location on the River Itchen that has been in use for various mills since the pre-Norman Conquest period. In the seventeenth and eighteenth centuries it was a paper mill run by Hugenot refugees. In the very early 1700s a young Henri Portal arrived from France to learn his trade. He founded his own paper-making business in Laverstoke and his company went on to print the paper used in British bank notes.

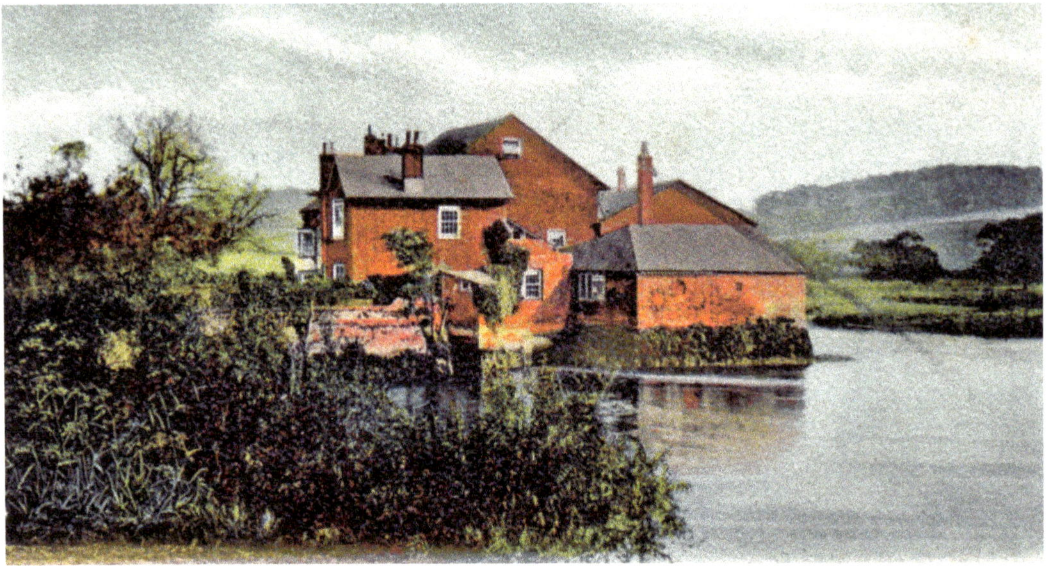

Woodmill

There has been a mill at this point on the River Itchen since medieval times. The mill is located at the juncture of the freshwater river and the tidal part of the river. In 1781 the mill was used by Walter Taylor, the block maker. It caught fire in 1825 and the building we see today was constructed after that. It last ground flour in 1950 and is now a water activities centre for young people.

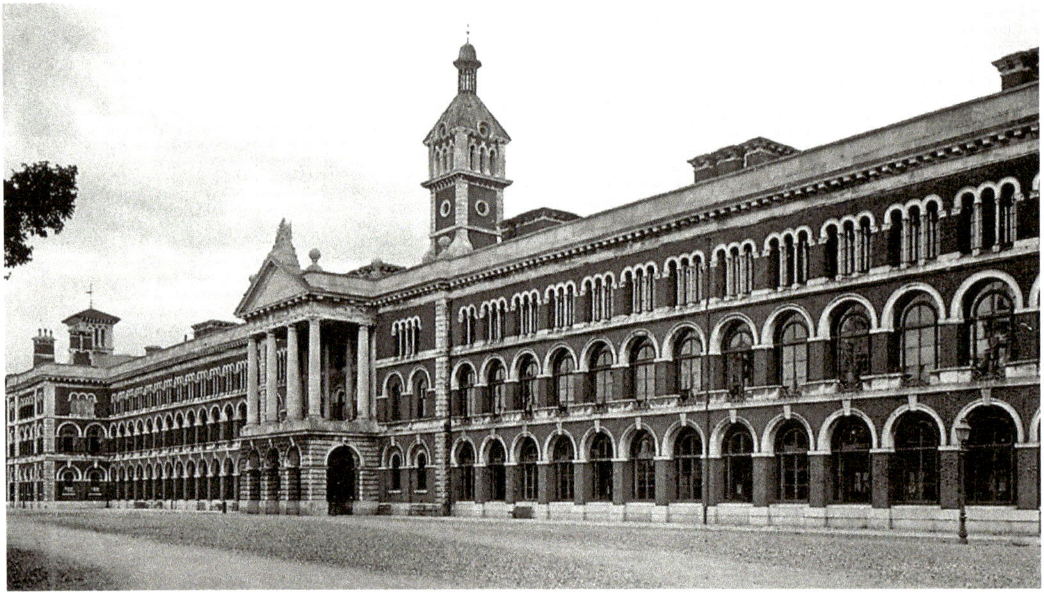

Royal Victoria Military Hospital

Built on land belonging to Thomas Chamberlayne's Netley Grange estate, the foundation stone for the hospital was laid in 1856. Although striking to look at, the building was deemed 'unfit for purpose' even before it was built, with architectural splendour taking priority over patient wellbeing. Plans were adjusted, but when the hospital opened in 1863, both late and over budget, it was still being criticised for being poorly planned.

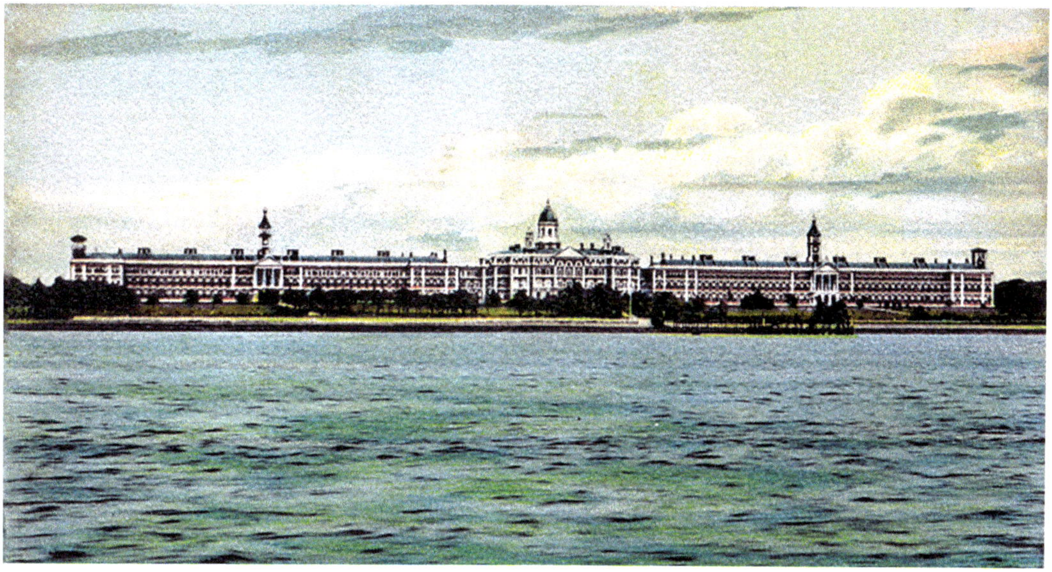

Netley Hospital

Work commenced on the huge Royal Victoria Military Hospital in 1856, in response to the appalling conditions troops had suffered during the Crimean War. The main part of the building, as seen in this postcard, was the longest building in the world at the time. After seeing service during the two world wars the main part of the hospital was demolished in 1966. It is now the Royal Victoria Country Park and is much appreciated by those who enjoy its peaceful location on Southampton Water.

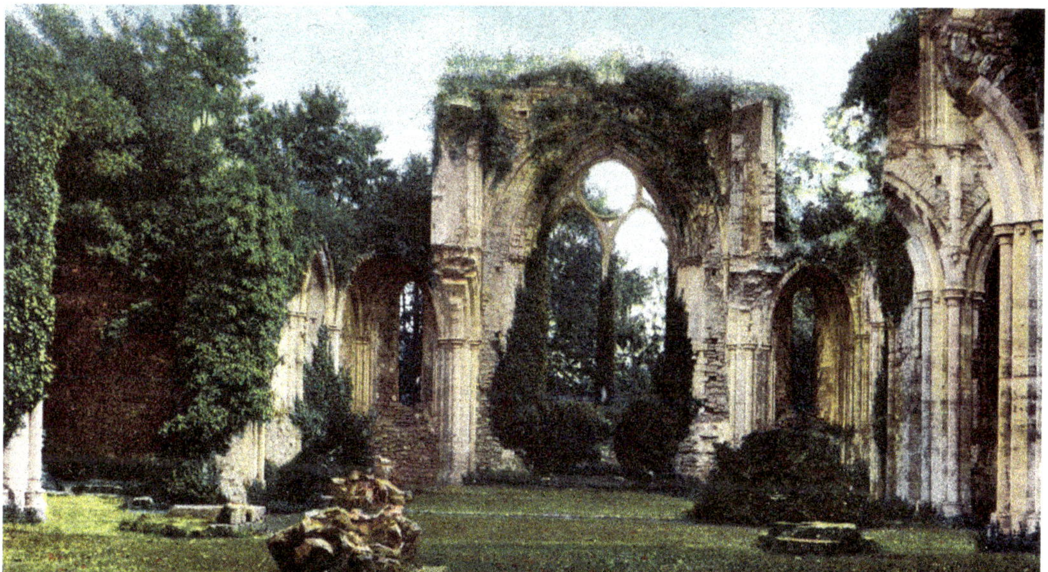

Netley Abbey

Founded in 1238, this Cistercian monastery was a powerful force in the area east of Southampton. However, in 1536, after the Dissolution of the Monasteries, Netley Abbey was converted into a mansion house. Eight hundred years on, the ruins of the abbey still attract visitors.

CHAPTER 4

NORTHERN PARISHES AND THE COMMON

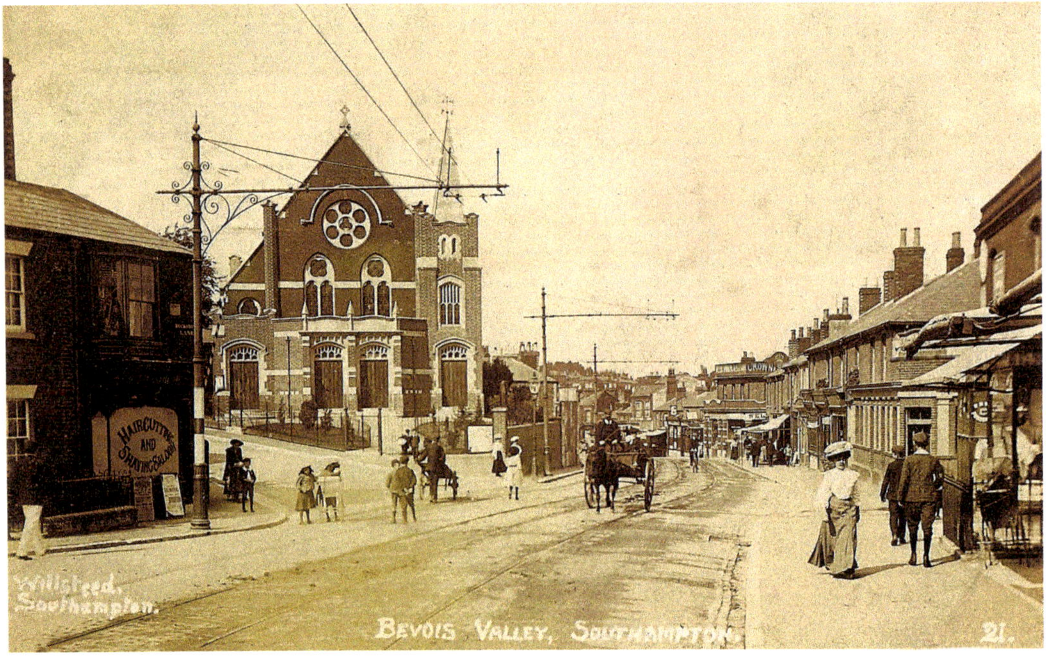

Bevois Valley

Onslow Road runs from the town centre through Bevois Valley towards the large suburb of Portswood. The areas in Bevois Valley include Bevois Mount and Bevois Town. The name commemorates the mythical hero of Southampton – Bevis of Hampton.

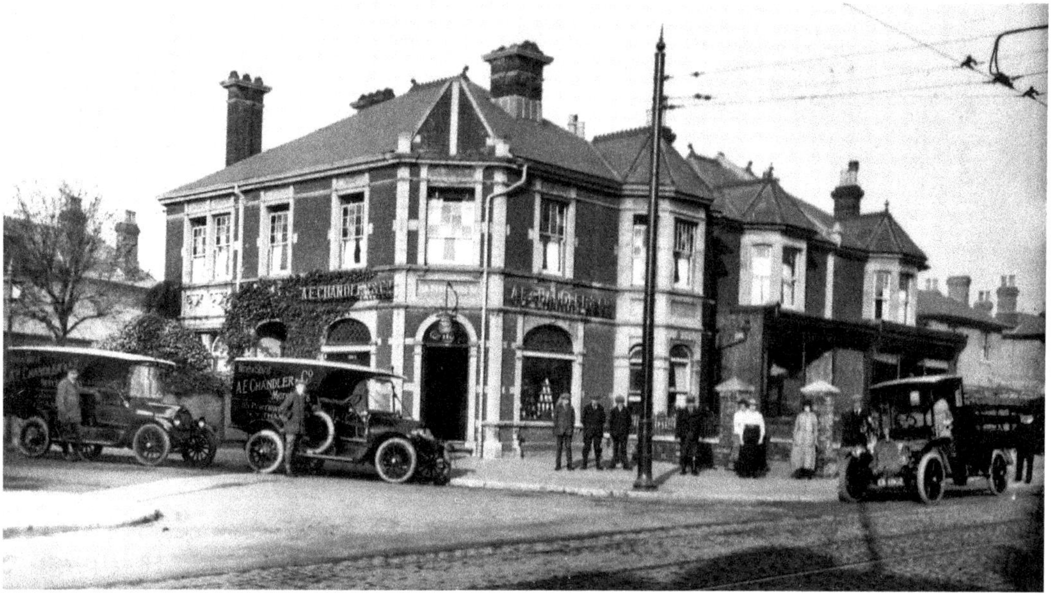

A. E. Chandler

In the early 1900s, A. E. Chandler was a very busy off-licence and wine merchant. Their fleet of delivery vehicles are proudly on show in front of the shop on the corner of Gordon Avenue and Portswood Road. Portswood and neighbouring Highfield were middle- and upper-class suburbs, and Mr Chandler had a good customer base in the immediate area.

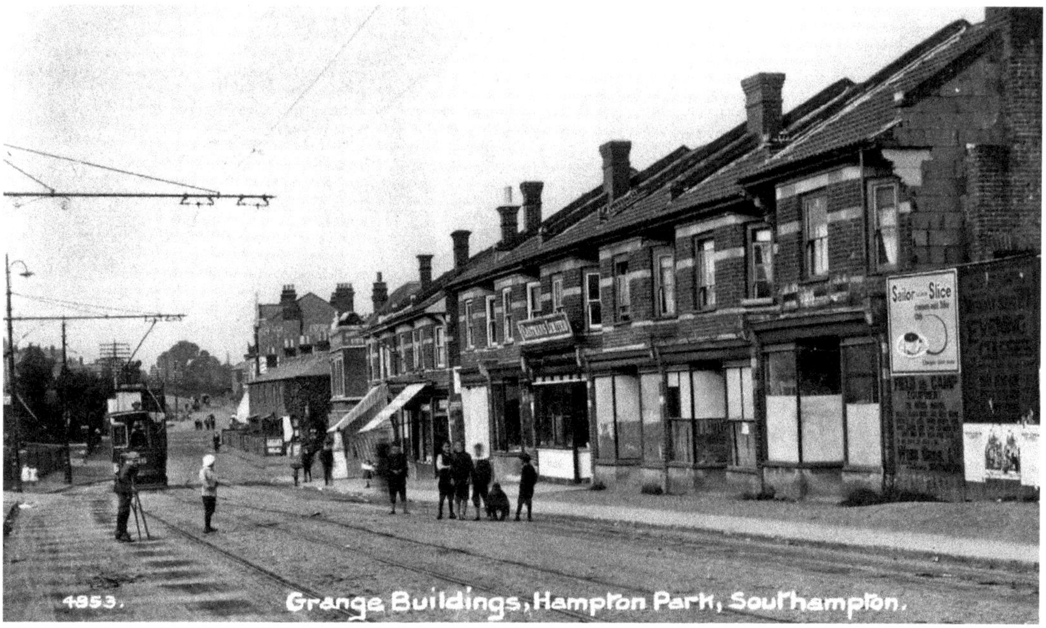

Grange Buildings

As the suburb of Portswood expanded during the Victorian and Edwardian period, more shops were strung out along the main road in the direction of Eastleigh. In common with all the other suburbs of Southampton, local shopping was paramount.

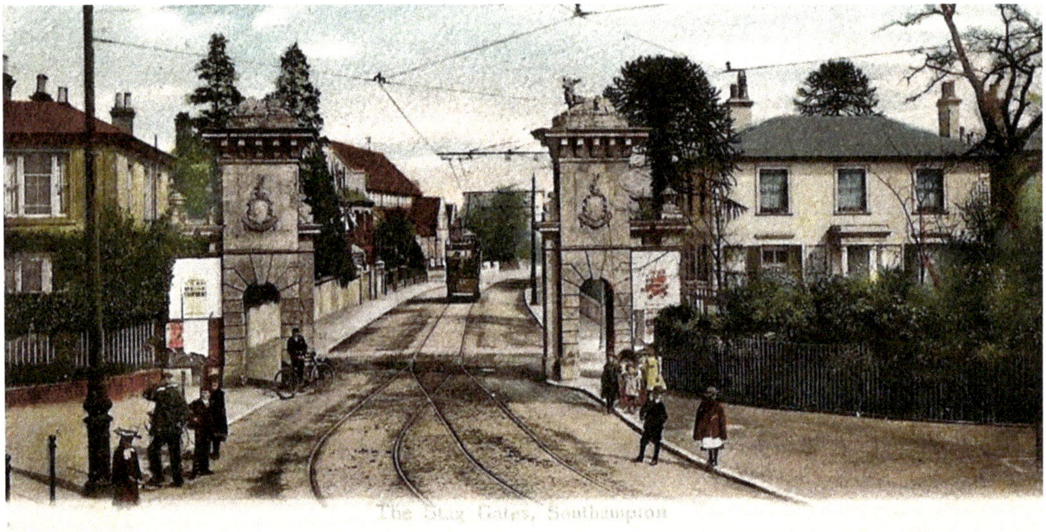

Stag Gates

Built in 1723 as the entrance to the carriage road into the Bevois Mount estate, these magnificent gates stood at the junction of Lodge Road and The Avenue. If you look closely at the animals on top of each gate pillar you will see they have no antlers. Should the gates really been called Hind Gates? In the 1920s the gates were in poor repair and this gave the impetus for the council to remove them and widen the road at this point. Although long gone now, the area in the immediate vicinity of the road junction is still referred to as 'Stag Gates'.

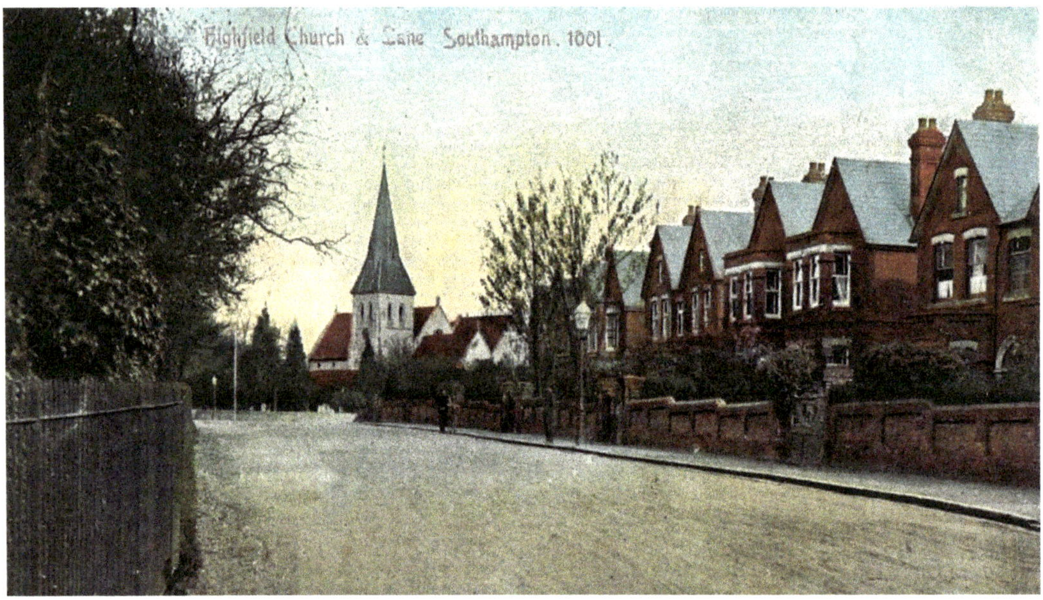

Highfield Lane, *c.* 1905

This area of high ground to the north of Portswood was agricultural land until the suburbs expanded. Farmland to the north of Highfield Lane, pictured here, was given up to provide a campus for Southampton University when it moved from its Lower High Street location in 1914. It now occupies a large amount of the Highfield area.

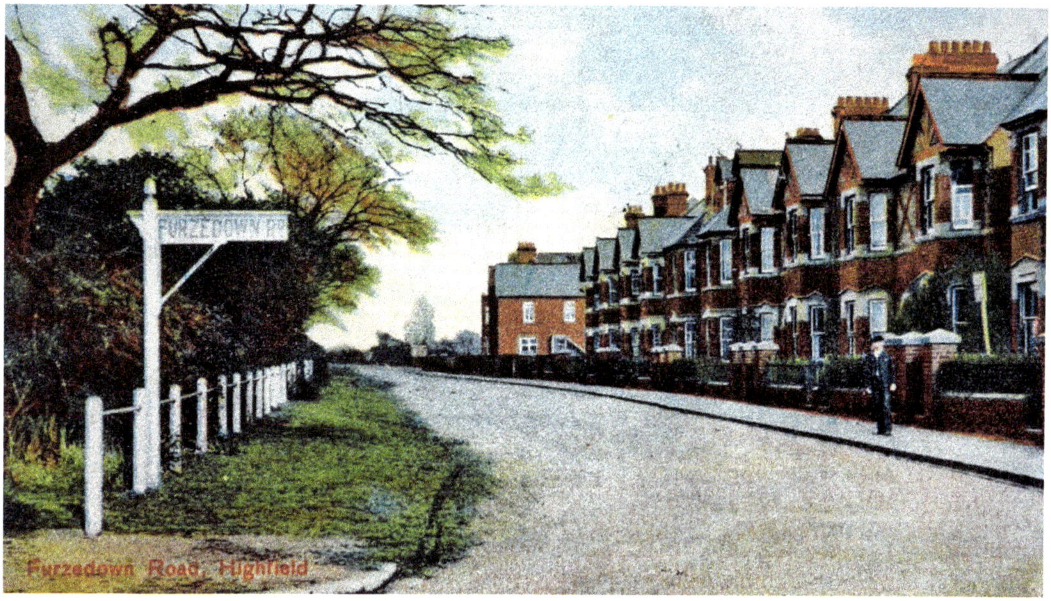

Furzedown Road, Highfield
Hay Field is believed to be the origin of the name Highfield. As a rural area in the 1900s, it was dominated by many large country houses, some occupied by naval officers. A prominent feature of the area is the distinctive Uplands estate, which was constructed by Herbert Collins. Furzedown Road, however, is one of the older Edwardian-style residential roads.

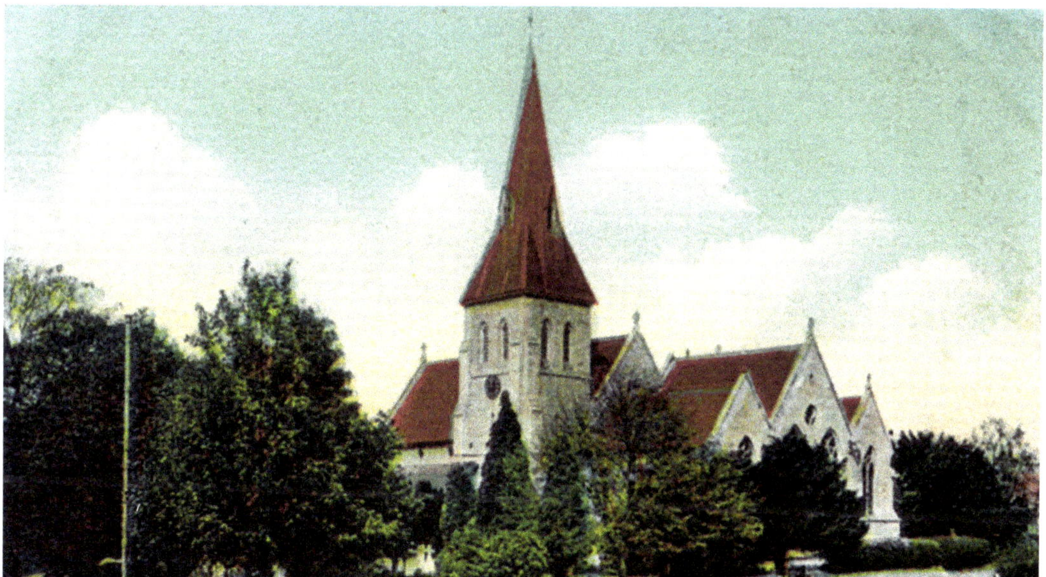

Highfield Church
Legally known as Christ Church Portswood, this 1846–47 church is known to all and sundry as Highfield Church. Its architect, Joshua Brandon, died before the building was complete. He now lies in the graveyard alongside his creation.

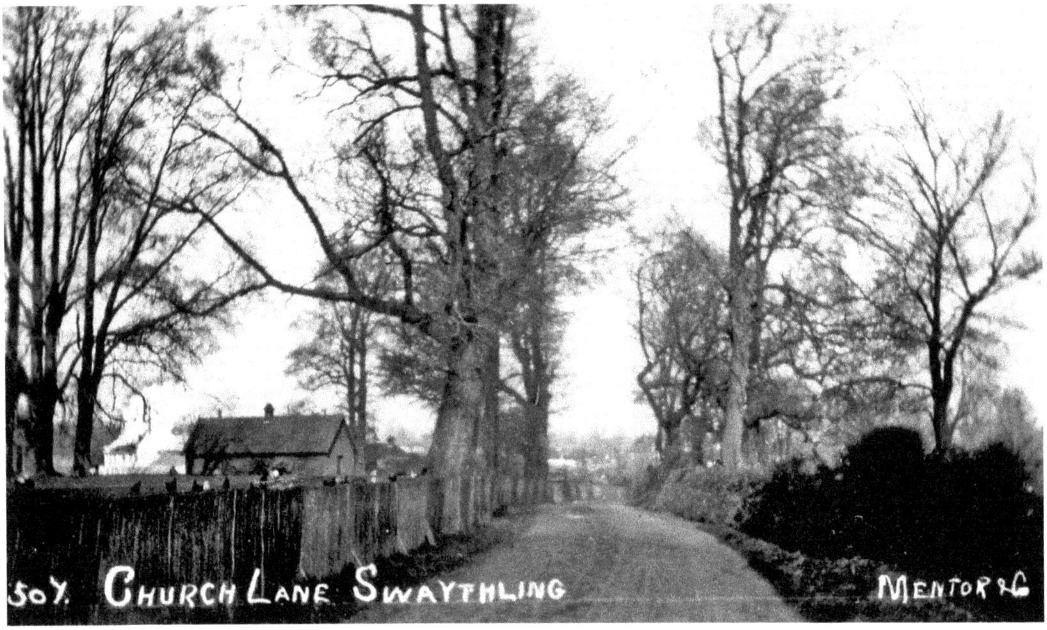

Church Lane, late 1800s
Church Lane is now considered to be firmly in the suburb of Highfield. It runs from Highfield Lane alongside the parish church, Christ Church. It dips down into a small valley and then heads uphill and becomes University Road. The rural feel has now long gone and this is today part of the wider university campus.

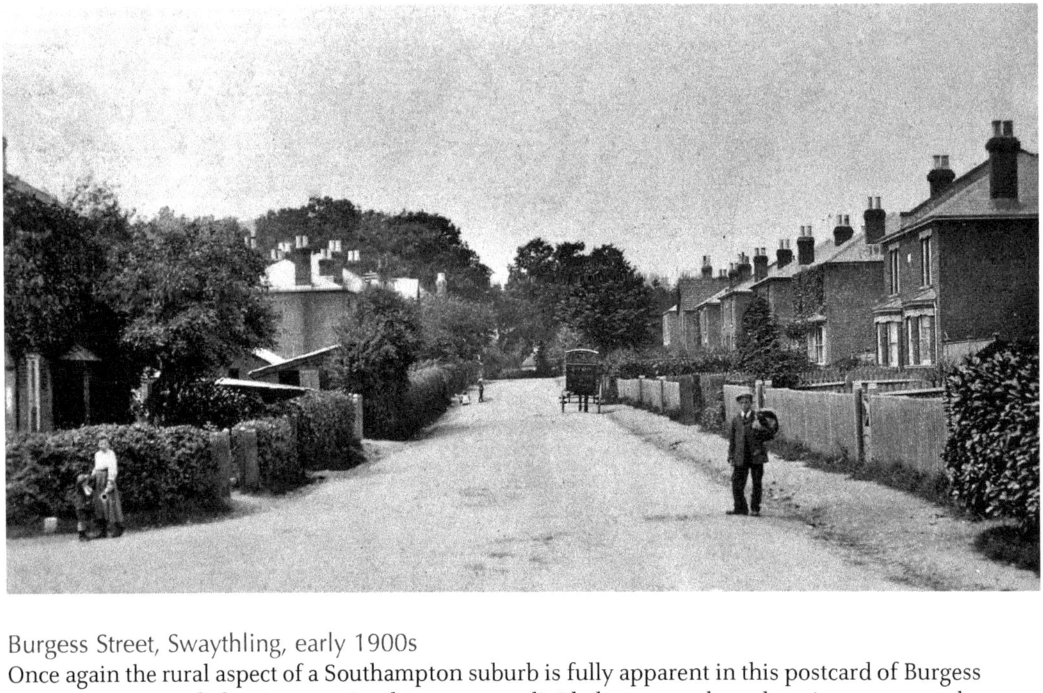

Burgess Street, Swaythling, early 1900s
Once again the rural aspect of a Southampton suburb is fully apparent in this postcard of Burgess Street. Now upgraded to Burgess Road, it creates a divide between a large housing estate on the north side and the sprawling campus of Southampton University on the south side.

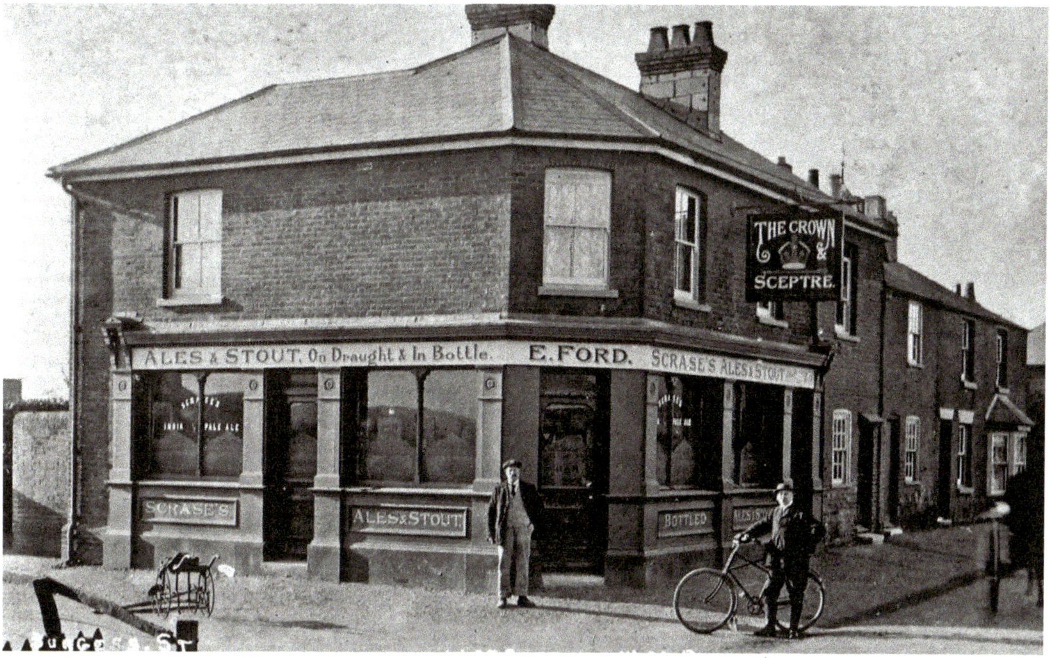

The Crown and Sceptre, Swaythling

This building was built in the early 1870s and originally had a beer licence only. In the 1930s the typical Victorian pub pictured here was demolished and a mock-Tudor version was built in its place. It is no longer in existence in any form.

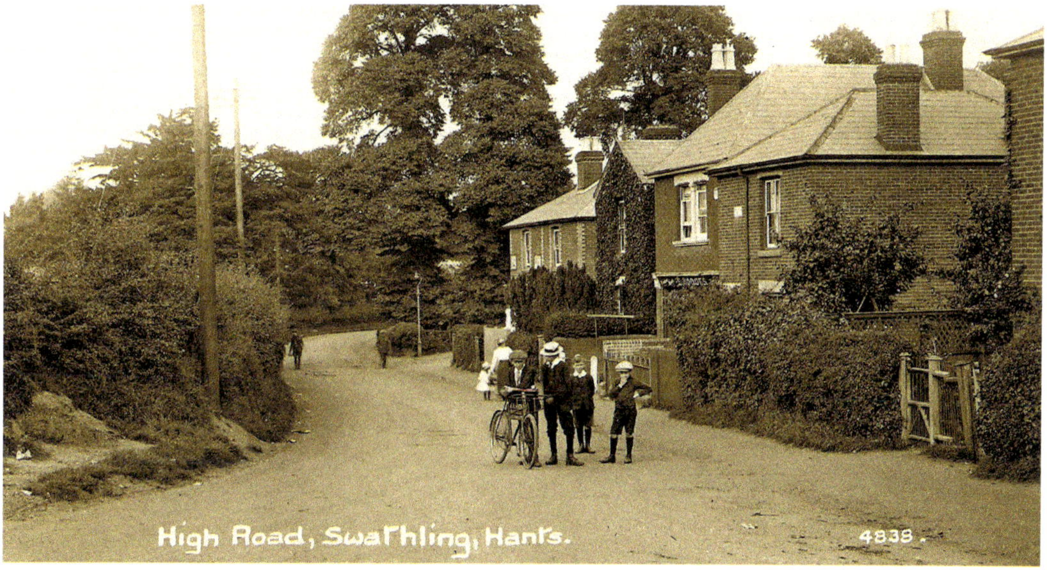

High Road, Swaythling, early 1900s

As with so many postcard images taken in every city and town in Britain during this period, the rural origins in this scene are very apparent. Those who have stopped for the photographer to take his shot have no fear of road traffic. Of course, the modern-day High Road in Swaythling is far busier.

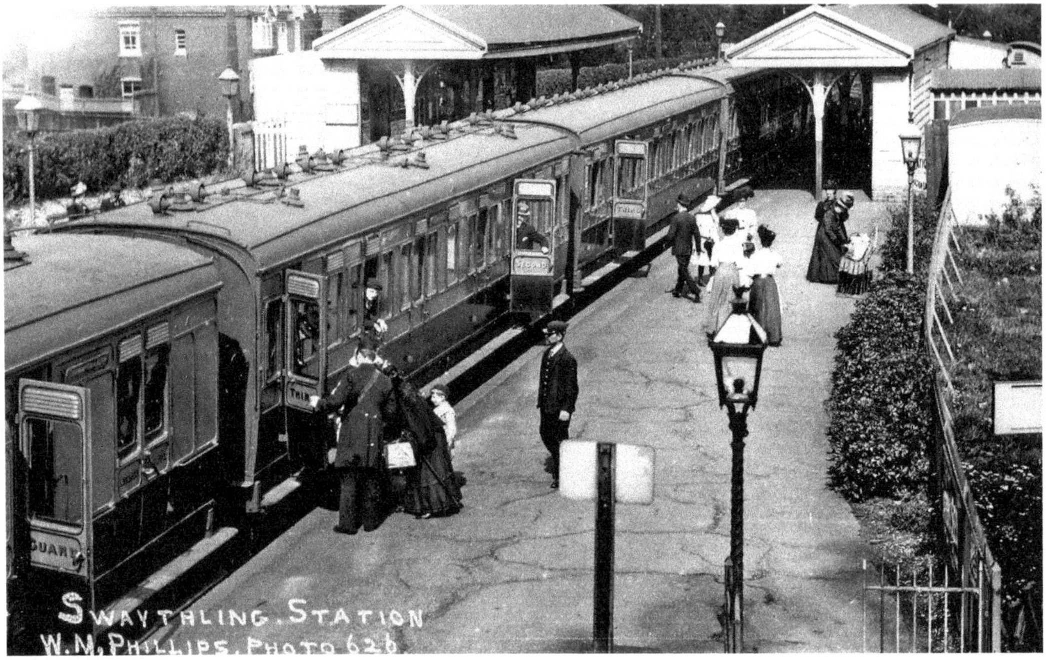

Swaythling Station

This railway station was built on the main line from Southampton to London in 1883. It proved to be extremely popular from the outset and saw a steady stream of passengers not only to London but also into Southampton. The station building still stands and is Grade II listed.

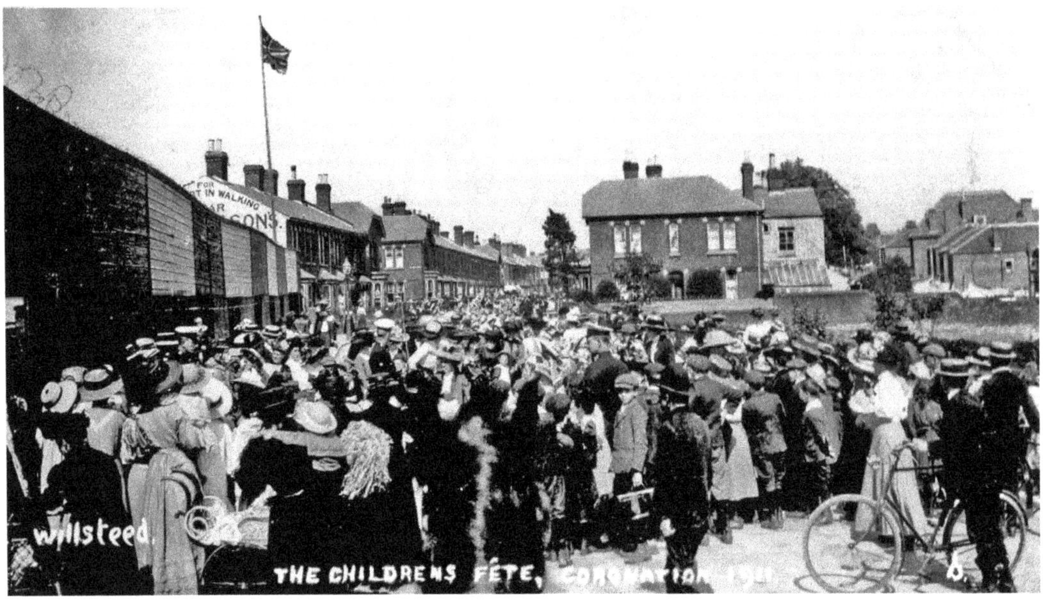

Banister, 1911

This postcard captures a bustling scene in which a coronation fête is being held outside The Dell, the old home of Southampton Football Club. Milton Road runs off to the left and Wilton Avenue is to the right.

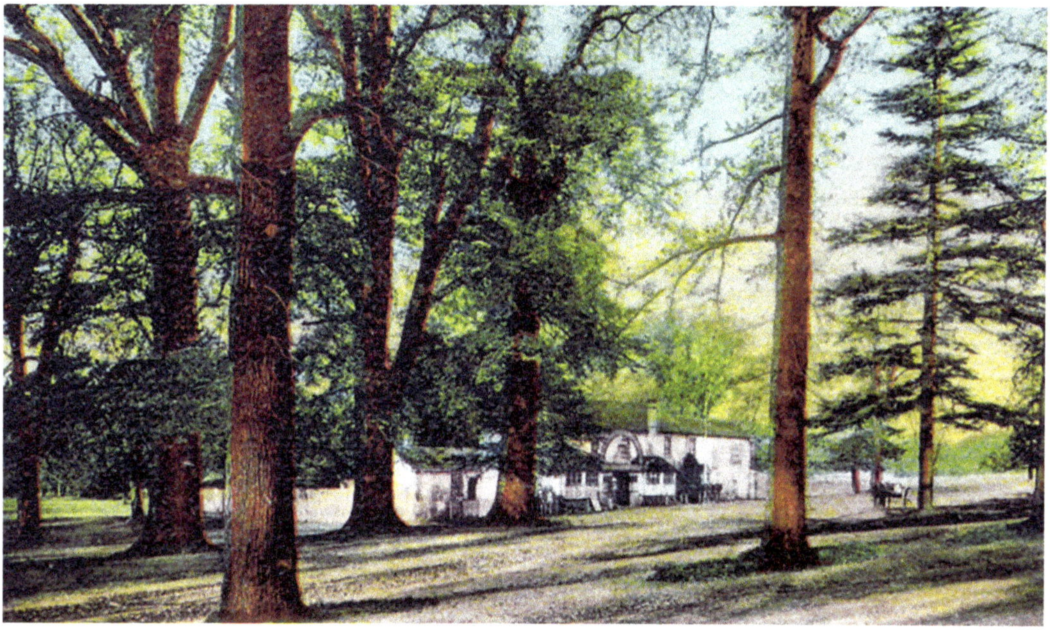

The Cowherds
The Cowherds public house. The core of the current building was built in 1762 on the site of an even older dwelling. It was the home of the man who oversaw the common land and it's grazing. In the eighteenth century the cow herdsman started to brew his own beer. Eventually the building was converted into a public house named The Southampton Arms. Local people remained stubborn and still referred to it as The Cowherds, and it again uses that name today.

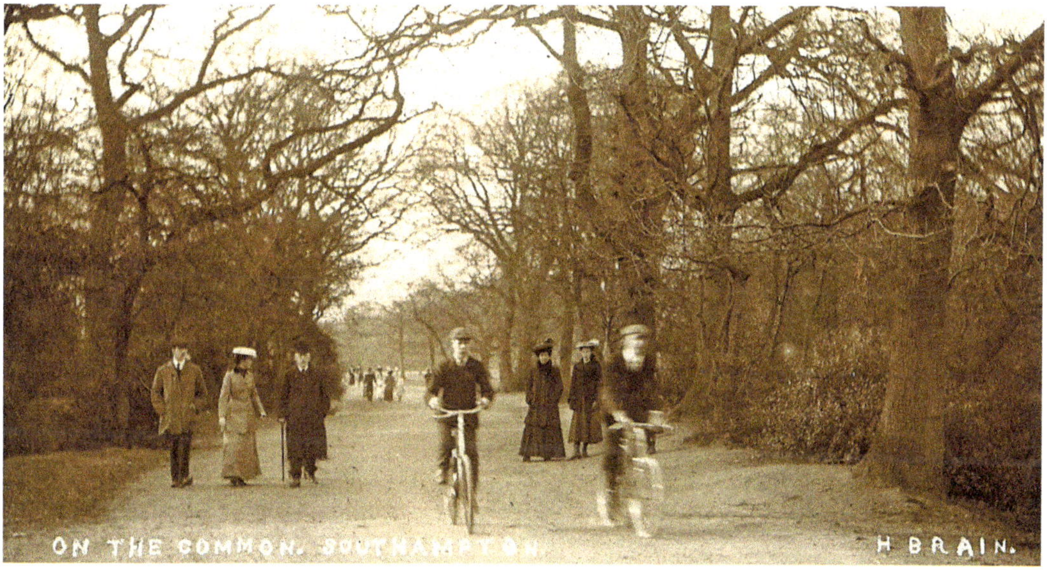

The Common, early 1900s
Originally common grazing land called Great Heath in the medieval period, the Common was slowly planted with trees. By the 1900s it proved to be a popular place to exercise and get fresh air at all times of the year. It is still used and appreciated for that purpose to this day.

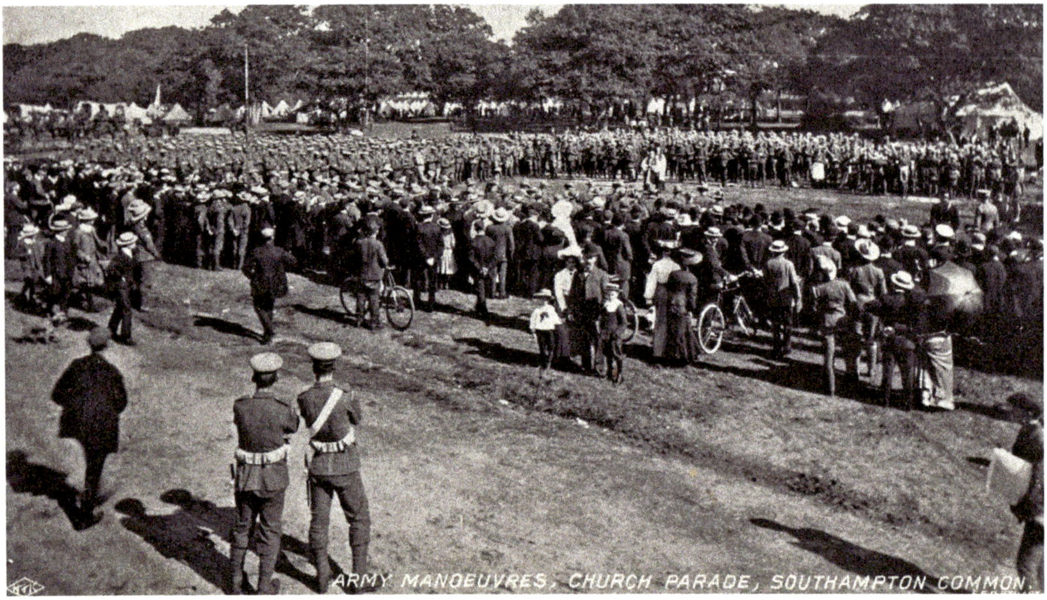

Army Manoeuvres, 1914–18

A crowd gathers to watch a church parade taking place among a huge army presence on Southampton Common. It is thought this postcard dates back to the First World War, when more than 8 million troops and equipment left for Europe from Southampton after it was named the top military embarkation port in August 1914.

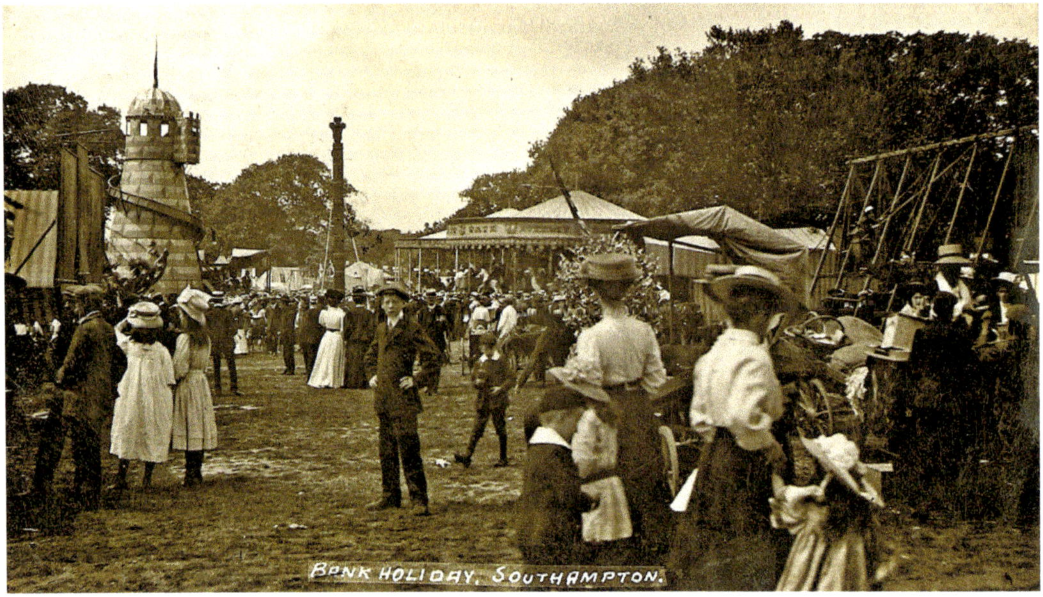

Bank Holiday Fair

A bank holiday fair on the Common has been a tradition since 1859 when the town council first granted permission for fairs to be held there. Large crowds have since gathered there, to be entertained with coconut shies, carousel gallopers, helter-skelters, boxing booths and to have their fortunes told.

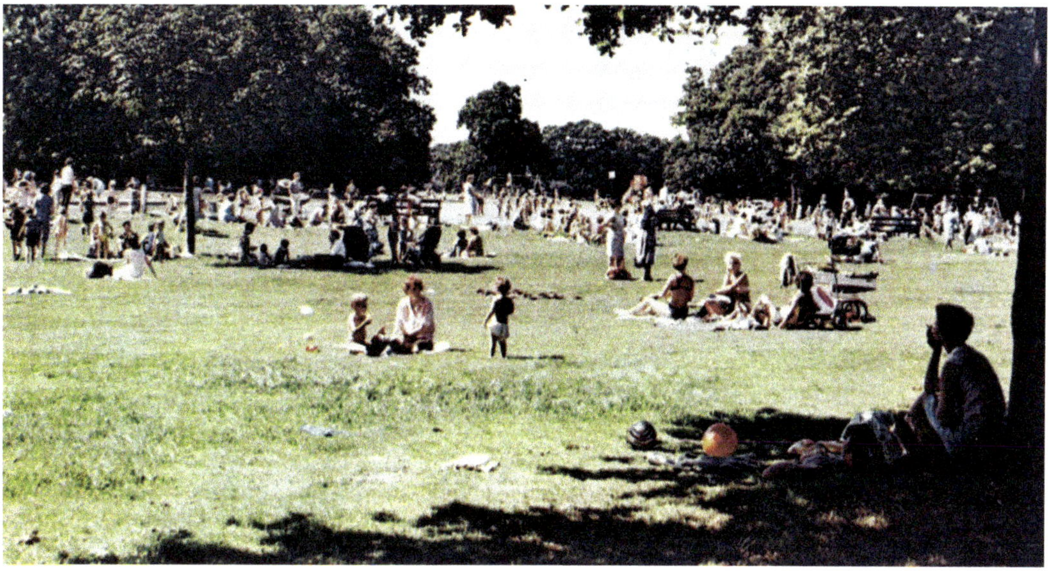

Paddling Pool, the Common, 1970s

The iconic paddling pool on Southampton Common was built in the 1930s when an unused reservoir that once supplied water to the town was filled in. Countless children will remember sliding around on the green, slimy concrete. It was later renovated and is pictured here during the long hot summer of 1976. In 2017, it was decided that as the pool was only open for three months per year it would be replaced with a new children's play area.

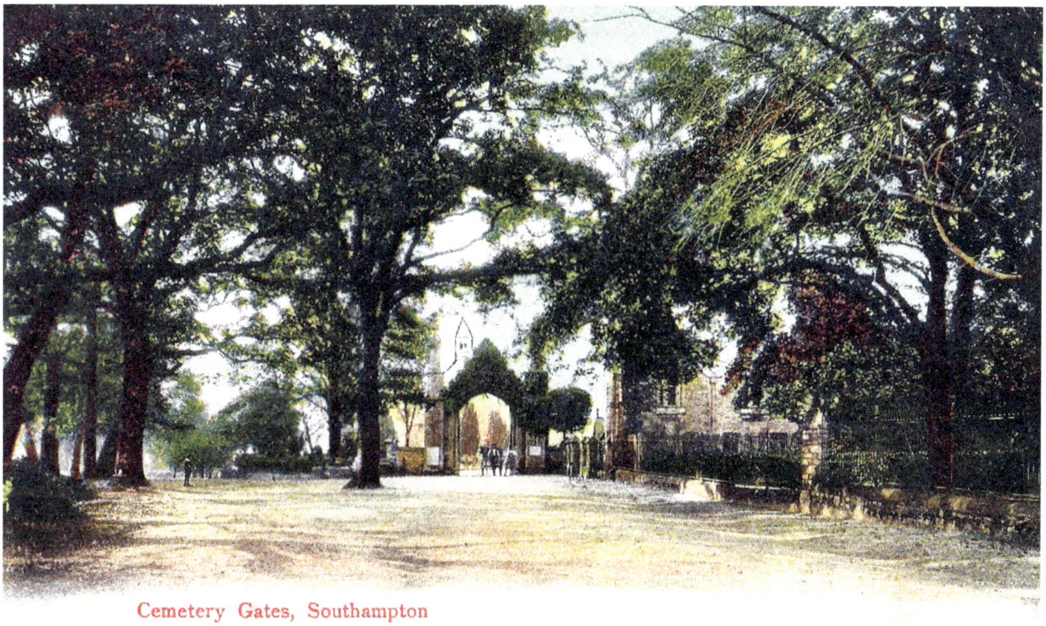

Southampton Old Cemetery

Southampton Old Cemetery occupies a site some 27 acres in size on former common land. Opened in 1846, it is estimated to be the final resting place of over 116,000 people from all walks of life.

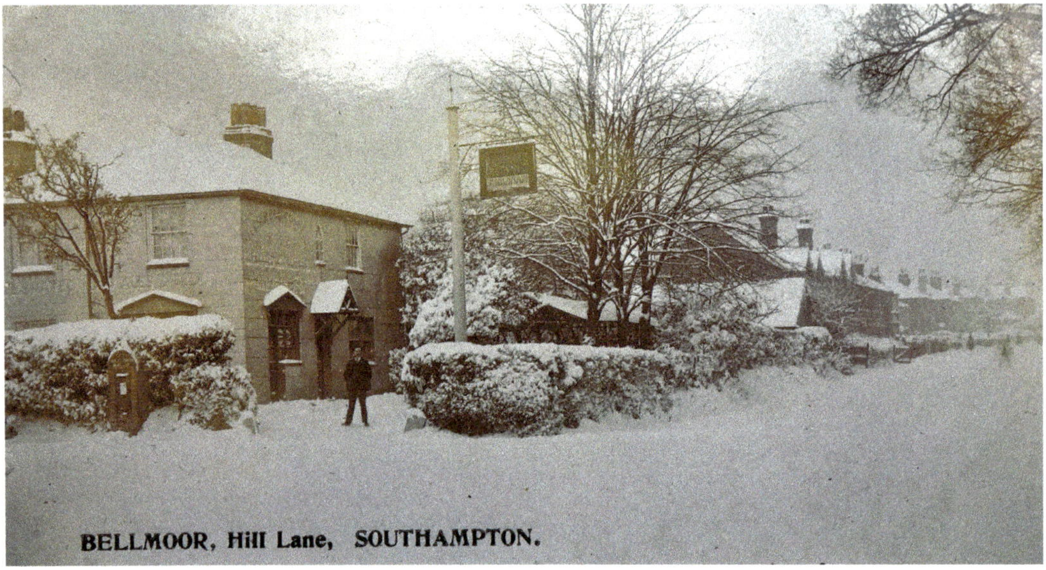

The Bellemoor Inn, Hill Lane

This public house was built in the mid-1880s and is located on Hill Lane, which runs north out of Southampton. The pub, close to one of the main gates onto Southampton Common, is always busy when bank holiday fairs are held there. At one time the landlord was the splendidly named Thankful Joy.

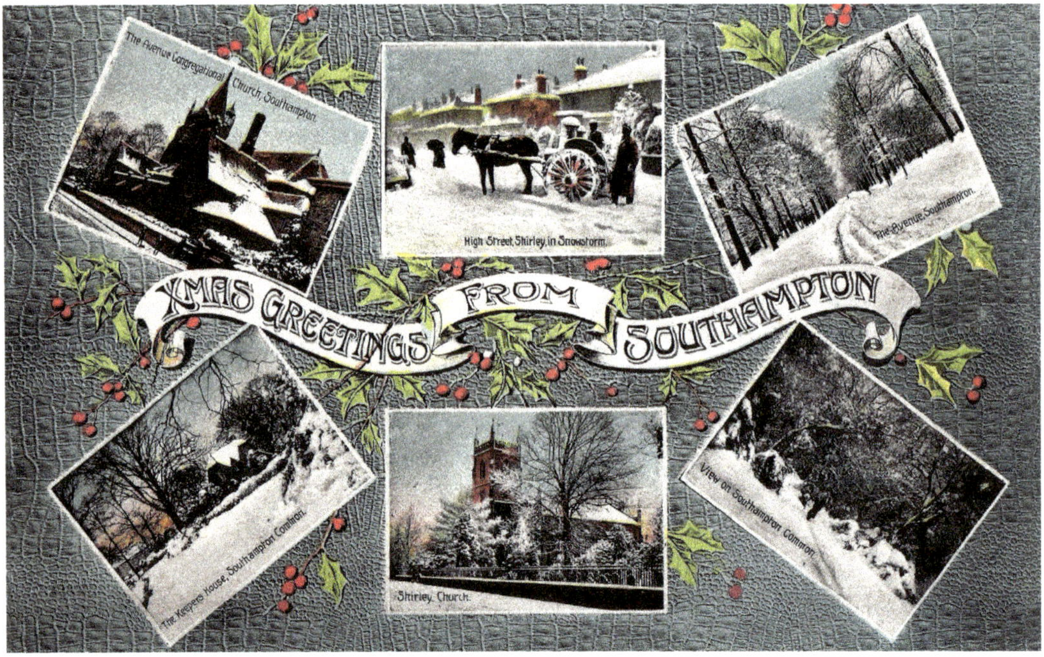

Snowy Greetings

As printing processes improved, postcards became extremely popular and sold well. This is a beautiful example of a Christmas postcard showing scenes around the town under a covering of snow.

CHAPTER 5

WESTERN PARISHES

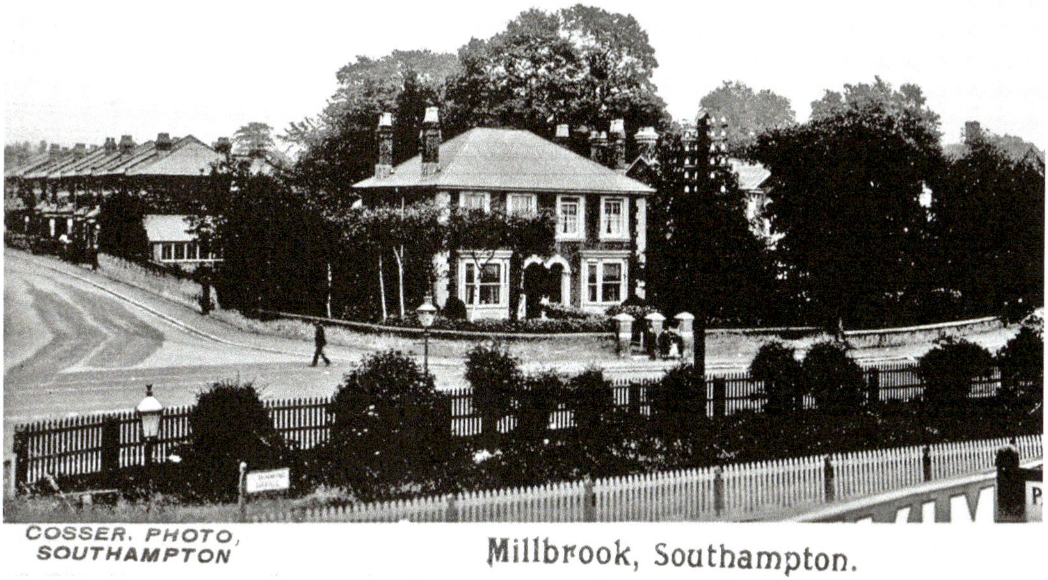

Freemantle

Confusingly in Millbrook Road, with Millbrook station in the right-hand corner of this postcard, Foundry Lane is pictured here on the left. To the right and the rear of the house is Freemantle Lake.

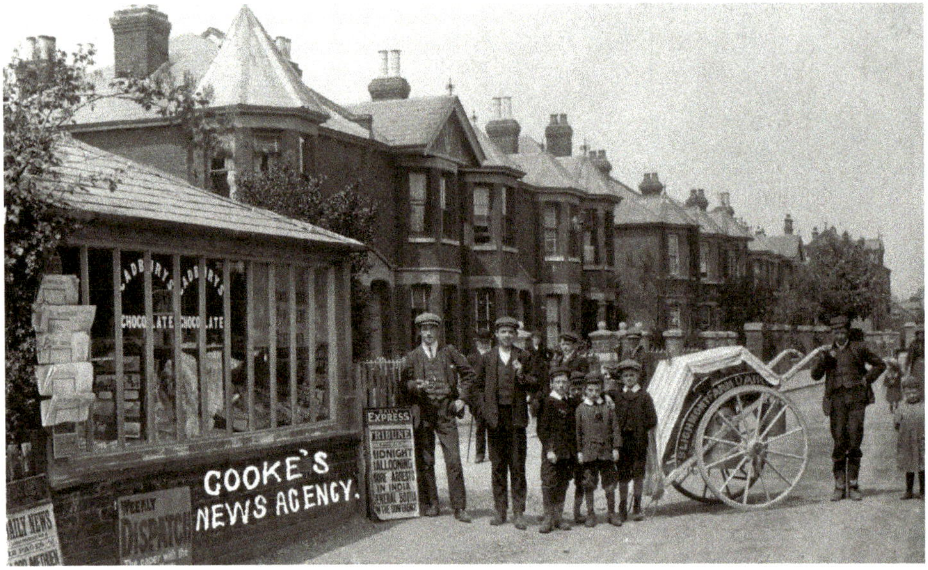

Foundry Lane, Freemantle
The newsagent's shop in Foundry Lane, Freemantle. The source of all news, both national, international and most probably locally. The billboards indicate the date as around the period of the Second Boer War. Lord Methuen was sent out to South Africa to become the senior British general; however, he made errors of judgement that resulted in his artillery shelling their own comrades. The dairy cart on the right belonged to the nearby Blighmont Farm. It is thought that the cover over the cart helped to keep the milk cool.

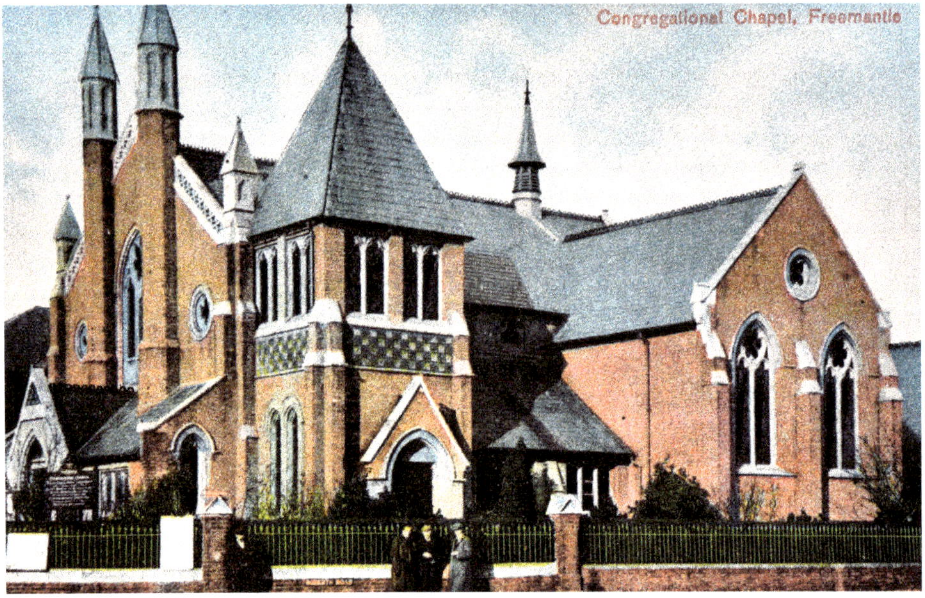

Freemantle Congregational Chapel
Freemantle Congregational Chapel was located on the corner of Roberts Road and Shirley Road between 1885 and 1940. The building met an abrupt end at the hands of the Luftwaffe, and today the site is occupied by residential flats.

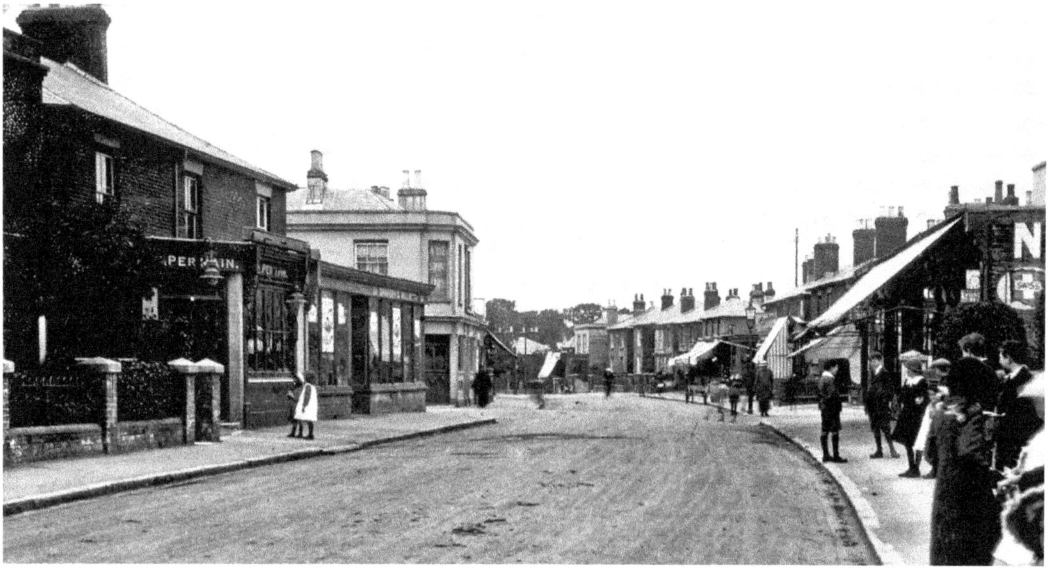

Park Road, Freemantle

Park Road in the parish of Freemantle, as with many Victorian suburbs, had something of a village feel. With a wide assortment of local shops, public houses, a school and places of worship, local people were well catered for.

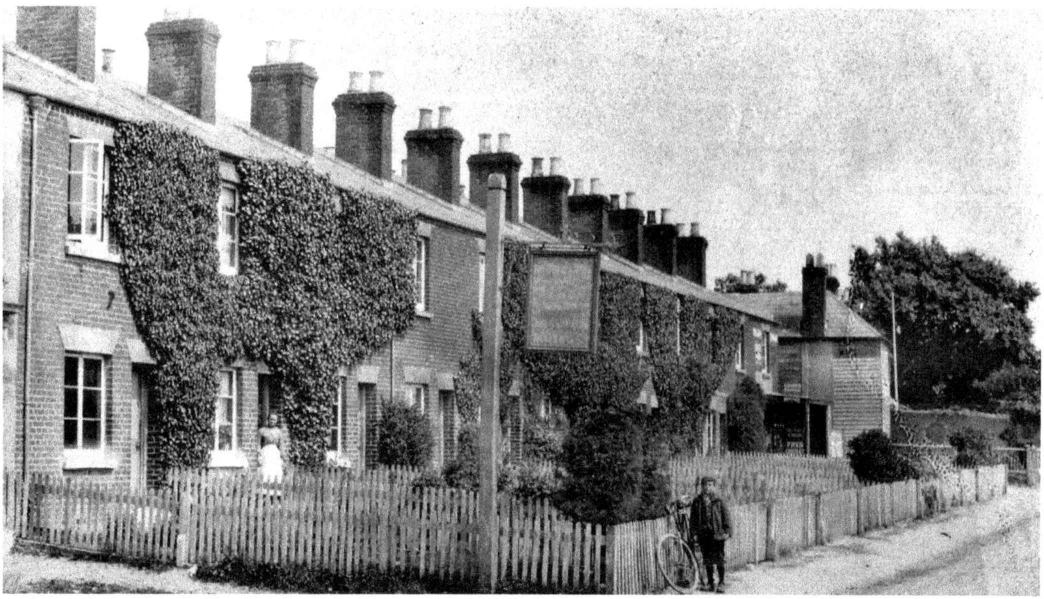

Vulcan Terrace, Millbrook

In the mid-1800s there was a thriving water-powered mill on the eastern bank of Tanners Brook. Engineer and iron founder Charles Kerman had set the business up and called it the Vulcan Foundry. Nearby, on the Millbrook Road, he built Vulcan Terrace as housing for his workers and their families. On the left-hand end of the terrace was a conveniently placed public house, originally named, aptly, The Vulcan Tavern. Its name was later changed to the Forest Inn as in its day it had a clear view of the edge of the New Forest across the River Test.

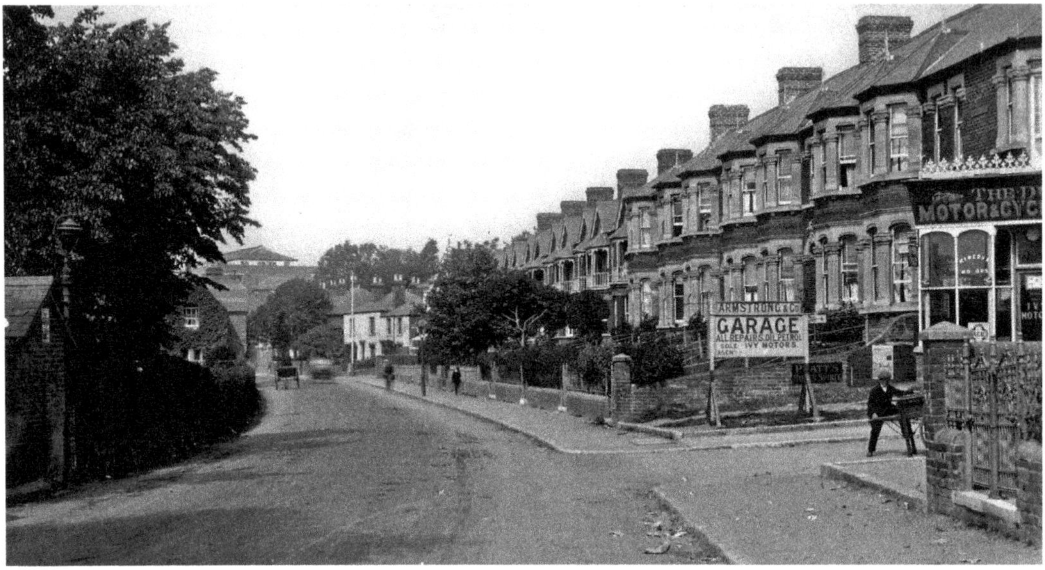

Testwood Terrace, early 1900s
Testwood Terrace on Millbrook Road. The occupants in that terrace of houses had a clear view of the River Test across the railway line. This was the main road west to Totton, the New Forest and all points west. In the distance looms the head office and warehouse of nurseryman and seed merchants Toogood's.

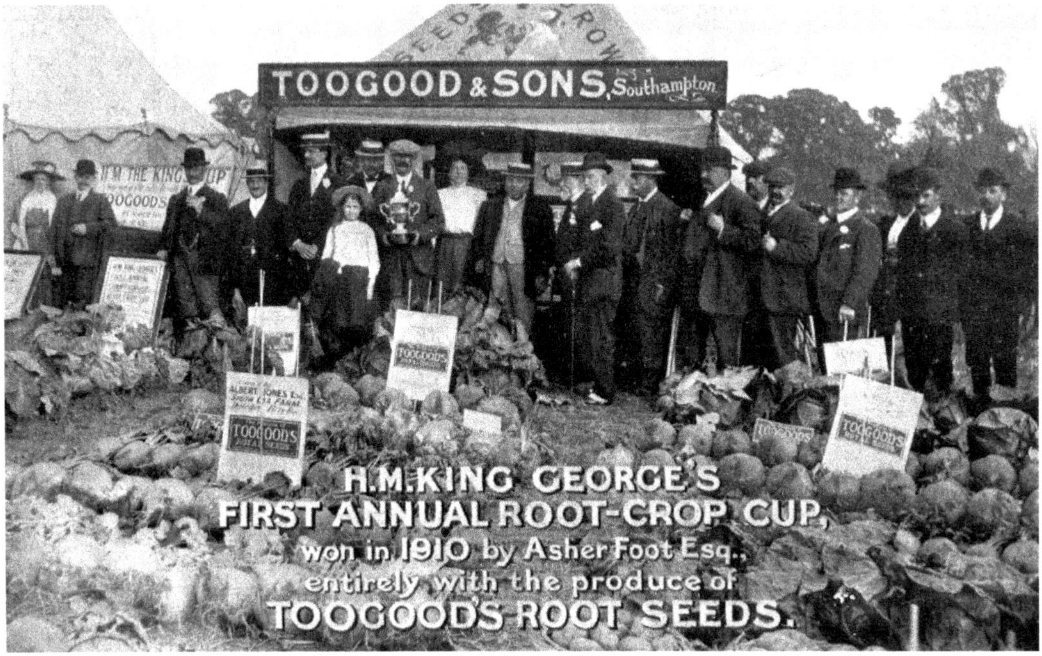

Toogood & Sons, Millbrook
One of Southampton's famous companies, Toogood & Sons prided themselves as being 'The King's Seedsman'. The seedsman and nurseryman had a shop in Above Bar Street, its main headquarters at Blighmont on Millbrook Road, and growing grounds at Nursling.

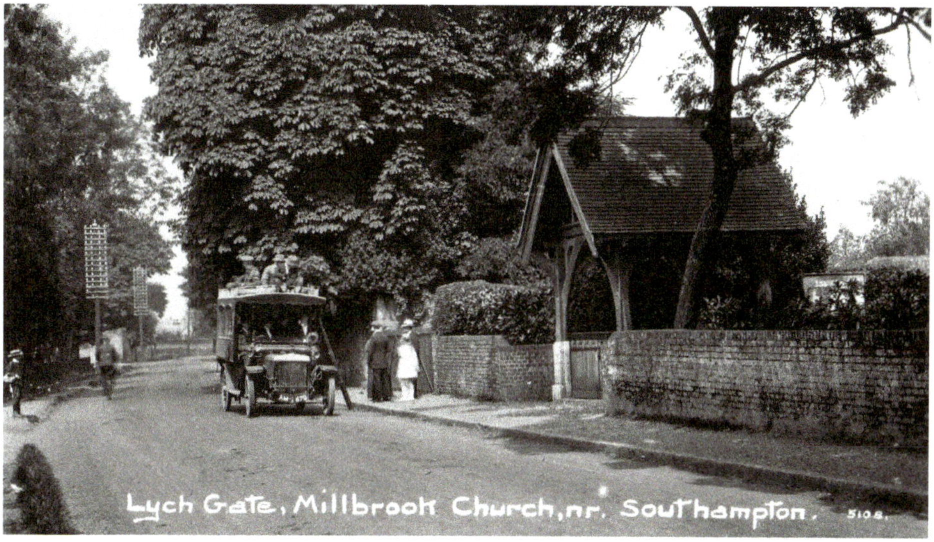

Holy Trinity Church, Millbrook Road, *c.* 1918

Considered to be the mother church for the west of Southampton, this church was built between 1872 and 1892. It replaced the dilapidated church of St Nicholas, which was a little farther east along Millbrook Road at its junction with Regents Park Road. Like so many old images of Southampton, the feeling of a rural setting is apparent. The church now sits alongside an extremely busy dual carriageway that takes traffic in and out of the city. The bus shown in the photograph had probably made the comparatively long journey around from the Hythe/Fawley area. Note the servicemen on the cheaper roof seats and the ladder alongside the vehicle to allow passengers to get on or off the transport.

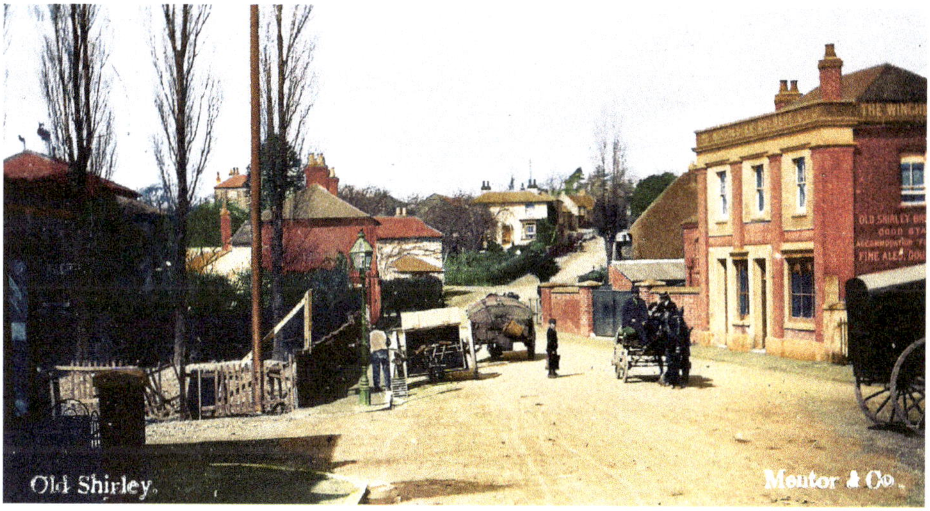

Old Shirley

From the 1200s, the small village of Shirley existed in the valley on the junction of Romsey Road and Winchester Road. With the advent of the railways and the growth of the docks in Southampton, the suburbs of the town expanded. Land on Shirley Common, between the old village and the town, was rapidly built on in the early 1800s. By 1900 Shirley Common and nearby Freemantle were covered with roads and housing.

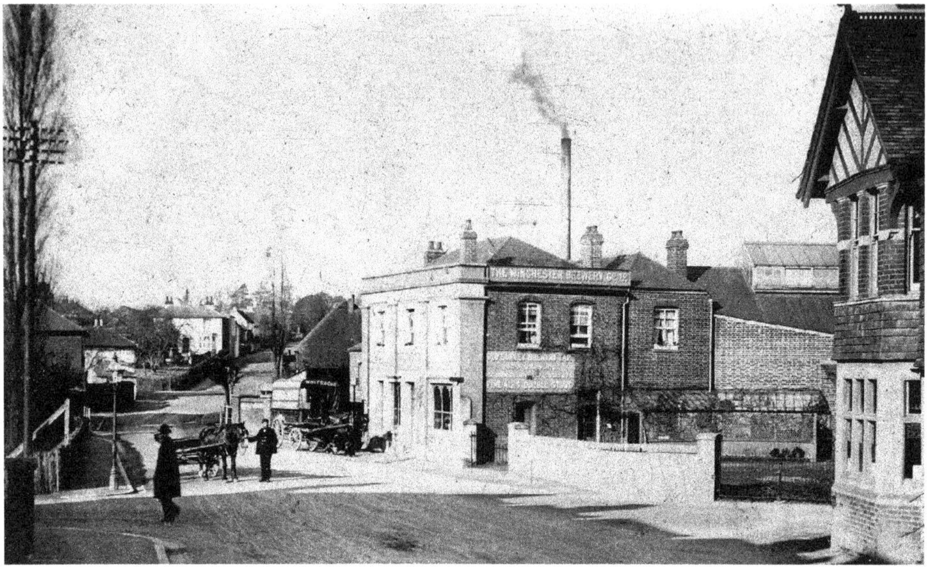

Romsey Road, Shirley, late 1800s

The main road from Southampton to Romsey ran through what had once been the original village of Old Shirley. On the immediate right The Blacksmiths Arms public house can be seen. The next building, with the tall chimney, was then the brewery belonging to the Winchester Brewery Company. Founded in the very early 1800s, the company ended up owning 108 public houses in the Hampshire area. The building the brewery occupied had been a mill and an iron foundry, then after brewing beer it became a laundry. Past the brewery the road runs up the hill towards Maybush and then on towards Romsey. The road passes the second public house in Old Shirley, The Thatched House.

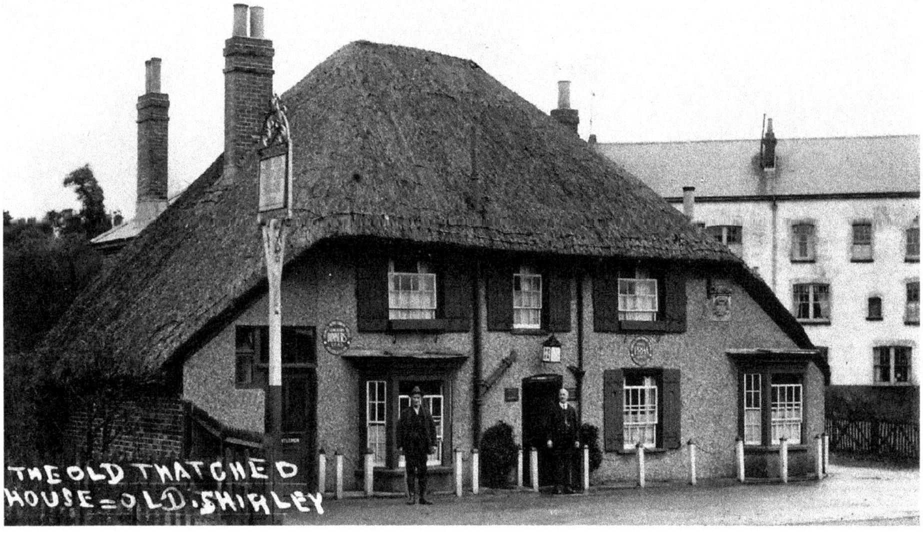

The Old Thatched Inn

The Old Thatched Inn public house on the Romsey Road. Built in the 1800s, the building, which still stands but is no longer a pub, is one of the last thatched properties within the city boundary. In the background part of Old Shirley Mill can be seen.

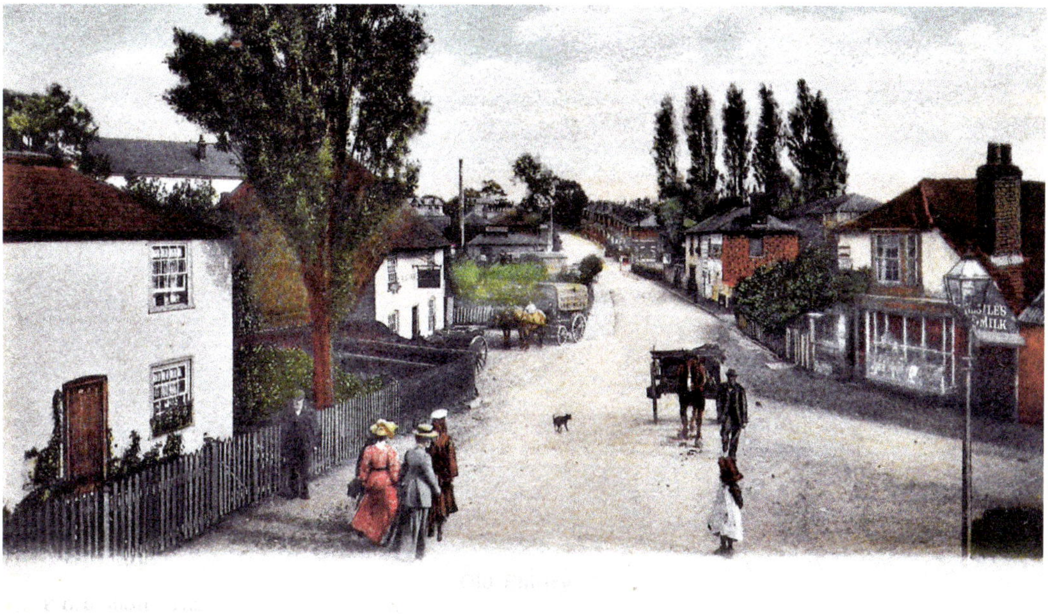

Old Shirley

The original location for the first village of Shirley. On the right is the old post office, to the left is Poppy Cottage and next to it is The Old Thatched House pub. Behind that are the old mill buildings, which at the time the postcard was printed was operating as a brewery. The hill in the distance leads up to where the modern-day centre of Shirley is located.

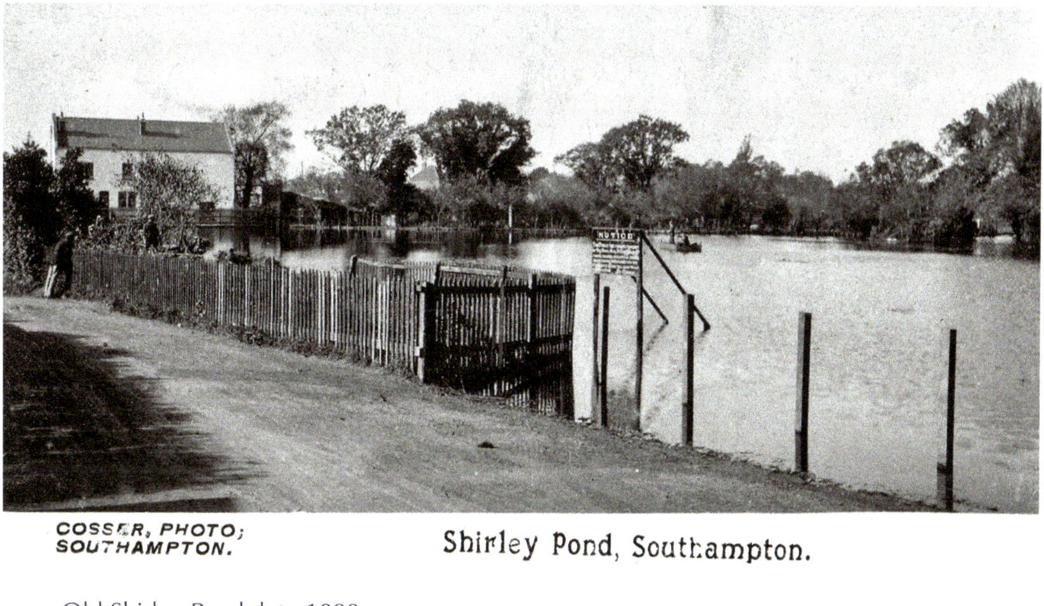

Old Shirley Pond, late 1800s

The large pond in the village of Old Shirley was its power source and water supply. The flow of water into the pond from the Holly Brook ensured a water source that drove the various mills along the stream from here to the River Test. The pond also supplied water for cooking and laundry and most probably drinking. The pond also served as a source of freshwater fish for food.

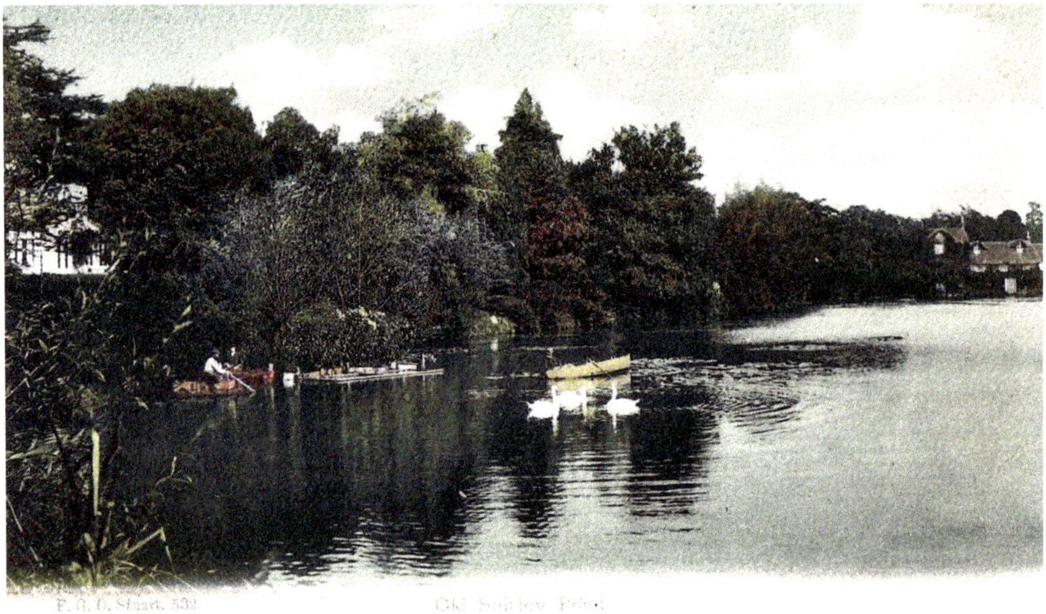

Old Shirley Pond

A sylvan view of Shirley Pond, at one time three ponds fed by the Holly Brook and Tanner's Brook. The water's power drove the pre-Norman Conquest mill on the site. It looked an idyllic location to live, complete with swans.

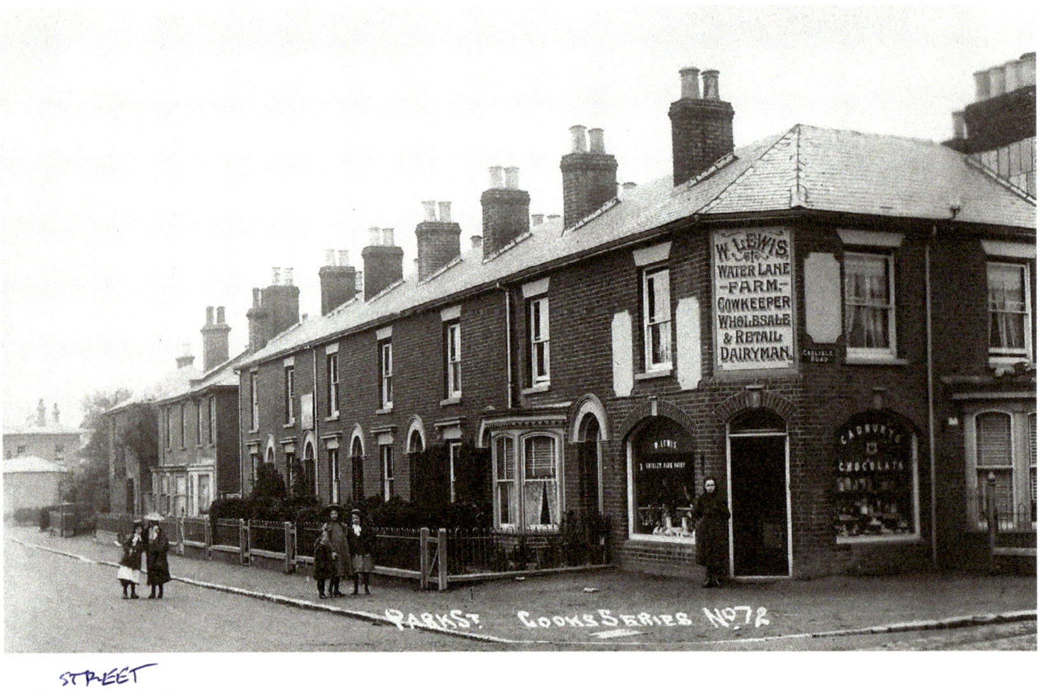

Park ~~Road,~~ STREET Shirley

This postcard shows Park ~~Road~~ at its junction with Carlisle Road. The enterprising Mr Lewis, who had his farm at Water Lane in Totton, branched into retail to sell his home-produced goods.

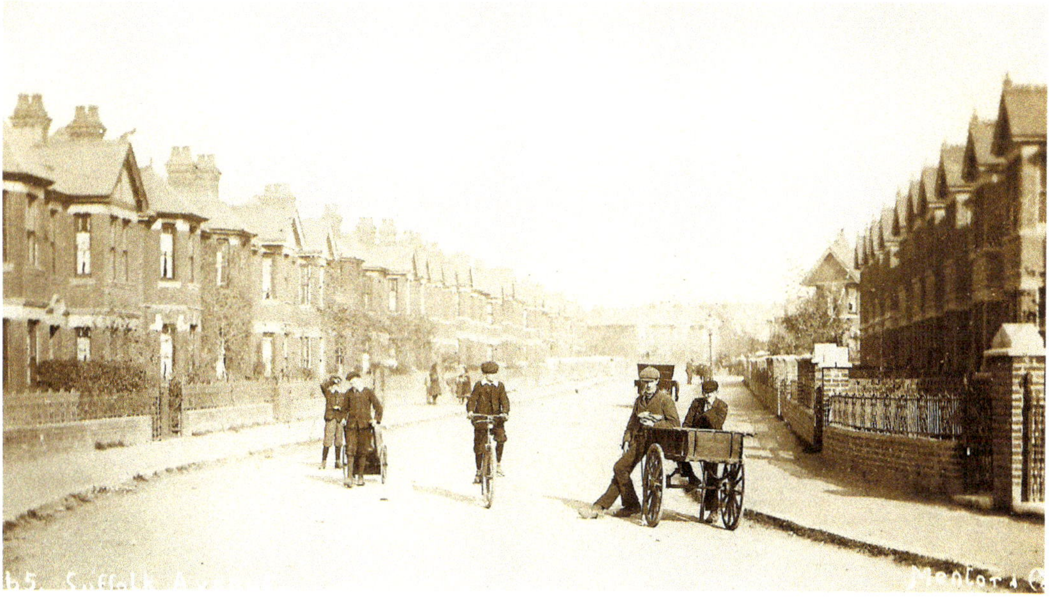

Suffolk Avenue, Shirley, late 1800s

The lads with the barrows are probably delivery boys, happy to take a break and gaze into the photographer's lens. So many goods were transported around towns like Southampton on handcarts and barrows.

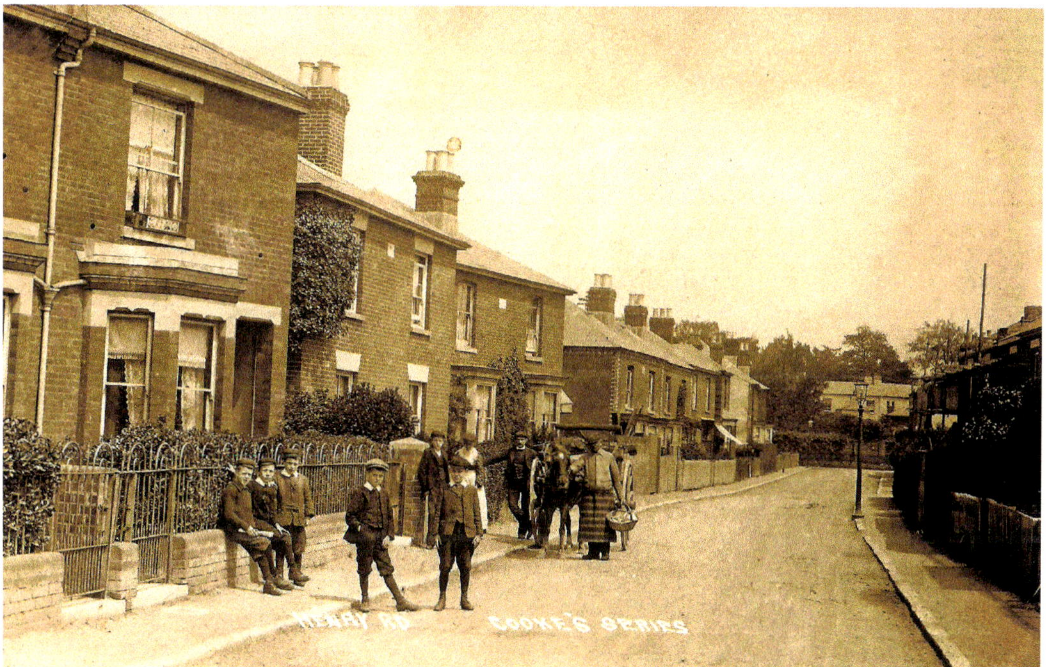

Henry Road, Shirley

Henry Road was a traditional Edwardian residential street. The local boys and the delivery man pose unsmilingly for the camera.

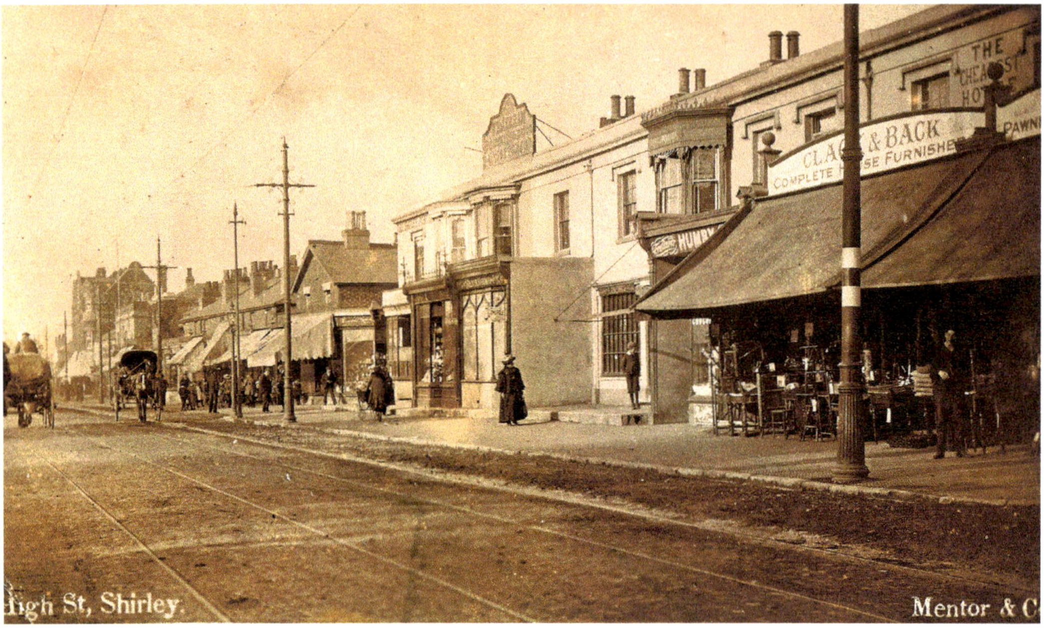

Shirley High Street, late 1800s
Shirley High Street in the Victorian era. The section of shops on the right, containing that busy furniture shop, is no longer there.

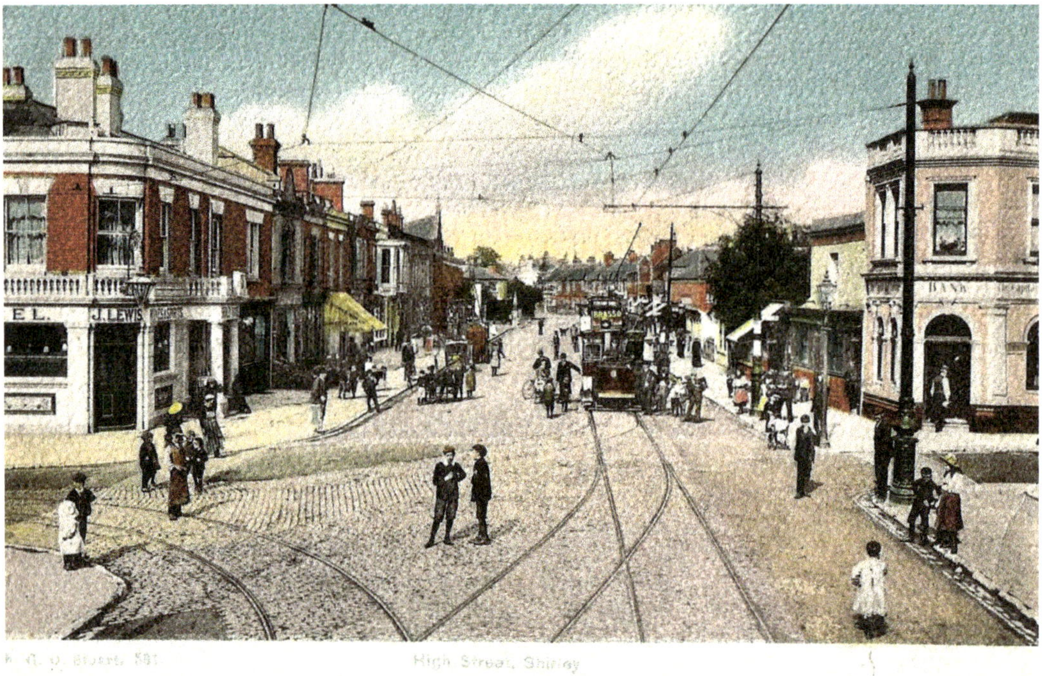

Shirley High Street
The High Street at its crossroads with Cannon Street on the right and Park Street on the left. Considering this was a busy tramline junction, the onlookers look quite happy to stand in the road.

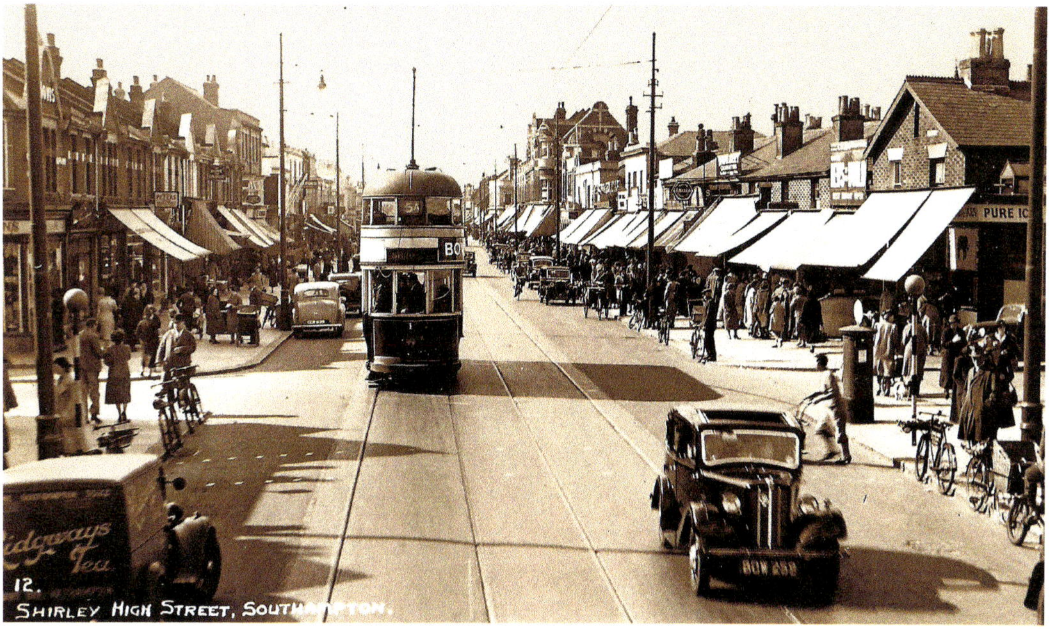

Shirley High Street, 1940s

Another familiar scene, but at a time when the motorcar began to appear in more and more photographs. The tram and the bicycle were still in evidence though. Many of the buildings in this view still stand, though the ground floors have changed a great deal.

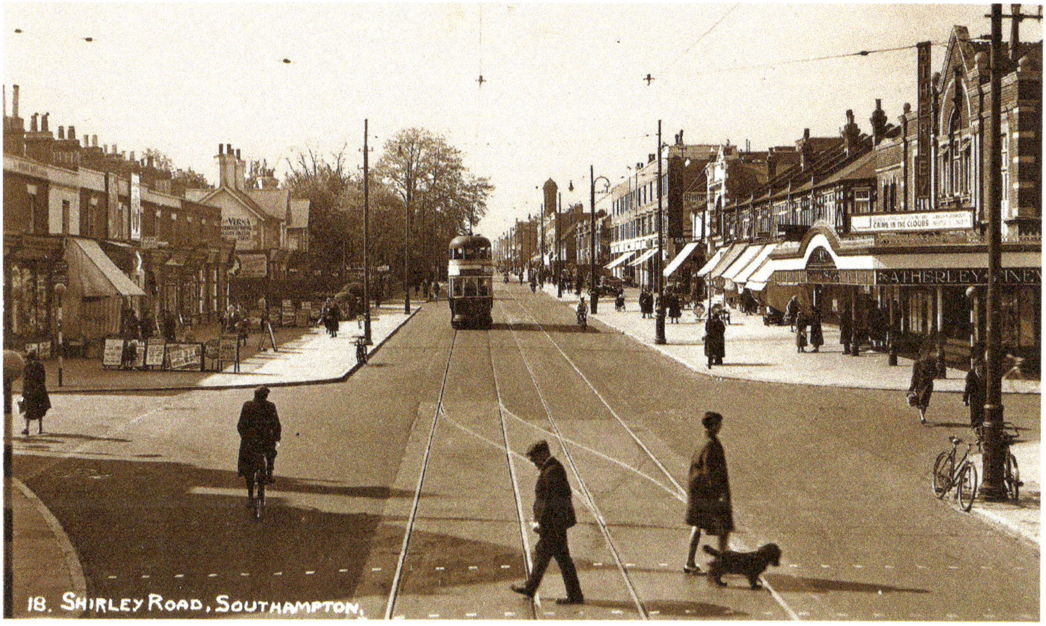

Shirley Road, 1930s

The tramlines run straight as an arrow along Shirley Road to the terminus at the north end of the suburb of Shirley. The Atherley Cinema, seen on the right, was the first purpose-built picture house built in the town.

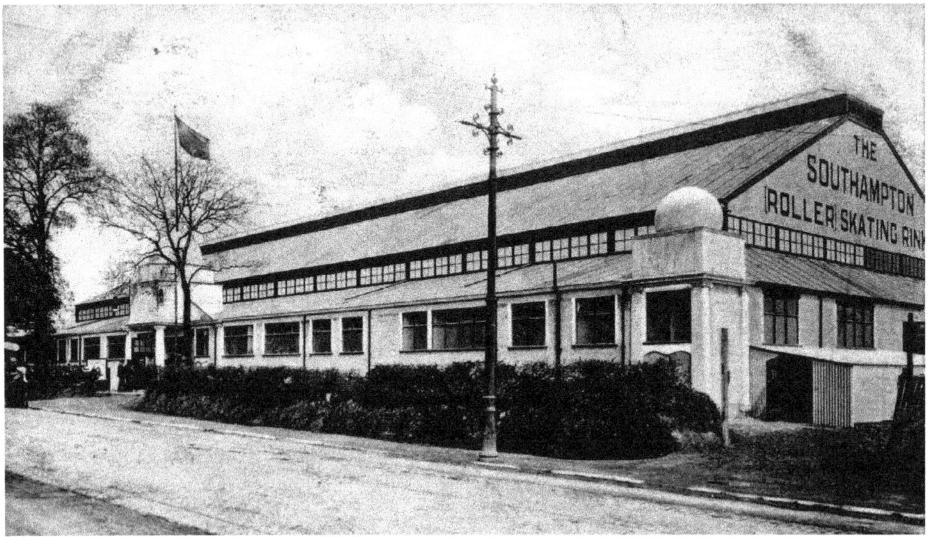

Roller Skating Rink, early 1900s
The roller skating rink on Shirley Road was situated at the junction with Janson Road. In the early part of the 1900s the building proved an extremely popular venue. It was said queues formed in the street for every skating session. During the First World War, the building was used as a transit camp for German prisoners of war. Post-war, the fortunes of the roller rink started to fail as cinemas started to gain a hold as a means of entertainment. The rink was sold and a large retail and apartment block, Burlington Mansions, was built on the site.

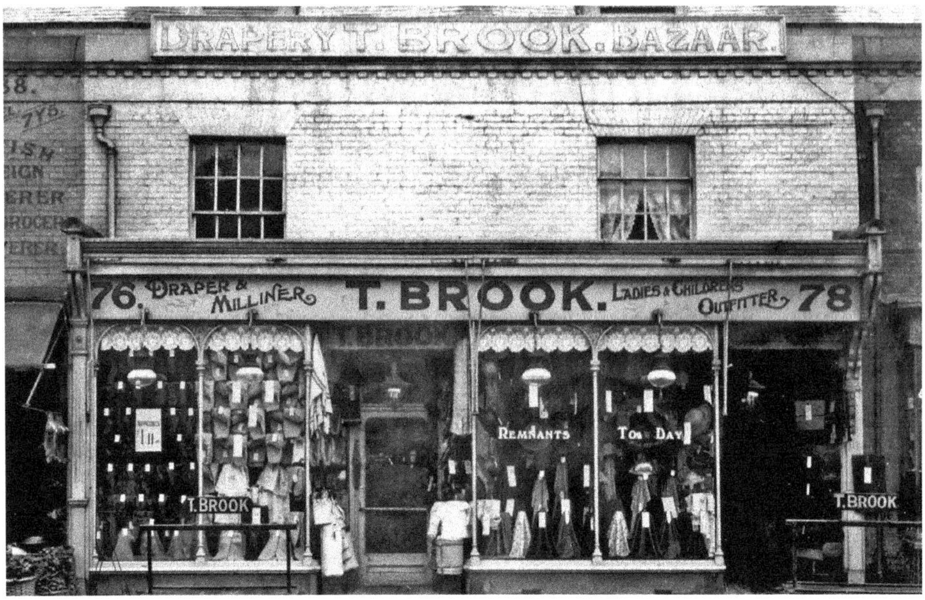

Brooks the Draper, Shirley High Street
Mr Brook had two busy establishments in Shirley High Street. At Nos 68, 70 and 72 was located his outfitters shop. At Nos 76, 78 and 80 was his drapery business. There is no indication on contemporary street directories as to the fate of No. 74, although a peek of it can be seen in this image, which was taken before Mr Brook expanded his businesses.

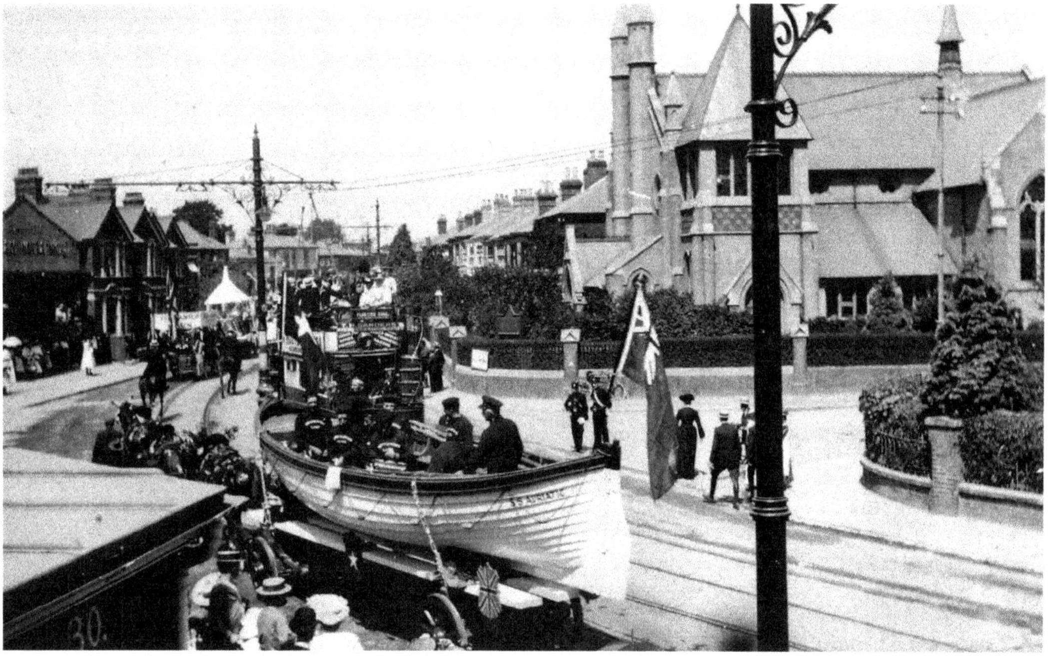

Lifeboat Parade, *c.* 1900

Shirley Road, at its crossroads with what is now Roberts Road and Waterloo Road. The occasion was the Lifeboat Parade, a fundraising street procession to collect donations for the lifeboat service.

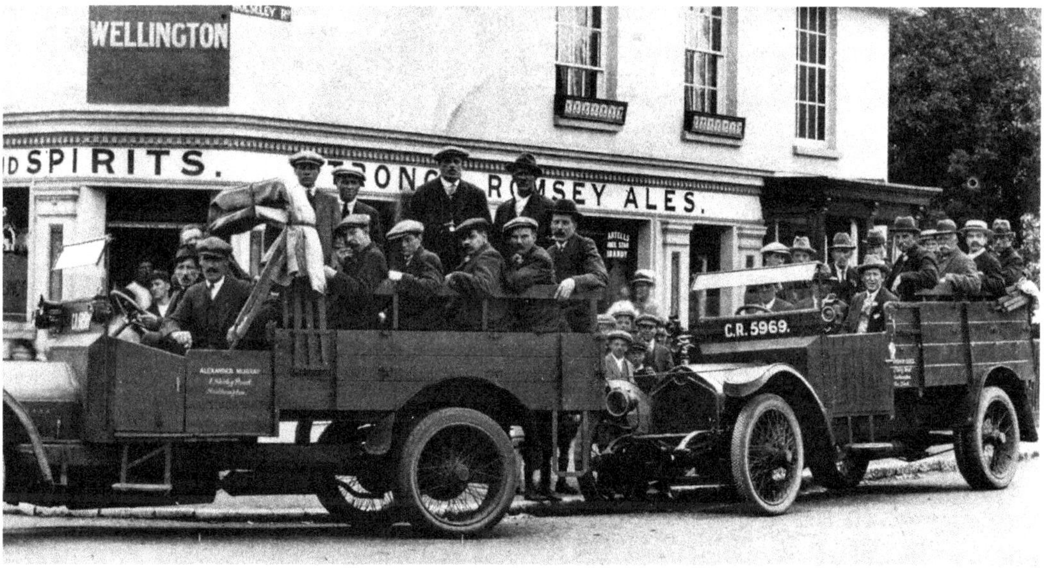

Duchess of Wellington

The Duchess of Wellington public house on the corner of Wolseley Road and Firgrove Road. This postcard is typical of many similar images taken in this period. The age of motorised group transport had arrived and day trips like this using charabancs or simply lorries with benches were the order of the day. Pub customers, church groups or just neighbours all enjoyed a day out to the seaside, the New Forest, or the races.

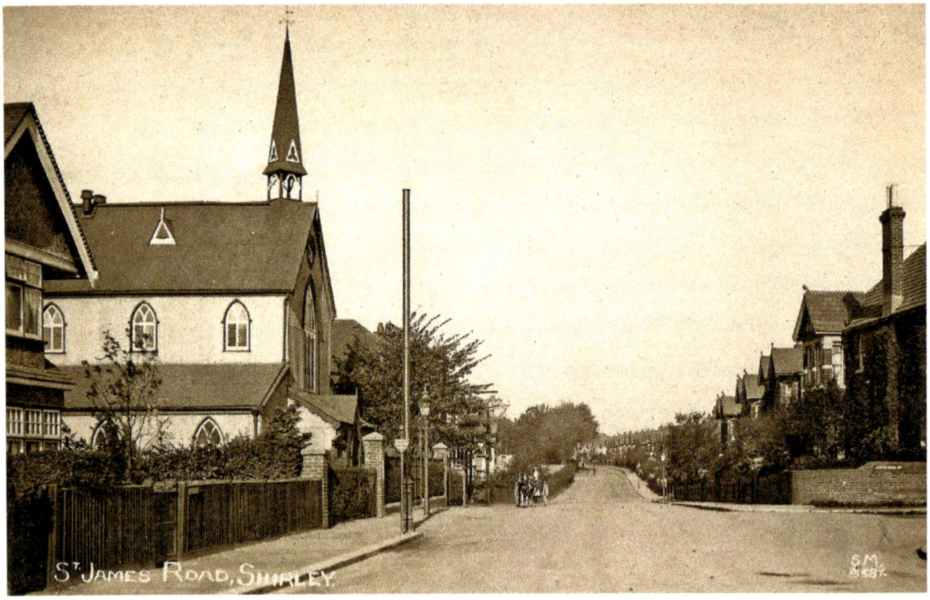

St James Road, Shirley, 1920s

St James Road runs through a typical Southampton suburb from Hill Lane to Winchester Road. On the left is St John's Church, the companion church to St James's Church a quarter of a mile along St James Road. St John's first opened its parish register in 1912.

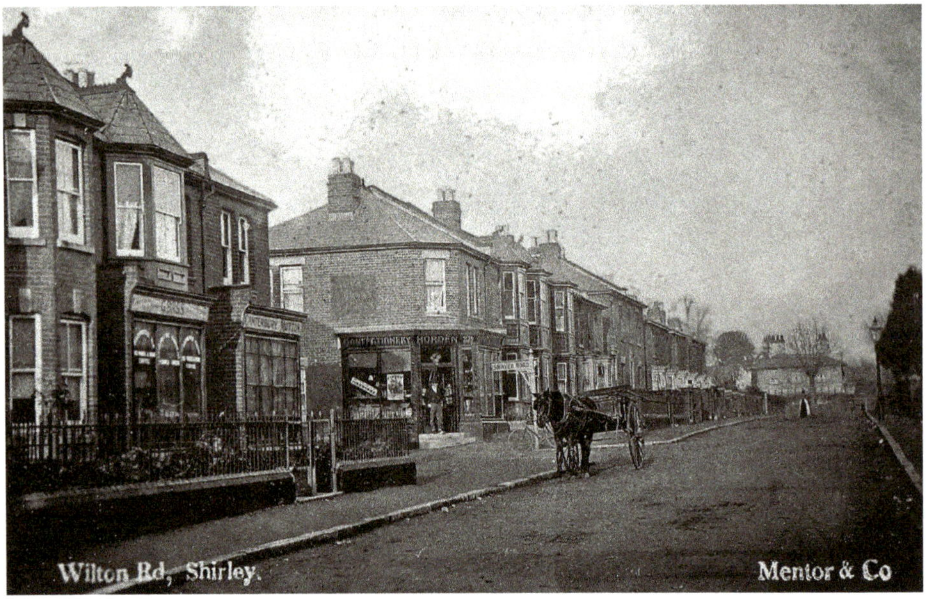

Wilton Road

Very little of what is shown in this image remains today. The houses and shops around the junction of Wilton Road and Shayer Road, plus all the houses at this end of Shayer Road itself, were demolished to provide extra land for use as playing fields by the adjacent Shirley Infant and Junior schools. In the distance, the grand Winchester Road residence has long since been swept away, the site now being occupied by a huge retail warehouse.

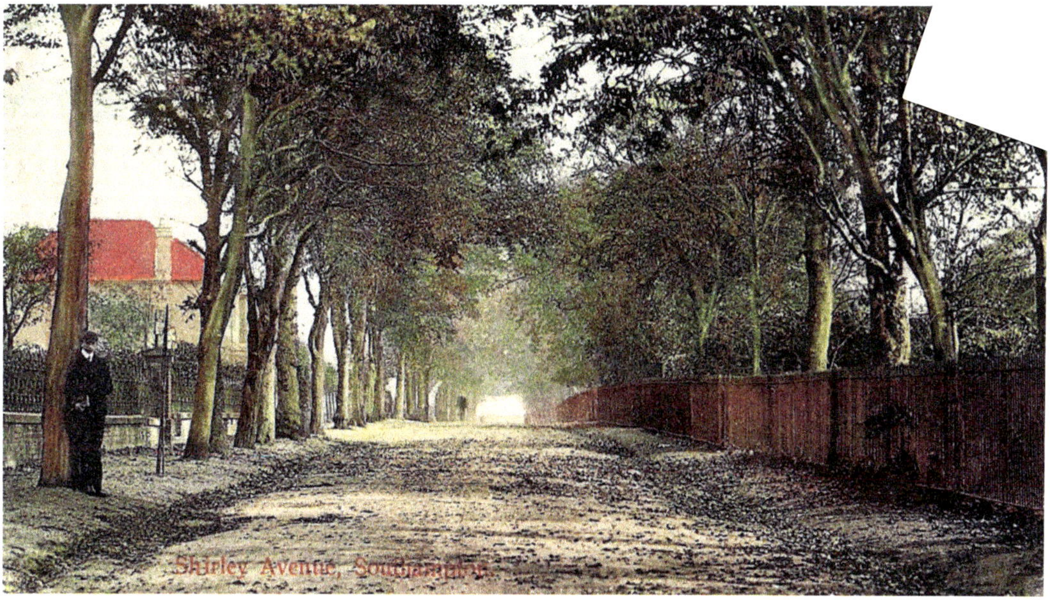

Shirley Avenue, *c.* 1905
The photographer stands towards the Shirley High Street end of Shirley Avenue, facing St James Road in the distance. Only the northern side of the road had housing at this time, and they face the open grounds of the Whithedwood Estate. This too was eventually built on, but the elegant scene pictured here remains recognisable even today, more than a century later.

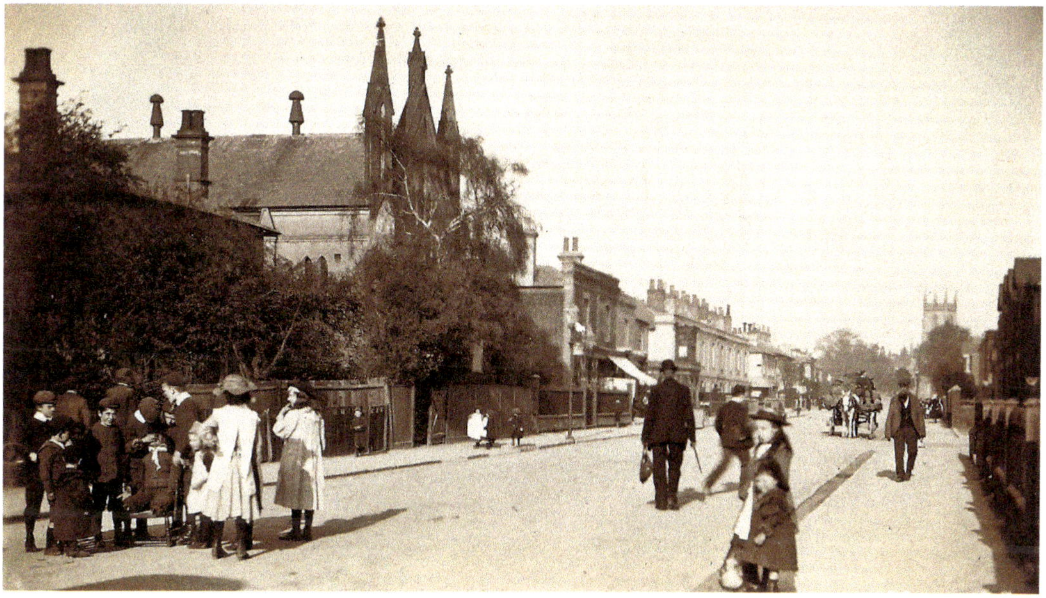

Church Street, late 1800s
On the extreme left the first Children's Hospital in Southampton can be seen, and it was also a dispensary for women. Next door to the hospital is the Wesleyan chapel. Although the exact year this Mentor postcard image was taken can't be accurately assessed, the time of year can. The group of children on the left are gathered around an effigy of Guy Fawkes.

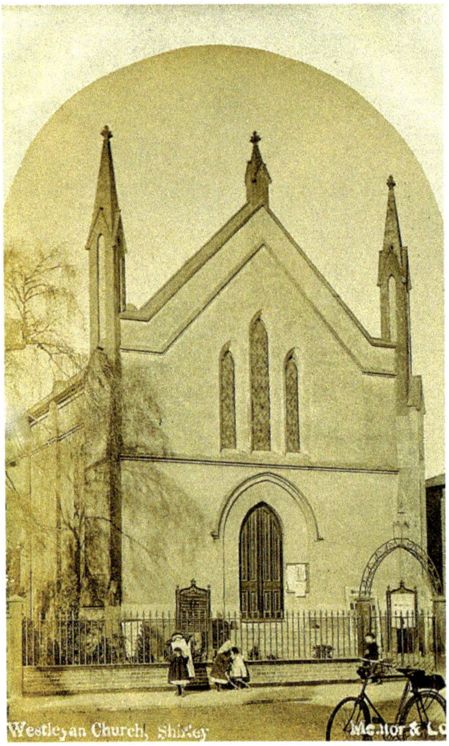

Wesleyan Chapel, Church Street, late 1800s
Shirley Methodist Church (Wesleyan chapel) was built in 1843 in the predominantly working-class area around Church Street. Somewhat a victim of its own popularity and faced with an increasing congregation, a new church was built in 1920 in nearby St James Road. The local Salvation Army took over the building pictured here, remaining until redevelopment in the late 1960s saw the building demolished and the Salvation Army move to a new location.

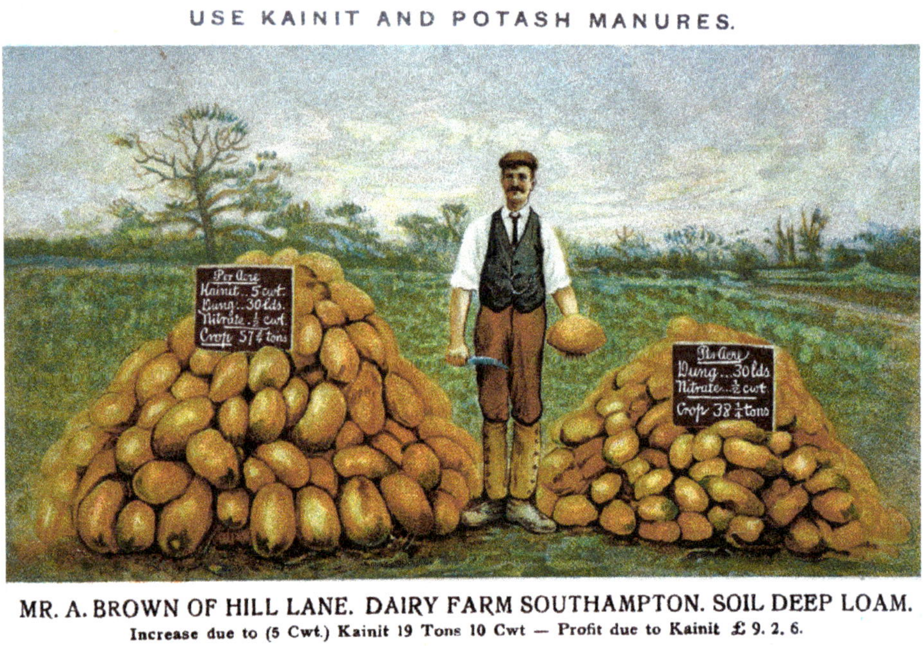

Brown's Dairy Advertising Card
In addition to the widespread practice of sending postcards for tourism or greeting purposes, some enterprising businesspeople used them for advertising. One such man was Mr A. Brown, whose dairy farm on Hill Lane was already well known in the area.

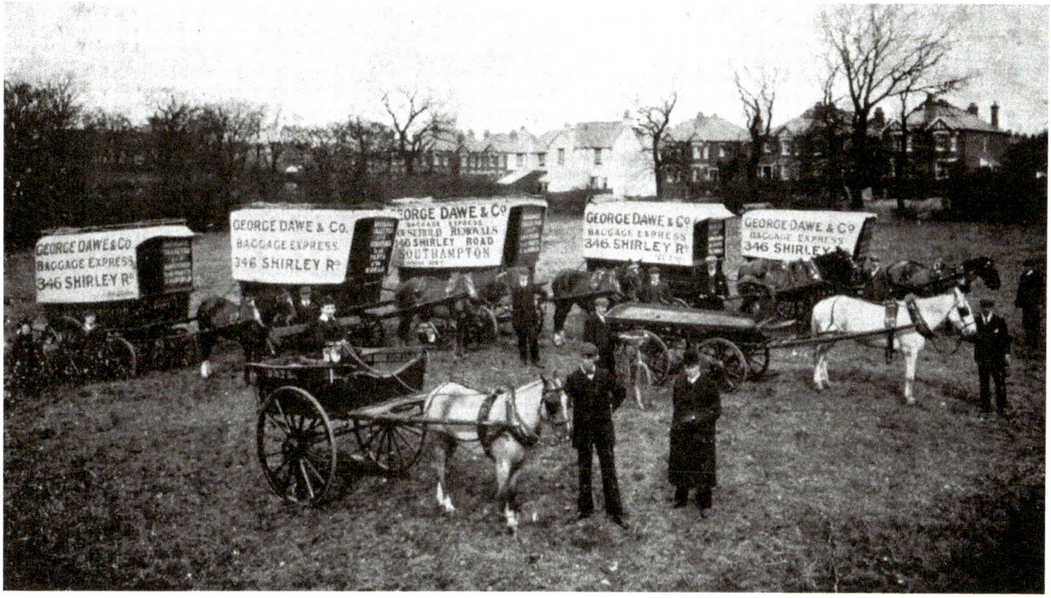

George Dawe & Co., Shirley

George Dawe & Co. proudly display their fleet of parcel and baggage horse-drawn delivery carts. In the background St James Road can be seen, and to the left is Gypsy Grove.

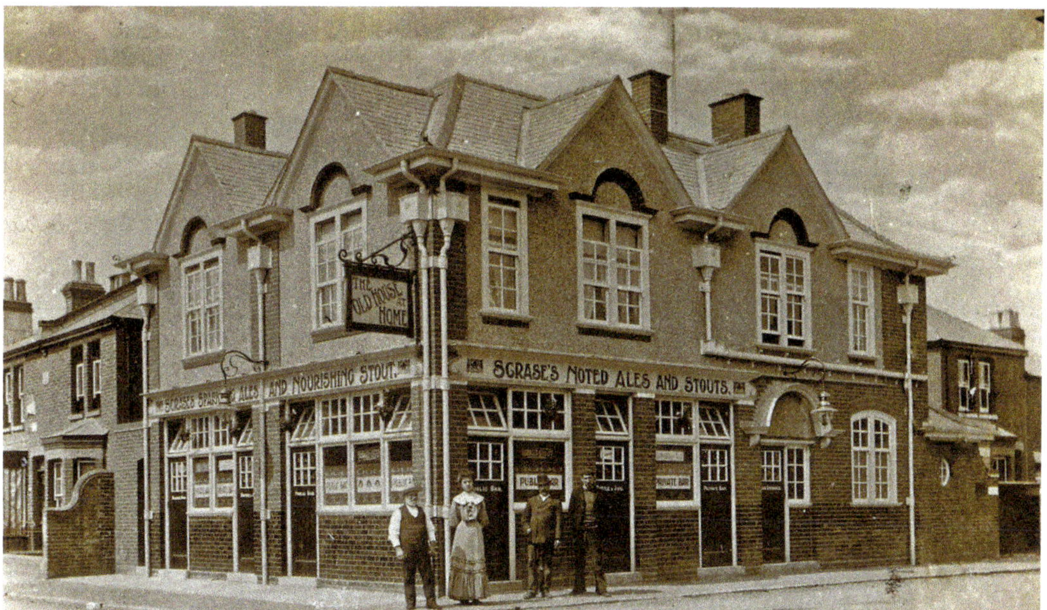

The Old House at Home, Shirley

The Old House at Home public house stood on the corner of Cannon Street and Milner Street. This large, impressive Victorian pub served this area of mainly working-class homes. The area, bounded by Shirley High Street on one side and St James Road on the other, contained a wide variety of drinking establishments. Most were demolished when the area was redeveloped during the 1960s.

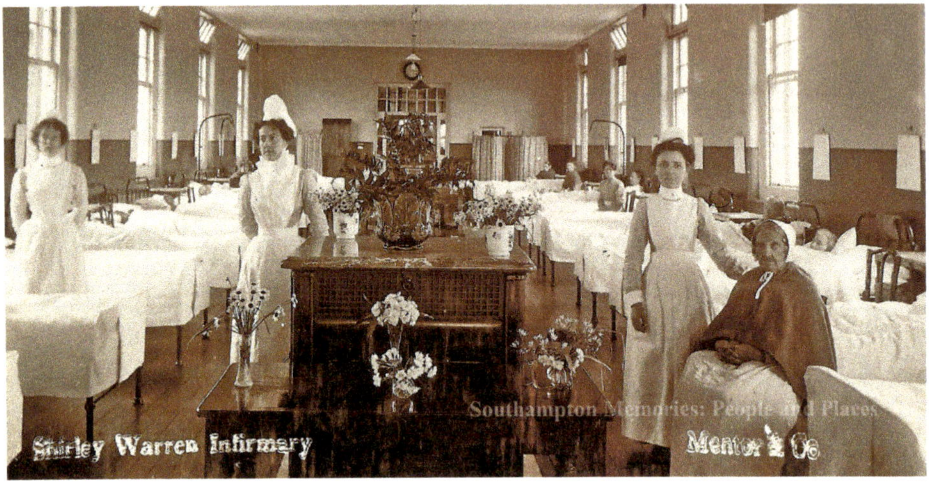

Shirley Warren Infirmary

The original Poor Law Union Infirmary was located in the workhouse adjacent to St Mary's Church in the town. In 1899 a decision was made to build a new infirmary and workhouse on the outskirts of the town. The incidence of infectious diseases in the town may have played a part in that decision. A large site was chosen on Chilworth Road (now Tremona Road) in the suburb of Shirley Warren. Although the planned poor house on the site never materialised, the infirmary continued to expand and is now known as University Hospital Southampton, which is one of the leading research and teaching hospitals in the British Isles. It provides health care for nearly 4 million people in the southern region and beyond.

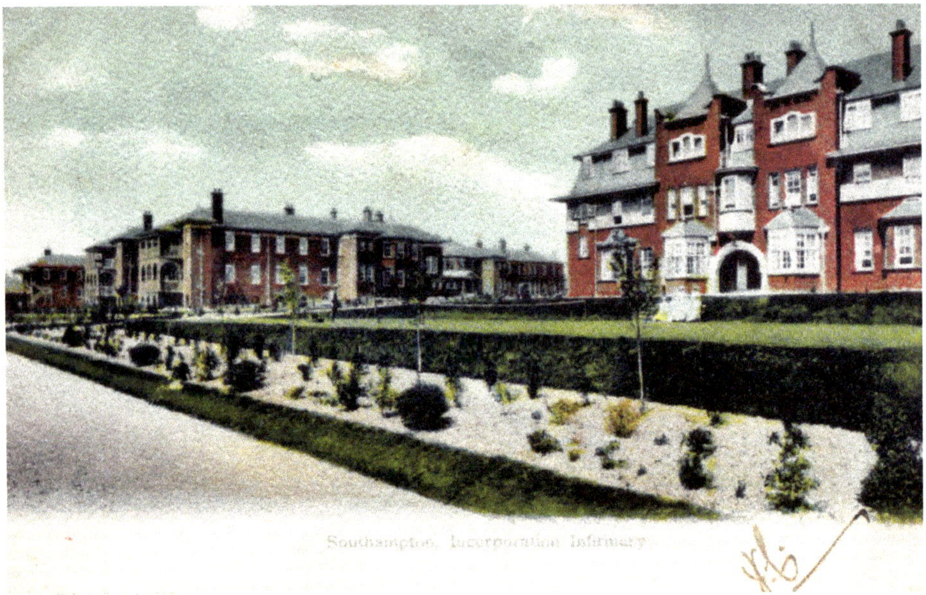

Shirley Warren Infirmary

Built on Hollybrook estate land and opened in 1902, the hospital relied heavily on charitable donations. In 1930 the hospital was taken over by the local council and was renamed the Borough Hospital. In the mid-1940s, when the NHS was founded, the hospital was taken under national control.

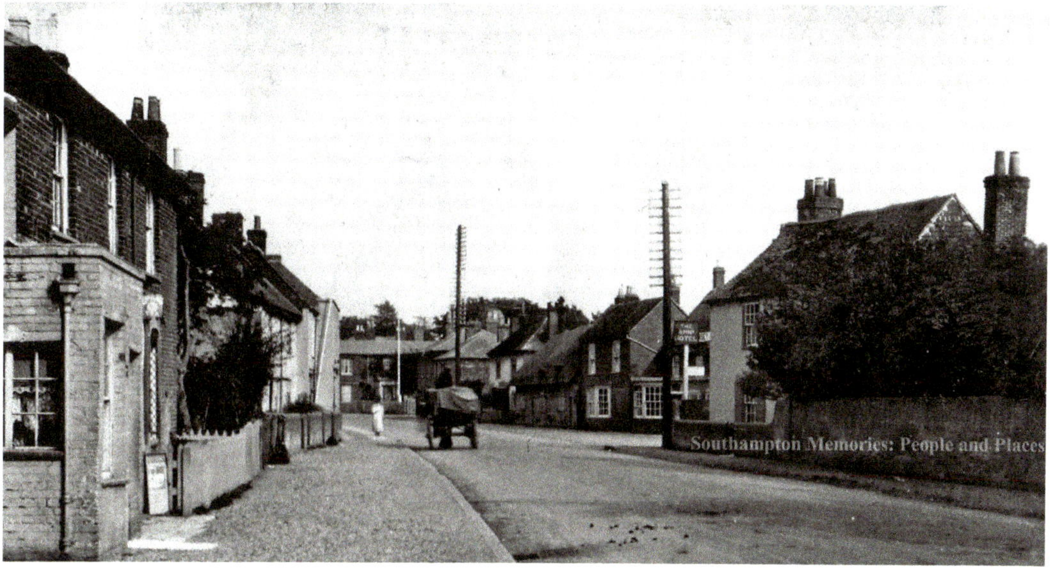

Redbridge, early 1900s

Redbridge is now a quiet backwater, bypassed by the main road west out of Southampton. It is situated at the point where the River Test meets its saltwater estuary. In the seventeenth, eighteenth and nineteenth centuries it boasted a busy trading quay and a well-respected boatbuilding reputation.

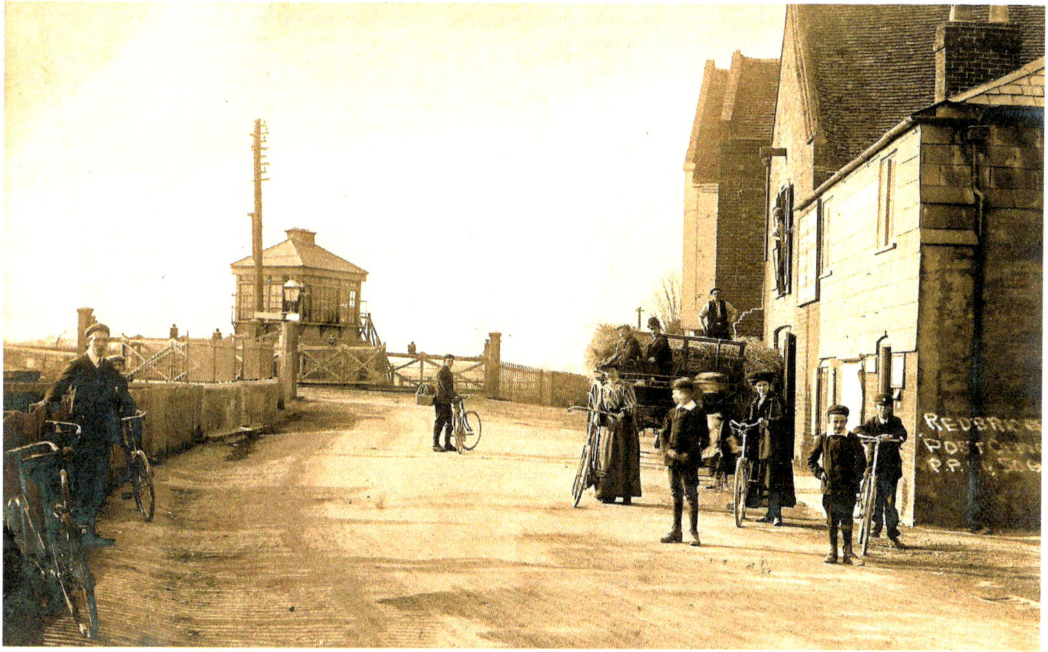

Redbridge, late 1800s

This was the main crossing of the railway and the River Test at Redbridge. Traffic to and from Totton and the New Forest had to wait patiently at the level crossing gates, which then, once the train had passed, allowed them access to the bridge over the river or the road into Southampton.

ACKNOWLEDGEMENTS

The authors would like to thank their friend and colleague Clive Sweetingham for granting permission to use his own photographs and copyright material in this book. A number of rare postcards from his personal collection have been used, and Clive's extensive knowledge has been invaluable in enabling us to tackle the task of putting this book together. We thank him for his unwavering support and friendship.

Every attempt has been made to seek permission for copyright material used in this book. However, if we have inadvertently used copyright material without permission/acknowledgement we apologise and we will make the necessary correction at the first opportunity.

Last but by no means least, we wish to thank Sue Andrews, Sue Wardall, Gill Waring, Ellie Keenan, Charlie Keenan and Ruby Waring for their constant encouragement, enthusiasm and patience.